Harvesting Coffee, Bargaining Wages

Linking Levels of Analysis
Emilio F. Moran, Series Editor

Harvesting Coffee, Bargaining Wages

Rural Labor Markets in Colombia, 1975–1990

Sutti Ortiz

●●●

Ann Arbor

THE UNIVERSITY OF MICHIGAN PRESS

2002 2001 2000 1999   4 3 2 1

A CIP catalog record for this book is available from the British Library.

Library of Congress Cataloging-in-Publication Data

Ortiz, Sutti, 1929–
    Harvesting coffee, bargaining wages : rural labor markets in
Colombia, 1975–1990 / Sutti Ortiz.
        p.   cm. — (Linking levels of analysis)
    Includes bibliographical references and index.
    ISBN 0-472-11018-7 (cloth : alk. paper)
    1. Coffee plantation workers—Colombia.   2. Wages—Coffee
plantation workers—Colombia.   3. Labor market—Colombia.
I. Title.   II. Series.
HD8039.C6382C716   1999
338.1'7373'09861—dc21   99-43137
                                                              CIP

To Ehud, to Dan
and
to the many hardworking laborers
I encountered in the mountains of Colombia

Series Introduction

The series Linking Levels of Analysis focuses on studies that deal with the relationships between local-level systems and larger, more inclusive systems. While we know a great deal about how local and larger systems operate, we know a great deal less about how these levels articulate with each other. It is this kind of research, in all its variety, that Linking Levels of Analysis is designed to publish. Works should contribute to the theoretical understanding of such articulations, create or refine methods appropriate to interlevel analysis, and represent substantive contributions to the social sciences.

The volume before you, *Harvesting Coffee, Bargaining Wages: Rural Labor Markets in Colombia, 1975–1990,* is an outstanding exemplar of the sophisticated articulation of local to national and international levels that advances knowledge. The growing of coffee, unlike with many other crops, requires each laborer to hand-pick each coffee bean, and to negotiate wages individually. However, those wages also reflect the large-scale forces of international commodity markets influenced as they are by climate, supplies from a large number of countries, and assessment of quality of the product. Coffee was an elite brew well into the twentieth century, when it became more popular and affordable. In recent years, concern with the health effects of coffee has led to a "herbal" revolution wherein herbal teas have taken a share of the market from coffee. In turn, gourmet coffees have brought some kinds of coffee to its elite status in the past decade, a status which requires that its cultivation, harvesting, and handling guarantee a high level of quality.

This book challenges many of the prominent economic models that assume that, left to their own devices, a multitude of buyers and sellers of labor will prefer to engage in bidding and arrive at a satisfactory wage arrangement. This study shows that bargaining is rare and that the negotiations embody complex social relations. What emerges is a more realistic image of coffee markets that will better inform policies such as the impact of minimum wage hikes on employment and the impact of labor market deregulation on production and welfare.

Harvesting Coffee, Bargaining Wages is rich in historical depth and detail. It builds on the excellent work on coffee of Roseberry, and goes beyond it by giving greater attention to the ethnography of social relations between farmers and laborers in bringing about a labor market that is full of the contingencies that characterize the human community. This ethnographically rich detail is all the more powerful because of the economic sophistication and rich data brought to bear by the author. It links ethnography to survey research in two municipalities in the context of the coffee markets of Colombia, and the world.

This work is in the best tradition of economic anthropology. It challenges that the structure of labor markets cannot be understood by focusing on supply, demand, productivity, costs, commodity prices, and risk, as economists all too commonly do. The relevance of these factors depends on the degree of competition between producers and between laborers, and on the extent to which social and political institutions support or hinder that competition. The role of Colombia's FNCC assured farmers of a buyer for their coffee, and protected them from extreme price swings. As a result, farmers did not have to compete with each other for market niche, thereby changing the competitive setting and local to international articulations. Job prospects of laborers have more to do with long-standing friendships and social obligations to a particular farm/farmer, the breadth of their information network, and the distance between their residence and the farms that employ them than on the wage rate itself. This is far from the open competitive bidding assumed in economic theory. As the author notes, "the market interaction is not between demand and supply, but between socialized and politicized individuals who only sometimes openly negotiate their interaction." The laborer has slightly greater power at the height of the harvest given the urgency and temporal limitations brought by manual harvesting, and the farmer has the upper hand the rest of the year. These shifting configurations of power are the product of past national policies, local institutional arrangements, and dynamic negotiations where supply and demand are only a part of a complex decision-making process. Local political ambitions of farmers, assurance of quality laborers during the harvest, and loyalty play no less important parts in bringing to market the highly touted quality represented by Colombian coffee.

It is my hope that this volume will encourage other scholars to examine other commodities in other settings, with the same combination of historical, economic, ethnographic, and political sophistication seen here. We encourage you to contact the series editor or other members of the editorial board to discuss your work and our possible interest in publishing it.

Editor
Emilio F. Moran, Indiana University

Editorial Board
John Bowen, Washington University, St. Louis
Conrad Kottak, University of Michigan
Katherine Newman, Harvard University
Douglas White, University of California, Irvine

Contents

Figures

Tables

Acknowledgments

Funding for the field research, coding, and analysis of the survey (1985–86) was provided by the National Science Foundation (BNS-8570614). A travel grant from Boston University made it possible to meet with Colombian colleagues to discuss the project during the summer of 1984.

This book would not have been possible without the collaboration of María Errazuriz. When I met her, she was completing her manuscript on coffee production in Tolima, yet she kindly redirected her efforts to help me with research on labor markets in Risaralda. Shortly after we began to work together, she became affiliated with Fedesarrollo and joined a research team engaged in a number of topics bearing on coffee production and rural employment, work that provided valuable insights into our joint endeavor. More practically, her efforts were instrumental in providing much of the data for this book: she assumed one of the trickiest aspects of the field research, the survey of the harvesters; she assembled and supervised the interviewers and the coding of responses; and she accompanied me on some of the field visits. I recall with fondness her companionship and enthusiasm. She generously shared information and ideas as well as her house and kitchen. Our many discussions over meals and coffee served to enrich my understanding of the issues raised in this book. My only lament is that work commitments did not allow her to join me in the analysis of the data and the writing of this book. The arguments and conclusions that I present are entirely my responsibility and I remain accountable for errors of information and interpretation.

Fernando Urrea shared his knowledge of employment in coffee agriculture and provided access to the questionnaire he used in his 1975 survey of harvesters. His ideas and experiences made our survey a more solid field exercise than it would have otherwise been. Carlos Becerra helped us to develop a useful and trustworthy questionnaire and to design a coding system that enhanced the analysis of the data. His considerable experience in rural surveys, some of them in the coffee-producing region, was invaluable. Jaime Forero and Guillermo Rudas also guided us through the initial difficult stage of designing the questionnaire and the survey. From them I learned a great deal about small farmers and rural laborers. Humberto Rojas helped us to understand coffee production in La Vega, where he and his students were researching peasant production. He also shared his team of collaborators and assumed responsibility for the survey of harvesters in that municipality. I regret that he was not able to participate more intensively in this project. José Leibovitch was most informative on the policies of the FNCC. Marco Palacios taught me a great deal about the history of the coffee industry in Colombia, which I had previously known about only from the perspective of poor Indian producers. There are many other Colombian historians, economists, anthropologists, and sociologists too numerous to mention who kindly met with me to discuss my work. Their comments and writings were extremely helpful, and I quote them throughout the text. Although previous fieldwork experiences in Colombia familiarized me with rural families, I owe to Virginia Gutierrez de Pineda my fuller appreciation of familial dynamics and to Roberto Pineda my greater understanding of rural life in the coffee region of the Grand Caldas. My trips to Bogotá would not have been as pleasant as they were without their encouragement, hospitality, and friendship.

I would like to thank the many individuals and institutions in Risaralda and La Vega who helped the various members of the research team. The FNCC's national, departmental, and municipal committees offered generous support and made available reports and census information that were key for our survey. Among FNCC personnel, Jairo Giraldo Valencia and Fabio Alzate Vallejo offered us considerable help on practical matters in the field and took the time to introduce us to local farmers and residents. I thank their team of agronomists, who corrected many of my mistakes and misperceptions. Lucero Henao and Zoraida Castaño introduced me to many farmers they had met when they worked in the FNCC's local offices. Antonio Ospina taught me a great deal about the history of many of the neighborhoods of Marsella while driving along long roads to meet farmers and laborers. He was a pleasant, knowledgeable, and kind companion. Jaime Marulanda, director of SENA in Pereira, drove us around and helped us select the municipalities. We owe much to his kindness and perceptiveness. In Boston, Suzanne Baker handled the very frustrating task of cross-tabulating the survey data. Anuradha Saxena helped me interpret some of the tabulated information.

Students and colleagues have commented on seminar presentations of sections of this book. I thank Emilio Moran for his general comments and for prodding me to introduce comparative data in my concluding arguments. Two anonymous reviewers offered helpful and careful comments on an earlier draft of this manuscript. Ehud Koch helped me with editorial revisions, and Dan Koch offered advice to improve the flow of the text. I owe much to both of them for their comments and their encouragement and to Ehud in particular for his patience and nurturing while I was working on this manuscript.

Chapter 1

Approaches to the Study of Rural Labor Markets

The wet mountain climate of the central Andes favors the milder-tasting coffee for which Colombia is famous. However, a cup of coffee would fail to capture its famous aroma if the berries had been carelessly harvested and processed. As the famous Juan Valdez television advertisements remind us, laborers must pick each bean separately, selecting only those that are fully ripe. Farmers then must promptly wash, hull, and dry the beans. Although the ads show magnificent views of the slopes and valleys where coffee is grown, the commercials distort the realities of farm work. The laborers—dressed in tattered clothing rather than in Valdez's quaint garb—often have to work long days on slippery, muddy, slopes, protecting themselves from the rain with sheets of plastic. The workers must carry their heavy loads without the aid of donkeys or trucks. Needing jobs, these men and women are willing to work despite difficult conditions and relatively low pay. In turn, farmers are willing to invest considerable care, time, and effort in maintaining trees and harvesting the crop. As long as coffee prices are high enough to bring an appealing income, farmers will continue with this labor-intensive production strategy to maintain the niche that Colombian coffee has gained in the international market. Thus, coffee farms are of interest to those of us who want to examine how the labor process and labor markets are structured in nonplantation, nonmechanized agriculture in which laborers must negotiate employment individually without any support from unions.

Although the laborers do not look like Juan Valdez, his image conveys an important message. He is not dressed like other Colombian peasants. He is a *paisa* from Antioquia, a department in the central coffee region of Colombia. He is a historic folk figure, an intrepid colonizer, hardworking and good at business. He was the farmer who, in the past century, opened the coffee frontier in the central region. The Federación Nacional de Cafeteros de Colombia (FNCC, the Coffee Federation of

Colombia) has chosen this image to bring the aroma of its coffee into U.S. and European living rooms. It is a pleasant image. People are charmed and respond with another purchase. Coffee drinkers in Europe and the United States are part of the chain of transactions that starts with the money paid for a pound of coffee and ends when a wage is paid to a laborer. Consumers' willingness or unwillingness to sacrifice other needs for a taste of expensive but fashionable brew will determine how fast stockpiles will dwindle and how fast the price of coffee will rise.

Coffee was first served as an elite brew. By 1900, it became cheap enough to be the drink of preference of the working population. It gave its name to on-the-job rest periods. But by 1920 coffee merchants had to contend with prohibitionist efforts to convince people that the drink was a danger to their health (Jimenez 1995b). The "herbal revolution" of recent years once more has affected consumption of coffee in the United States, which has decreased from an average of 2.3 cups a day per person in 1953 to 1.37 cups in 1986 (Junguito and Pizano 1993: 47).

The annals of coffee history demonstrate how the price of luxury commodities can rise and fall at unexpected rates. This history also points to the impact of tastes, preferences, and trade wars on these rates. Ultimately, these global currents reverberate down the chain to farms and affect what the harvesters earn. Yet, as chapter 7 shows, wages do not necessarily respond directly and do not always drop when the market slumps. The chain of events is much more complex. In Colombia, as in other countries, there are many mediating steps that help to ameliorate global market conditions and protect workers and farmers alike. Governments can reduce tariffs, alter export duties, and set foreign exchange rates. Industry-wide associations can lobby for protective policies, mobilize investment funds, and organize commercial cooperative ventures. In Colombia, the Coffee Federation has influenced policy, helped producers, and, with the aid of Juan Valdez, sold the image of Colombian coffee abroad (see section 2.5). This case study illustrates the dangers of overgeneralizing the impact of global trade by disregarding the role that national institutions may play as mediators in trade and abaters of market shocks.

Roseberry makes a similar observation when comparing systems of coffee production in various Latin American countries. In his introduction to *Coffee, Society, and Power in Latin America,* he notes that despite the fact that Latin American coffee-producing countries are incorporated in the same international markets, they share neither the same social relations of production nor similar approaches to how they mobilize or extract surplus labor (1995: 6). I would add that these intercountry variations also appear within the regions of any one country. In Colombia, the FNCC policies do not have the same impact across all coffee-producing regions or reflect equally the farmers' interests. Some regional FNCC committees have a greater voice in national decisions and are better endowed than others. These regional variations are significant because it is at the local sites, where coffee is sold and laborers are contracted, that political power, economic resources, market advantage, and government policies play out and determine what farmers gain and what workers earn. Prices and policies become most real when farmers, laborers, and consumers enter local stores, local banks, merchant houses, the offices of the municipal committee of the FNCC, or go to work on a farm. If the conditions they encounter are discouraging or detrimental to their well-being, farmers and laborers will use whatever power they have to challenge them. If they have limited power to assert their claim, as is so often the case for laborers, they at least try to work out a solution that shelters them from misfortune. Therefore, it is not surprising that one can note considerable variation in wages from region to region and even from one locality to the next. Indeed, while labor markets are structured at the national level by international and national conditions, they are structured at the regional level by conditions that obtain in each region and by conditions that pertain to the local market. But even within these minimal conceptual units there is no homogeneity. Indeed, different types of farms offer different contractual options and even different pay rates. This books seeks to examine how macro and micro processes can be integrated to reveal a comprehensive understanding of the labor market of an export crop, such as coffee.

Harvesting and tending coffee trees is not a highly skilled occupation. Hence, this labor market can justly be classified as unskilled. Some economists will then expect it to share the characteristics of their idealized market models: perfect mobility and a technologically driven demand. Both of these assumed characteristics rest on the postulate that markets are information centers about supply and demand and the equilibration of preferences. This portrayal of the market disregards the complex set of sociopolitical institutions that influence how traders come together, how exchange is generated and regulated and how preferences are outlined and negotiated. The assumption that this complexity can be reduced to a simple model that integrates a few stylized facts is misleading. It has encouraged economists to imagine the possibility that exchanges can approach an equilibrating state (the perfect market). In the case of the labor market, competitive equilibrated relations are expected to enhance the flow of labor from less productive farms to more productive farms that pay higher wages. In this argument, a competitive market can help to improve workers' welfare. The questions raised by economists then concern what conditions hinder the supply-demand relation and productivity consideration and how these hindering obstacles can be removed. In contrast, I believe that it is more important to ask how the exchange proceeds, what considerations affect the relation between transactors, and when and how demand and supply affect negotiated contracts.

One of the goals of this book is to offer a way of looking at this exchange process, by examining the needs and concerns that bring farmers and laborers into the exchange and by incorporating the role played by other actors and institutions in the exchange. This way of looking at the process helps integrate micro and macro processes affecting labor exchanges.

This approach seeks to avoid a central weakness of many economic models: the assumption that, left to their own devices, a multitude of buyers and sellers of labor will prefer to engage in a bidding negotiation and will arrive at a satisfactory exchange. A second aim of this book is to encourage scholars to shift their attention from specific contract formats and wage cycles to the nature of the negotiating process. This case study illustrates that bargaining is rare and that the exchange is circumscribed by the conditions encapsulated in the negotiations. A third aim of this book—an area often neglected in the literature on agricultural labor—is to show that the prevalence of a particular seasonal contract cannot be discussed out of the context of policies geared to stimulate production. This work also illustrates that scholars must consider how each contract relates to the use of other contracts and managerial strategies. For example, piece-rate contracts are best suited to pressured harvest conditions because they preempt the need to screen workers, but they are appropriate only if the farmer can afford to supervise the work.

The more realistic image of a market, as developed in this book, should help policymakers identify the potential ramifications of policies that are presently debated: the impact of minimum-wage hikes on employment and the possible impact of labor-market deregulation on production and welfare.

1.1   Modeling Labor Markets

Economists have represented the market as a configuration of demographic and economic factors. In these neoclassical models, farmers and laborers are portrayed as bidding competitively for productive power and jobs. The end result of this competition is an exchange of labor for a bargained compensation. It is argued that willingness to participate in the labor market depends on the wage that is offered, the marginal product of alternative activities available to the potential laborer, and the fixed costs attached to working for a wage. The demand for laborers, in turn, depends on the utility of the farmers' maximizing or "satisfyzing" calculus. They can choose to increase or decrease production according to the value of the crop. Farmers are also likely to use fewer laborers if the marginal cost of hired hands is higher than the marginal cost of machinery, chemicals, or new agrotechnology. Farmers will then either mechanize production or use chemicals instead of laborers to weed their land.

These models succeed in representing realities and concerns such as the impact of shifts in supply and the productivity of labor. However, these models assume that farmers in advanced agricultural economies will find solutions to these problems "in the market" instead of using nonmarket institutions to attract more laborers, decrease the marginal cost of human labor, or improve its productivity. For example, fruit and vegetable growers in California, who also faced sharp seasonal shifts in required labor inputs, solved their needs by co-opting the state to import laborers (Galarza 1964; Daniel 1981; Fisher 1953; Tootle and Green 1989).

Since marginal costs are believed to be instrumental in determining contractual options, economists expect that in advanced economies farmers will give up less productive arrangements and hire laborers only when needed. Not surprisingly, economists have been intrigued by farmers' continued reliance on permanent workers even when they are underemployed for most of the year. Noting that these permanent workers often receive lower wages than do occasional laborers, scholars have tried to explain this apparently "traditional" behavior as a clever "rational" economic strategy to insure a readily available, cheap supply of labor during peak season. Economists have also argued that these lower-paid laborers profit because they reduce the risk of income loss during periods of unemployment. While there is considerable evidence that this is the case in India, where laborers with large families face sharp changes in employment opportunities throughout the year (Bardhan 1984: 73–85), in the coffee regions of this study farmers paid permanent laborers the same wages as other workers. Reasons other than cost explain why Colombian coffee farmers hire permanent workers (see chap. 7). More recently, economists have added another clause to their argument: attachment may continue because it buys the loyalty of the laborers. While such may sometimes be the case, as chapter 7 shows, attachment can also breed resentment.

Economists have also argued that the common practice of mobilizing harvest labor supply by extending loans before the start of the season can be regarded as a market transaction that benefits both parties and can thus be analyzed as part of the economic calculus of market actors. Farmers profit because they assure themselves a timely supply of laborers without having to offer high wages or engage in high recruitment costs. Laborers profit because they gain access to credit at a lower interest rate than what the open market would charge. But for both farmers and laborers to profit, the wage has to reflect the interest that the laborers would have to pay and the interest that the farmers would forgo as moneylenders. Because the wage, in this argument, is expected to reflect interest rates, these exchanges are labeled *interlinked contracts.* Following the logic of the economic calculus, these contracts are expected to pervade in regions where credit markets are tight and farmers need considerable numbers of seasonal workers (Bardhan 1984: 86–95). While such seems to be the case in the more technologically advanced agricultural areas of India, there is no evidence of interlinked contracts in coffee agriculture, despite the fact that both conditions also apply. In a recent article, Pal (1996) argues that the model is too tight and that preferences other than security or credit may be responsible for the attractiveness of interlinked or permanent wage contracts. Hart (1986) has made a more damning critique of the microeconomic explanation. She demonstrates that labor tying is not always present when expected—that is, when demand becomes sharply seasonal—and the paradoxical finding that such tying flourishes in Java under slack labor market conditions. Bardhan has recognized the weight of these arguments in a later publication (1989).

While these microeconomic arguments have opened the models by including other bargaining considerations—for example, laborers' preferences for secure income and farmers' concerns for a timely supply—and have helped to highlight how demographic and economic factors impinge on wages and contractual arrangements, these contentions fail to explain why farmers sometimes do not choose the best market options and why other nonmarket arrangements are sometimes used to achieve the same ends. Economists blame "externalities" for inadvisable nonmarket choices—that is, barriers to mobility, limited information, inappropriate social rules, and so forth—but they cannot incorporate these realities into their models. Thus, while these arguments help to evaluate the potential economic significance of particular contractual arrangements, these propositions cannot predict use of such arrangements. The more encompassing sociological models may also have limited predictive power, but they can encompass a wider range of agencies and events. A major goal of this book is to incorporate some of the elements that economists have identified as instrumental in the choice of contracts but to do so without losing sight of laborers' limitations in bargaining. These choices must then be analyzed within a wider framework that includes the sociopolitical scenario of negotiations and/or labor exchanges.

In an attempt to broaden the scope of these models and to account for otherwise apparent irrational market behavior, economists have incorporated two other variables: job-search costs and unemployment risks. The willingness or unwillingness to accept or to continue to search for work is said to be related to information flows, the cost of gaining more information, the cost of searching for other offers, and the risks of failure in pursuing such action. While these considerations have served to humanize the model of the market, very few of the job-search realities faced by unemployed workers find expression in mathematical models (see chap. 6).

A more helpful approach was the one pursued by past labor economists (Kerr, Lester, and Reynolds) who saw the market as a social institution with "rules, procedures, and circumstances under which buyers and sellers are brought together, affect the performance of the market, its price, and quantities transferred" (Dunlop 1988: 48–49). These economists encouraged their students to continue to examine case studies and to integrate personal observations and experiences with their general theories about wages and employment. Although it is difficult to transpose their findings to coffee agriculture because they worked mostly in urban and industrial labor markets, this study shares one of their central assumptions: the bargaining of wages, choice of contracts, and hiring practices are affected by government policies, ideas of what is proper, and the political power of unions and of producers' interest groups (Marsden 1986).

These admonitions do not imply that supply and demand conditions are irrelevant. On the contrary, market conditions are clearly in the minds of laborers and farmers when negotiating. If laborers know that jobs are plentiful, they are likely to wait until they are offered attractive wages. If not, they will accept any offer above their reservation wages—that is, a wage that would warrant working for someone else. If farmers are aware of a queue of workers by their farm gates, they might lower the offering wage and see if there are any takers. However, supply and demand only set the stage; they determine neither the offering rate nor its acceptance. A central assumption in my portrayal of the market is that to understand wage rates, one must consider not only cost, returns, and market conditions but also the social conditions and cultural perceptions that impinge on the formulation of the offering wage. Furthermore, I assume that cultural and social norms also influence when and how to bargain. Solow ends his sketch of bargaining economic models with an important sociological observation: bargaining is not an abstract quantitative process but a complex social process:

> What actually happens is altogether different [from the ideal Hobbesian competition]. I presume that experience and reason lead to the emergence of social norm. We do not compete for each other's job by nibbling away at wage levels because we have been taught that it is unfair to do so, or demeaning, or unacceptable, or perhaps-self-destructive. . . . I do not know how those norms get established, historically speaking, but once established they draw their force from shared values and social approbation and disapprobation, not from calculation. (Solow 1990: 48–49)

This book will show how both social values and market conditions affect the ability of laborers and farmers to bargain and consider the bargaining situation's effect on the labor process and on contractual arrangements. But three important questions must first be answered: How do laborers arrive at their reservation wages? How and when do laborers and farmers bargain and negotiate a wage? And does the wage relate to other privileges, services, and benefits that laborers receive?

Some economists have resolved the first question by using unemployment insurance as an approximation of the reservation wage. But this is not a viable approximation for rural Latin America since people there are not covered by social security benefits. Other economists have argued that the baseline from which sellers and buyers of labor bargain is the basic cost of laborers' subsistence. However, agricultural wages are often not sufficient to cover the cost of subsistence. Yet when no other jobs are available, workers will not voluntarily remain unemployed. In this book I argue that the more fluid concept of fair wage proposed by Akerloff (1990) is more appropriate for an understanding of bargaining in a labor market. My interpretation of a fair wage is a cultural construct based on subsistence needs weighted by acquired social responsibilities and remuneration previously received.[1] Following this interpretation, I argue that coffee workers in Colombia in some circumstances will withdraw their services from the market if the prevailing offers are not considered appropriate but will only do so if they can afford it. For example, young men sometimes stay home rather than accept what they consider to be low wages. In contrast, their fathers, trapped by family responsibilities, cannot afford that luxury. Older men have limited job offers and must take what is offered. These married and older men respond, however, by adjusting work performance to what they consider to be commensurate with the wage they receive. I address these issues in chapters 7 and 8.

Scholars have also avoided the second and third questions, which are harder to answer because the information is usually elusive and anecdotal. By taking into account farmers' financial condition and relating it to the laborers' accounts of job-search experiences, I describe how both farmers and laborers manage the labor exchange. What happens during these exchanges determines how many and what benefits are offered to laborers. During the coffee harvest, when supply is tight and unemployment limited, laborers bargain openly. Farmers are forced to quote a rate and allow laborers to reject offers and keep the bargaining going until rates considered suitable by the laborers are quoted. Thus, the harvest wage is a competitively determined market rate. It is also quite high compared to the wages received by other agricultural laborers in Colombia. However, in contrast, workers are powerless after the harvest. They do not dare to question farmers, who prefer to view the hiring process as under their control. Many laborers receive very little information about the terms of the exchange and must deduce it from hints and past experiences. They start to work without having had the chance to bargain their wage and contract. In other words, it could be argued that the postharvest wage is not a market wage even if one follows Solow's more social vision of the market and Akerloff's fair wage concept. Only when there is a balance in power or when the supply-demand relation favors the laborer is the contract likely to be truly negotiated. Power is thus an important determinant of market transactions.

To understand how the postharvest rate (with or without benefits) is determined when open bargaining is not permitted, I have turned to the anthropological conception of social transaction and Akerloff's notion of partial gift exchanges (1982, 1990). Following Mauss (1954), anthropologists assume that a gift—in this case, a work effort of given intensity—is eventually reciprocated in appropriate manner. While quoting Mauss, Akerloff (1982: 549) relies more closely on Homans's representation of exchange reciprocation as more appropriate for the wage labor situation he analyzes. The postharvest labor-wage exchanges fall somewhere in between a wage contract and a gift exchange. Laborers give their effort, expecting or hoping for a fair return—that is, a fair wage—but it is understood that a lower figure is equally acceptable if followed by other rewards, such as promises of longer employment or other fringe benefits. As in a gift exchange, the return transaction (the wage) is not openly discussed. It is set by farmers based on what they consider to be culturally appropriate and what they believe they can afford. If the wage meets with the earnings anticipated by the laborers, the transaction is considered satisfactory and complete. If not, laborers quietly accept it, but they do so with the expectation of receiving subsequent favors, just as in a protracted gift-exchange transaction. However, unlike in some of the classic examples in the anthropological literature, coffee laborers keep track of what they receive and, if dissatisfied, react negatively; for example, they may reduce their work effort next time they are hired by the same farmer. Since farmers and laborers do not always belong to the same social class, their respective evaluations of what constitutes a fair wage do not necessarily match. Thus, while farmers can get away with paying unacceptable wages, they must be prepared to tolerate low productivity and tensions (see chap. 6). Hence, in Akerloff's notion of partial gift exchanges, both transactors can be cheated if one has more power and the other is intent on maximizing return.

The key feature in all examples cited in the literature that conform to the format of an exploitative partial gift exchange is that they share an oversupply of impoverished agricultural workers. The laborers, as a result, suffer dire consequences. Breman, for example, is surprised to note that in Western Gujarat "wage settlement has taken on the character not so much of a business transaction, as that of granting of a favor. On returning from the land, the laborer hangs around on the farmyard for a while and it is very common for the farmer to make him wait. . . . The farmer then deducts money given for loans without any explanation" (1985: 277). The immigrant laborers during the Mexican-American bracero program suffered a similar fate. Wages were set by a commission that took into account information about the customary wage in the region. Laborers and farmers were not allowed to negotiate according to local market conditions (Galarza 1964).

It should be kept in mind that not all farmers in the municipalities of this study adopt postharvest hiring practices that impede bargaining and obscure information. Farmers in better financial positions make it clear what the offering wage and working conditions are, thereby opening the door to possible bargaining and to market transactions. However, when farmers retain social control over the terms of the exchange and cut costs by inhibiting bargaining, they fail to fulfill one of the central conditions of a market exchange. Microeconomic models then cannot function properly and cannot be used to explain contractual strategies. To understand the differences between these two groups of farmers, the analysis of market and partial-gift exchanges must be set within the wider context of the labor process in coffee agriculture. By the term *labor process* I mean to include all the means used to appropriate natural resources and transform them into commodities: agrotechnology, market and nonmarket transactions to acquire means of production, range of management strategies used for an orderly combination of means and resources, and social relations during the process of production. Although there is no need to always encompass the full labor-process scenario, it is important to incorporate in the model or argument a sufficient number of these conditions to explain deviations as well as central tendencies. It is not helpful to relegate a large number of conditions to externalities, as some economic arguments do.

There is yet another reason for focusing on the labor process and the nature of labor exchanges. Farmers are just as concerned with the costs incurred because of low productivity of labor as they are with the actual wage. They are aware that productivity can be influenced not only by offering a fair wage but also by closely supervising laborers' work or by engaging them in a patron-client relation (Bazzoli, Kirat, and Villeval 1994; Platteau 1995). Managers of large coffee farms use a combination of these strategies. Some managers gain the loyalty of a few resident workers through patronage and then use these workers in a supervisory capacity. In turn, these supervisors may be considerate with their crews, but they may also insure high productivity through ruthlessness and exploitation. Other managers intervene more directly and try to foster commitment by being helpful to laborers and by offering to employ them during most of the year. Chapters 3 and 8 explore some of these differences in attitude and consider them in relation to farm size, financial constraints, and farmers' sociopolitical perceptions.

In general, exploitative managerial tactics and inattention to the concern of workers often lead to open confrontations, social movements, and unionization. These formally or informally organized groups impinge on the behavior of farmers, who either try to regain control over the labor process or contract out some agricultural tasks. In California, for example, strawberry growers reintroduced sharecropping contracts in areas experiencing high union activity (Wells 1984). By delegating the organization of production to sharecroppers, farmers distanced themselves from the organizing efforts of union activists. Tomato producers in California (Friedland, Barton, and Thomas 1981) and sugarcane plantations in Argentina have instead mechanized some productive activities (Whiteford 1981).

Although there has recently been no organized labor activity in coffee agriculture in Colombia, tensions are obvious and are verbalized by farmers and laborers alike. All farmers and administrators try to handle the situation as best they can. No single strategy prevails. Some farmers engage in a close interaction with laborers, others offer better wages and working conditions, and still others become very ruthless. A few have begun to offer attractive working conditions for women. The only shared element of these varied strategies is the continued general tendency to shift away from long-term contracts with laborers and to hire individuals for short, unspecified periods of time. When laborers have to shift from farm to farm to be fully employed during the year, they have difficulty carrying out organized stoppages. Whether the shift to occasional labor crews is not only intended to reduce costs but also to minimize confrontations remains unclear.

Thus, the labor market in coffee agriculture is highly structured, much like industrial agriculture in the United States (Friedland, Barton, and Thomas 1981; R.J. Thomas 1985). In the case of Colombian coffee, the labor market is structured by costs of production, financial markets, seasonal crop requirements, diversity of productive enterprises, the network of relations that serves to transmit information and leverage political power, institutional supports and regulations that facilitate certain management strategies while circumscribing others, and supply conditions. Subsequent chapters examine how these factors interact with the social and cultural baggage that laborers and farmers bring to the market.

My analysis of labor markets shifts away from tight predictive and depersonalized neoclassical models to more complex actor-oriented arguments that also incorporate power, political conditions, and culture (Ortiz 1992; Kevane 1994). This analysis encapsulates the logic behind farmers' and laborers' strategic choices about contracts, management, and jobs. This logic is grounded in the attainment of multiple objectives: security, independence, social standing, well-being, returns, and/or income that surpasses costs and falls within the experienced normal range (Ortiz 1983). I do not assume that farmers calculate marginal utility, since to do so they would have to carefully document all costs and returns. Most coffee farmers keep rudimentary account books at best, and only on the larger enterprise farms do managers track all expenditures and the yield per plot. Managerial decisions are made by people with field and personnel experience but limited investment expertise. Almost none of the farmers had any training in agronomic research. They consulted with the agronomists of the local branch of the FNCC, but they did not routinely evaluate the worth of their technological practices.

The logical principles that guide strategic choices and the conditional requirements for their implementation do not fully explain the array of management strategies and contractual arrangements. Each choice stands on the shoulders of antecedent strategies and the cultural-historical memory of those experiences. Farmers' decisions to avoid or allow bargaining of postharvest wages rests also on the memory of earlier attempts to elicit productivity and compliance from laborers. Bad experiences generate either stronger confrontational managerial tactics or bargained contracts, depending on whether the farmers regard laborers as enemies or potential allies.

I propose in this volume a wider, more encompassing paradigm. Microeconomists may object to the complexity and openness of my argument. However, their tighter logic and narrower set of assumptions fail to explain the realities of this case study and of similar events involving agricultural labor. Their approach also does not help in comprehending the transformations observed. I believe that to understand the labor process and the dynamics of the labor market—in this case, Colombian coffee agriculture—it is necessary to examine market exchanges within a wider gamut of interpersonal relations contextualized within local conditions.

1.2   Labor Markets as Localized Exchange Process

A 1975 national survey of Colombian coffee harvesters revealed that migrant laborers were hired only after all locals who were available were contracted (Urrea 1976). The crews of local harvesters included women, children, teachers, and many men who had other occupations during the rest of the year. Many of those who came from elsewhere did so because they had some connection to the region, either having lived there in the past or having kin and friends in the area. The local community was the context within which jobs were searched and bargained. It was clear that the survey that we were to carry out should also use local markets as the units of analysis. The validity of this decision was confirmed by our own findings and by a later national survey and analysis of wages.[2]

Geographers have argued for some time that economic activities are spatially organized. Lösch (1959) and Christaller (1966) pointed out that differential transport costs lead to the clustering of exchanges around equidistant centers. They also argued that commodities, which are more costly to market and have more irregular demand cycles, are likely to be sold only in strategically located centers. The competitive advantage of these centers was expected to foster their growth at the expense of other regional market centers. Skinner (1964) and Smith (1974) introduced some of these ideas to anthropologists, who have since used this framework to outline the historical transformation of commercial networks, the economic and political ascendancy of these centers, and the emergence of market communities. Sociologists have also assumed that labor markets are spatial units in their study of urban labor markets. However, these scholars have been more concerned with the limitations that costs and social identity have set on spatial mobility than with the hierarchy of labor markets. Horan and Tolbert (1984) have reviewed many rural and urban labor markets and have emphasized the importance of approaching the study of labor markets as localized exchange processes. Such studies reinforce the important implications of the idea that exchanges are geographically circumscribed by the cost incurred in the search for either jobs or laborers, by the cost of commuting to work, and/or by community identity. The geographic circumscription of supply implies that the availability of laborers is finite and demographically determined unless producers assume the added cost of transporting, financially enticing, or forcing laborers to work in areas beyond commuting distance. At the same time, since the significance of costs depends on the expected return, qualified workers who are seeking better-remunerated jobs are expected to be willing to travel further afield. In such an argument, the scope of local supply area relates to job qualifications: the area is greater for administrators than for unskilled laborers and greater for better-paid harvest jobs than for lower-paid maintenance work. (I am concerned in this study only with the two lowest tiers of the market, harvesters and field-workers.)

It would be an error to concretize the concept of locality and reduce it to transportation costs. As discussed in chapters 5 and 6, mobilization costs can be reduced through social relations. Laborers do not look at maps when they decide to go to another harvest. They call friends and relatives and bear in mind considerations other than costs and wages in their final decision. When they enter a market, they bring their own social identity, which may or may not differ from that of the harvesters who reside in the area. In other words, labor supply is not homogeneous or impersonal. It is internally differentiated into unknown outsiders, familiar migrants who come regularly, and local residents. Given that unknown outsiders are distrusted and even feared, degrees of identification with a locality are as significant as transportation costs. Laborers are likely to look first for a job in coffee agriculture within their local market area, then search for other unskilled jobs within the same area, and travel elsewhere only as a last resort. They also go mostly to areas that are both accessible and familiar to them.

The concept of local market, as Horan and Tolbert (1984: 11) point out, negates the notion of perfect labor mobility and allows the incorporation of social and cultural variables when mapping job searches, migrations, and seasonal intermarket linkages. Another advantage of a socially meaningful spatial framework is that it permits viewing rural and urban labor markets as integrated and for recognizing the significance of rural job opportunities for urban growth, and vice versa. Although the towns within the local markets selected for this study are too small to examine the role played by agriculture in the growth of commerce and industry, this issue must be kept in mind when analyzing coffee labor markets that are centered near industrial cities.

There is yet a more fundamental argument for grounding the analysis of labor markets within spaces or localities. If, as I have argued, labor markets are in part structured by political and social institutions, they will operate in different ways in unrelated social and political spaces. In his recent book *Work Place,* Peck forcefully argues for the incorporation of a spatial framework in the analysis of labor markets:

> Engagement with geographic contingency marks a step closer to the objective of explaining the workings of *real world* labor markets. This is important not least because labor markets are *lived* locally (see Han-

son and Pratt, 1995); playing a significant role in workers' lives. This matters theoretically because it concerns both how labor markets are experienced and how they work. What is at stake here is the status of the local labor market as a conceptual category . . . akin to a data-collection unit or a case study area. In fact, the local labor market has a real claim to theoretical status. (1996: 86)

If the daily social experience of laborers and the embeddedness of markets in political institutions are arguments for using a spatial framework, then the geographic identification of local markets must take these realities into account. Hanson (1992) suggests that the market region should encompass not just the sites where work is performed (in this case study, the coffee farm) but also where the labor is reproduced (the family), the social conditions of each, and the nexus between them. To do so in the case of coffee agriculture, the bounded local market must encompass the homes of year-round laborers and the geographic spread of their networks of close kinsmen. Hanson adds that it is also important to take into account the spatial distribution of sources of political control and the location of service centers. In Colombia the municipal townships have the capacity to administer and police their own rural areas. Banks, stores, coffee buyers, central government service centers, and FNCC agencies are located in the administrative centers of the smallest political unit, the municipalities. Even the lowest administrative tier of the FNCC consists of a group of coffee farmers in each of the municipalities where the crop is intensively grown.

For this study, I used municipal boundaries to identify the farms that fall within the local market. Year-long laborers also live within this area. The harvest does bring workers from further away, and, strictly speaking, one should include these seasonal satellite supply areas as part of the local market area. I did not do so because it would have been difficult to draw the boundaries before I was able to determine where the migrants lived. Furthermore, these workers come from similar families that share the same cultural background and work as coffee laborers in their home sites.

A regionalized description and analysis of labor markets opens the possibility for comparative analysis. Local market contrasts also help "elucidate the geographically varied forms and consequences of supposedly universal labor market processes" (Peck 1996: 110). Once the configuration of each local market is mapped, it is possible to examine market dynamics not just from an individual perspective of buyers and sellers of labor but also from an institutional perspective (Horan and Tolbert 1984: 34). Although the two local markets intensively examined in this study did not differ enough in their configuration to yield a rich comparative analysis, this tool was nevertheless useful in gaining a better understanding of such factors as the differential participation of women in harvesting labor crews and the use of contractors for the expansion of coffee groves. In the future, it would be useful to select and contrast local markets where farmers have differential access to power. All of these contrasts enrich the understanding of the dynamics of management strategies within the labor market. However, to pursue this point, researchers will have to develop a more precise methodology. Sociologists have done so for urban markets (Horan and Tolbert 1984), but rural sociologists and anthropologists are barely recognizing that labor markets in commercial agriculture are often localized, even when acknowledging, for example, that English farmers know the laborers they hire (Newby, Bell, and Saunders 1978: 156) and that "an overwhelming majority of hired hands in the state [of California] are residents of the communities in which they work" (Barnett 1978: 21). In the case of American agriculture, the omission results in part from a desire to examine the role of growers in the legislation facilitating the importation of cheap workers and to expose the distressing condition of migrant families. In the process, however, readers are left with an image of an agricultural labor force with no community identity. Studies of the organization of labor in coffee, cotton, banana, and sugar plantations or farms in Latin America say even less about labor supply unless it is mediated by contractors and brought in from elsewhere.

Bardhan and Rudra (1986) noted the fragmentation of rural labor supply areas into village markets in Bengal. In turn, Rao faulted economists and anthropologists for not fully considering the localization of supply and the regional integration of labor markets: "Even when economists reject the notion that the market is the sole arbiter of labour exchanges, the village is rarely recognized as one of the institutions influencing wage earnings, labour allocation and employment" (1988: 238). He added that conversely, "anthropologists and others tend to treat the villages as nearly autarchic entities whose internal rules shape the terms and types of labour exchanges" (238).

The special particularity of locality may not always be relevant. The modernization of commercial agriculture is likely to blur whatever local markets existed before, as has been illustrated by Etxezarreta for Spain (1992). Even in traditional agricultural systems, there may not have been any localized labor markets if contractors brought laborers and supervised their performance. A more recent variant of this strategy occurs when farmers enter into agreements with companies that assume full responsibility for the harvest and bring workers from elsewhere. It is well to keep in mind, however, that in the United States, a country with large commercial farms, migrants currently make up only between 10 and 20 percent of the agricultural labor force (Martin 1988: 74–98) and that most field laborers work full time and live near where they work (Buttel, Larson, and Gillespie 1990: 102–3; Barlett 1986). It is thus quite possible that some labor markets in advanced capitalist agricultural sectors are also localized or fragmented and that the movement of migrants may, at least in some areas, correspond to the geography of kinship and social networks (Attanasio and Schioppa 1991). Griffith (1993: 226) illustrates this point with a case study of a strawberry camp in California. In the local markets of Griffith's study, resident laborers perform 62 to 64 percent of the annual labor required. Wells (1996: 16) alludes to local markets to explain managerial tactics and styles of contestation by laborers in California's strawberry industry. Van der Ploeg (1992) echoes Wells's arguments, suggesting that the unifying tendencies of technological development and commercial centralization are often countered by differentiation at other levels. Generalized technological knowledge requires an understanding of local conditions. Following Van der Ploeg, Torres (1997) dramatically illustrates his point with the case of tomato production in Mexico: only local supervisors grasped how to contextualize new technology and how to make it work in that particular ecological and social niche. While Van der Ploeg and Torres use a more abstract rephrasing of the localization process than I do, they, among others, have recognized that localization does not necessarily disappear with modernization of farm management and capitalization of production. What, then, explains the coexistence of local markets with markets in which the supply areas are amorphous and the locus of the administration is not centered in the production area? A definitive answer awaits more information on labor supply sources and how those markets intersect.

The localization of coffee markets in Colombia has historic roots and relates to the strategy of using tenants and sharecroppers to clear forests and plant coffee trees. In chapter 2, I recount the relevant part of that history. In a way, this strategy was similar to the system used in Brazil after slavery. The only difference was that in Brazil, many of the tenants were Europeans brought specifically for that purpose rather than peasants from other areas, as was the case in Colombia. Once settled, the tenants became the localized labor force even when they left a particular plantation or farm. The other Latin American countries where coffee production was mostly in the hands of plantation owners or large commercial farmers were Puerto Rico, Guatemala, and El Salvador. In the first two countries the supply of labor was highly politicized through laws that forced Indians and peasants to work for wages on farms. In El Salvador peasants lost their land with the expansion of coffee agriculture and the abolition of *ejidos* (Williams 1994). They became dependent on plantations, sometimes near their place of residence. The emergence and sustainability of localized labor supply thus rests on a combination of the following realities: the demographic structure of the localized population, political power of farmers to co-opt the state to import laborers or to appropriate property, the cost of supervising occasional workers, the cost of attaching laborers to the farm, the economic return of share contracts, the productivity of laborers acquired through contractors, credit markets, and risks in commodity markets. In some cases farmers encouraged tenants to settle on or near a particular piece of land because they represented a political following.

The preceding list of contingencies narrows the definition of localization to the place of residence of laborers. It ignores the possible role of farmers' local culture in the determination of the labor process. Local producers often form tight cliques and share a perception of what is proper in labor relations and what contracts can be easily sanctioned. Local farmers often also share belief about what population sectors should be allowed to work. In other words, the producers themselves contribute to the definition of the supply area and the range of contracts that will characterize their producing region. For example, sharecropping has been adopted as the most viable production strategy by vegetable producers in the province of Buenos Aires except in those communities where most of the farmers are of Portuguese descent. They prefer other management strategies (Nemirovsky et al. 1997). Van der Ploeg and Torres imply this meaning in their use of the term *local market*. I add two other elements to my definition: most labor is performed by local residents, and these laborers have an attachment to the place where they reside.

1.3 Linking Levels of Analysis

Much has been written in recent years about the impact of the globalization of food production for rural laborers and families. Industrialized fruit and vegetable farms, using generic mechanical and chemical inputs, are becoming vertically integrated with processors and exporters that have become the key actors in the financing of production. In their drive to reduce costs and retain their competitive advantage and with the support of a rising neoliberal political elite, farmers opt for more economical workers hired only for the duration of a task who do not receive fringe benefits of any sort.

While this characterization has some relevance for this case study, there are significant differences. From its beginning, coffee production in Colombia was intended for export. The crop was initially introduced by owners of very large tracts of land. These landowners raised the money to grow coffee and hire laborers by mortgaging their property or by obtaining loans from merchant houses. From 1920 to 1940 most of these merchant houses were foreign monopolies that bought directly from producers and transported the coffee to specific foreign cities (Palacios 1983). Historians of coffee agriculture have documented the impact of international events and national policies in great detail. Eventually, the power of private merchant houses was curtailed by the FNCC as it gained wealth, national power, and international presence. The Coffee Federation became one of the major architects of the international coffee agreement that served to control the export of coffee (Bates 1997). While the collapse of the agreement curtailed the FNCC's ability to shelter coffee producers from the vagaries of the international market, the federation still has the capacity to help growers finance, export, and commercialize the bean. The FNCC also has continued to assume responsibility for research and training.

There is no magic formula for an analysis of local markets that incorporates local, national, and international developments, as Sanabria points out (1993: 195). In the past, Marxist scholars offered a framework, but it was overdetermined and could not account for variation in the historic trajectory of coffee production. In analyzing coffee laborers and labor markets, I propose that local labor markets should be studied using various perspectives that incorporate specific regional, national, and global processes as key factors that structure local markets rather than as externalities.

The first perspective is a historical account of coffee production for an international market. Although each of the farmers in this study has experienced but a fraction of this history, the collective representation of the most dramatic moments of that history remains for each of them as a text full of warnings and admonitions. Coffee historians have provided detailed accounts for each Latin American country, and chapter 2 briefly summarizes some of the historical realities most relevant for the regions of Colombia discussed in this study. These histories, as Roseberry points out, provide pictures of the internalization of the external (1995: 7). Political forces emanating from the centers of the world economy—London, Hamburg, New York—were reinterpreted in terms of local experience and retained as collective perceptions of what it means to be a farmer or a laborer working under the aegis of a national polity that can set the rules of the game and an international market that set the rules of trade. These perceptions shape farmers' trust in their own trade organization, their government, and their laborers. Likewise, these perceptions define how laborers view farmers, government agencies, and labor courts.

The second perspective can be gained by analyzing the different fields of power wherein farmers, traders, and laborers operate, as Roseberry suggests (1995: 7). Contestations at regional, national, and international levels are considered in relation to the discussion of prices, policies, and services provided by the government and the FNCC (see chaps. 2 and 7). The most powerful farmers, paradoxically, are not necessarily the most exploitative ones. To understand who uses power to bias contracts in their favor we have to examine the totality of the labor process. In chapter 3, I introduce the farmers and laborers who operate in each of the local markets. Although it was not possible to examine in great detail their local political connections and networks, a very sensitive subject, I do discuss some relevant information. I identify the farmers who have greater access to financial resources and are intimately connected with the personnel of FNCC's local committees.

Coffee production has specific requirements that constrain the management options available to farmers. These requirements also bring market power to laborers during the harvest. As Sanabria (1993: 196) suggests, a historically grounded approach must be contextualized within the specific dimensions of the required material conditions of production and reproduction. This third perspective is incorporated in chapter 3, where I describe the ecological setting, the technical requirements of coffee production, and the demography of labor supply. Of particular relevance are the technological constraints that were introduced when the FNCC encouraged farmers to adopt a new variety of seedlings and a new technology of cultivation.

This introduction has commented on a fourth perspective. It examines the impact of prices and policies on the management choices of farmers. It also considers how workers respond to wages and policies relevant to contracts and how they try to affect them. This study was timed to capture the impact of costs and prices on the management of the labor force. The 1980s were a worrisome time for farmers, who were still trying to cope with the abrupt drop in the price of coffee between 1977 and 1979. There was little hope of a change in prices despite some improvement for a short period in 1986. This study examines how farmers and laborers reacted to the changes in the commodity market and how farmers countered a loss of revenue. The initial assumption that price changes would affect wages and contracts in the labor market proved too simple, as I discuss in chapters 2, 7, and 8. While institutional arrangements were mobilized to shield the farmers from some of the consequences of these market developments, farmers were reluctant to openly tamper with existing labor-management strategies. Laborers were equally reluctant to abruptly change their job-search strategies or move away from the region. Instead, they honed their information networks, tried to consolidate relations with farmers, and suffered through. Neither farmers nor laborers stayed in these municipalities simply to invest or to sell services. They grew up in these communities where they have family and friends, and where they know how to play their social and political ambitions. Their responses to crises are thus complicated and protracted.

Although macro policies and shifting market conditions have affected the labor-demand cycle and agrotechnology, they have had no direct impact on the array of contracts used. Only the incidence of particular arrangements changed. Some farmers reacted to the market changes by increasing the use of occasional laborers, while others subcontracted tasks to a group of laborers. The managerial adjustments were adopted slowly and piecemeal. Ultimately, all farmers did reduce the number of resident laborers, but it took almost eight years and another slump in prices for enterprise farms to change some of their hiring practices and begin to seriously limit labor inputs.

Average real wages have remained relatively stable during the past decade despite decreasing prices. These paradoxical consequences of the articulation of the local and the global market are related in part to the FNCC's equally puzzling policy of subsidizing the expansion and intensification of coffee production (see chap. 2). The official average figures do not reveal, however, the wide dispersion of wages during the maintenance season due to the adroit manipulation of hiring practices by some farmers.

The FNCC policy of encouraging renovation of coffee groves has also led to a year-round demand for labor. Landless families have returned, offering farmers a supply of familiar helpers. Few have settled near the farms; rather, there is a tendency to move to towns and cities, where schools are available and where some family members may find other employment. These developments thus contribute to the linkage of rural and urban labor markets.

1.4   Commodity Analysis of the Labor Process

A commodity framework may not be appropriate for mixed agriculture, but it is warranted when studying labor markets in the region selected for this study. Travelers do not need census figures to grasp the significance of coffee agriculture for rural employment in Risaralda as they view slope after slope covered with coffee trees. It is hard to imagine local residents doing anything other than tending coffee trees and harvesting the berries. Urrea's 1975 national survey of the harvest labor force (1976) confirms the casual observation: 80 percent of harvesters listed coffee as their major occupation; only 7 percent said they worked most of the time in other agricultural activities. Although several crops were grown on these farms before the 1970s, historians have pointed out that managers did not always shift laborers from crop to crop. If laborers are not rotated from crop to crop within a farm, they will not profit from year-round employment opportunities that might open up if farmers follow the recent FNCC policy of agricultural diversification.

Regional specialization is not the only reason offered by scholars for centering the analysis of labor-market dynamics on specific commodities. Economists have convincingly argued that the levels of labor input and remuneration, two aspects of labor-market dynamics, relate not only to general economic conditions but also to conditions specific to the commodity in question—commodity prices, quality of labor required, and cost of technological improvement and inputs. Microeconomic models have provided powerful tools for examining for each commodity the appropriate level of labor input, the advisability of capital-labor substitution, and the likelihood that growers will be interested in technical innovations (Padfield and Martin 1965). Similar studies of coffee agriculture in Colombia suggested that growers are only likely to expand production and increase their demand for labor if the farm-gate price for coffee increases by 20 percent or production costs decrease significantly (Federación

Nacional 1985). It has been suggested that production costs can be diminished with a 10 percent reduction in wages and a 10 percent currency devaluation (Landell Mills Commodity Studies 1990: 11–15). Farmers also need the stimulus of and access to research organization if they are to expand production (Friedland 1984).

The agronomic characteristics of the crop also have an impact on the technology of production and on the use of wage laborers. Mann and Dickinson (1978) argue that capitalist agriculture is more likely to emerge in crops with short production cycles and in regions where diversification is possible. Capitalist farmers only engage in the production of crops with long cycles when the demand for labor or machinery is evenly distributed through the cycle. Crops with long cycles and intermittent labor demands are more likely to be grown by peasants, family farmers, or sharecroppers. Capitalists will be interested in these crops only if they can use a "marginalized wage labor force that is vulnerable to inequalities arising from ethnicity, citizenship status, and gender, and thus subject to greater control" (Mann 1990: 39)—and lower wages.

The botanical characteristics of coffee have had a decisive impact on the economic behavior of producers but not necessarily in the ways suggested by Dickinson and Mann. Farmers must wait three years after they plant new trees to realize returns on their investment, and there is a thirteen-year cycle of increasing and then decreasing yields. The seasonality of labor requirements adds another burden: it is difficult to attract sufficient laborers for the harvest when they cannot be offered employment the rest of the year. Yet both capitalists and small farmers have engaged in coffee production. Furthermore, they have not targeted a marginalized labor force. Instead, they have used a number of other labor-management strategies to cope with the problems mentioned by Dickinson and Mann.

A commodity approach must not be restricted to technological and agricultural constraints. As Mann (1990) points out, it must also consider governmental and institutional policies geared to control the production of certain commodities or to ease the burden and risks faced by farmers. For example, tariffs, export duties and international trade agreements have had an important effect on coffee production. Friedland adds that this approach must also include an analysis of labor-management practices, the social organization of growers, the organization of research and extension activities, and the structure of marketing and distribution networks (Friedland 1984). Several Colombian historians who have focused on coffee agriculture have used a broadly based commodity perspective to explain some significant transformations in the labor process. Machado (1977) has outlined the role of land and labor legislation in the eviction of tenant farmers from coffee farms; Palacios (1983) has examined the role of inflation, devaluation, taxes, and commercialization in the labor process; Arango has offered a careful study of changes in cost of production and financial policies on demand and wages (Arango, Aubad, and Piedrahita 1983). Their findings and explanations have provided a useful background for this study. A commodity approach to the study of labor markets in coffee agriculture that is more closely related to this study is Urrea's (1976) sociological analysis of the changes in the labor process occasioned by the introduction of *caturra* coffee trees to Colombia. These trees have a slightly different vital cycle, and the agrotechnology that FNCC agronomists recommended demanded higher labor inputs during the maintenance season. Urrea pointed out that these technological changes brought higher incomes: wages increased, and seasonal unemployment was reduced.

There is a danger of relying too heavily on a commodity perspective. A salutary exercise is to recognize that the labor process in coffee production differs in each Latin American country. There are, for example, some striking variations in how the labor supply sector is tapped, the extent of the demand for wage laborers, and the level of investment in labor-substituting technology. In Brazil, sharecroppers and attached laborers were familiar figures on coffee farms some thirty years after they disappeared from Colombian coffee agriculture. Although most of the upkeep in Brazilian plantations is now carried out by wage laborers, 57 percent of the laborers in the state of São Paulo were permanent workers in recent years (Welch 1990: 162), which is a much higher rate than for most farms in Colombia. Another striking difference is that in Brazil the nonresident occasional laborers are brought to the farms by labor contractors, who also serve as supervisors (Stolcke 1988). In contrast to Colombian farmers, Brazilian growers have adopted several labor-saving techniques (dry processing of beans, strip-harvesting, and mechanization) that, together with low wages, have made it possible for them to secure the lowest production cost in Latin America (Landell Mills Commodity Studies 1990). In Costa Rica, where coffee production is carried out on smaller farms than in Brazil, labor costs are reduced by using family workers as well as by centralizing the processing of beans in mechanized plants owned either by cooperatives or by private companies. These strategies have allowed Costa Rican producers to adopt new technologies and to attain by 1980 the highest yield per hectare in Latin America (Errazuriz 1989a). Coffee is also central to the economy of El Salvador, where the coffee farms on average are larger than those in Costa Rica and Colombia. As in Colombia, Salvadoran coffee growers rely mostly on nonresident wage workers and have well-maintained coffee groves. However, in contrast to Colombia, Salvadorans have managed to keep costs of production low by controlling wages and maintaining higher yield (Paige 1997). Guatemala, the Latin American coffee-producing country with the lowest yield per hectare, has managed to reduce production costs without modernizing the technology of production by tapping and exploiting a vulnerable Indian population neighboring the coffee producing region (Bossen 1982; Landell Mills Commodity Studies 1990). Coffee farms in Guatemala are much bigger than those in Colombia and the rest of Central America and are managed using a large number of permanent laborers (Errazuriz 1989a; Paige 1997). Some of these differences reflect the historical roots of landed aristocracies in each country and the state's ability to curtail or enhance their power. Other differences relate to growers' control over the commercialization of coffee and the significance of their exports in the international market. Brazil is the only country where the producers are protected by an organization comparable to Colombia's FNCC (Bates 1997; Zuleta et al. 1989). In the other Latin American countries, coffee organizations have either comparably less power and resources or represent only a sector of the producers. In Costa Rica, coffee growers are supported in part by the state and in part by processing and marketing cooperatives (Gudmundson 1995). In El Salvador, coffee processors have a separate organization from the one representing growers. Although producers have considerable political power, they have had to contend with government efforts to nationalize the export of the bean (Paige 1997). In other Latin American countries, the coffee producing sector does not play such a crucial national economic role, and their respective organizations do not have a significant presence in either the national or the international scene.

1.5   Design of the Research

I chose coffee as a commodity in part because it is a crop in which many farms specialize in the central region of Colombia. Equally relevant to my choice was the large amount of information available about present and past production costs, types of farms, and farming practices. The FNCC had carried out production surveys and farm censuses that I could use to delineate trends and to situate a regional study within the wider national perspective. A still more decisive influence was the existence of Urrea's nationwide study of the coffee harvest labor force. He carried out his monumental study in 1975, during the height of a coffee boom that revitalized the industry. With Urrea's guidance and that of many of his team members, we selected a number of possible field sites during the summer of 1985. After visiting several of them, two municipalities were chosen in the department of Risaralda, one of the major coffee-producing departments. Distance from the department's capital was an important consideration in the choice of sites for this study. Marsella had been surveyed by Urrea in 1975 and could be used to measure changes. Belén is located further away and is less accessible to laborers from other departments. Another important consideration was the willingness of local authorities to collaborate in our endeavor. We added a third municipality in Cundinamarca, a coffee-producing area that is more diversified than Risaralda and that has a different cultural tradition and history. Humberto Rojas was to supervise the survey of Cundinamarca, and a group of his students who were investigating farming issues were to interview farmers and laborers there. As it turned out, the task proved too burdensome given his previous commitments, and only partial information was gathered in this third field site. Consequently, I limit my detailed descriptions and analysis to the two municipalities in Risaralda and use the third municipality only to comment on our Risaralda findings. Although the information for Cundinamarca is limited, it offers a useful perspective since this department has a more mixed rural economy and is located near several major industrial centers.

The first step of this study was to repeat Urrea's harvest survey to determine what changes had taken place during the ten ensuing years. This period was critical because during that time more farmers had adopted the new higher-yielding technology that required considerably more labor input, and prices of coffee had begun to plummet. María Errazuriz and I designed a questionnaire to be administered to harvesters in Risaralda. A total of 388 harvesters were surveyed in Risaralda (217 in Marsella and 170 in Belén), and 105 were surveyed in Cundinamarca during the peak harvest period. In November 1985, we allotted two weeks for survey work in Marsella and another two weeks in Belén. The vagaries of weather affected the number of people interviewed in each municipality—it is hard to interview harvesters in a downpour. No attempt was made to prolong the interview period to capture the same number of workers in each municipality. The peak harvest period was coming to an end, and many migrants were returning to their homes. Had we extended the survey period in the second municipality, we would have captured a different moment of the harvest than that captured in the first municipality. The findings would not have been comparable. The harvest survey in Cundinamarca took place in April 1986. We repeated some of Urrea's questions to detect changes and possible trends. However, our questionnaire was much longer than the one he administered. Our survey included questions about residence, background, experience, migration, job searching, and employment history as well as information about the occupational history and experiences of other members of harvesters' families. Most of the questions were closed-ended to facilitate the administration of the questionnaire. However, questions intended to capture opinions, and preferences were left open-ended.

We sampled the farms where the interviews took place rather than the harvesters on those farms. For this purpose we used the farm registers kept by every FNCC municipal committee. Although the farm registers may not be complete, the omissions are not significant because they are likely to disregard only smaller farms that do not hire many laborers. We grouped farms in the register according to the size of their coffee groves rather than the size of the farm (5–10 hectares, 10.1–15 hectares, 15.1–50 hectares, and more than 50 hectares). Seventeen farms had less than ten hectares in coffee, eleven had between ten and fifteen hectares, nineteen had between fifteen and fifty hectares, and five had more than fifty hectares. We also considered whether the farms had traditional shaded coffee groves or groves planted with *caturra* bushes under sun or partial shade. If more than 35 percent of the coffee grove was planted with the new variety, the farm was considered technified. (An arbitrary proportion had to be used since conversion is progressive and few farms had totally replanted their trees.) Out of the fifty-two farms selected for the survey, fifteen fitted our definition of traditional and three were considered to be in an intermediate category. The other thirty-four farms had a high proportion of *caturra* bushes. Of the farms selected for our study, thirty-six were located in Risaralda and sixteen were in Cundinamarca. The proportion of each type of farm (by size and degree of technification) reflected the distribution of farm type in the farm register. The distribution of types of farms selected for our survey was as follows: seven traditional and seventeen technified in Marsella; three traditional and nine technified in Belén; and six traditional and ten technified in Cundinamarca. Finally, we also tried to balance the selection of farms to reflect their locations in terms of distance from the main township and altitude, two variables that are critical for the timing of the harvest, the competition for available hands, and the population of harvesters that could be attracted.

There was one deviation from our established selection procedure. We added one farm in Belén because it had reintroduced all-women harvesting crews. We wanted to look at that population given the relative absence of women in the harvesting population. However, I have excluded this farm from tabulations in the text where I discuss the activities and strategies of all harvesters. I use it only to consider gender issues in coffee agriculture.

Once the farms were selected and permission was obtained, the harvesters were interviewed as they rested or waited for the weighing of the coffee they collected. To ensure that no biases were introduced in the selection, all harvesters on each farm were approached until at least half of the harvesters on each farm were questioned. A team of trained assistants under the supervision of Errazuriz interviewed the harvesters in this survey. No statistics were kept on rejections, which were more likely to be motivated by tiredness and irritability than by reluctance to talk. Farmers, administrators, and resident laborers were interviewed separately during the harvest.

I spent two months in Risaralda in June–August 1986, the period of maintenance and unemployment. Errazuriz accompanied me during the first month of this field stay. We interviewed local laborers and their families in their own homes. With permission, some of these interviews were taped. No attempt was made to reinterview the laborers who had been surveyed. The laborers interviewed at this time were selected by their availability, making sure to cover different neighborhoods in each municipality. We were able to meet with thirty laborers and/or their wives in Marsella and with twenty-one in Belén. We talked to them about their work histories and their experiences in the past year. When possible, we tried to gather information about their parents. We also reinterviewed some of the administrators or owners of the farms in our sample. Again, some of these interviews were also taped with the interviewees' permission. To protect their privacy, I have changed the names used in this book. To gain a more complete picture of labor demand, we also interviewed a number of small farmers (twenty-eight in Marsella and fifteen in Belén) who owned five hectares or less in coffee.

Much of my time in Risaralda was spent reading documentary information locally available and meeting with residents familiar with town events. However, we made no attempt to reside on a farm. By not living in a farm and not working alongside other women, I may not have gained the full flavor of farmer-laborer relations; still, I hope that my experiences and close association with town residents who were laborers allow me to convey a relatively full picture of the structure of the labor market. I quite consciously avoided gathering information on the subtleties of local politics and how they reflected the management strategies of some farmers. Such an attempt would have compromised my position of neutrality and limited my access to information. Although my story is not complete, lacking much about the connection between power and management, and may not have the personalized flavor of many anthropological studies, it is an attempt to gain a wider vision of labor markets from the perspective of two carefully studied local markets and one brief view of another.

Chapter 2

Coffee and Labor in Colombia

The early coffee farms were manned by tenants and resident laborers (*agregados*). Fathers and older sons worked throughout the year planting, weeding, and maintaining the trees. Wives, daughters, and younger children helped during the harvest. As the trees matured and the harvest increased, occasional laborers were recruited to help pick the crop, but they were an incidental contingent of men who were relevant only during good years. Not until the third decade of the twentieth century, in response to rural violence and syndical movements, did landlords choose to shift from a predominantly resident labor force to crews of workers hired on a day-to-day basis. This change in strategy marks the beginning of what I call the second period in the history of the labor market in coffee agriculture. The memory of rural violence has made many landlords fearful of labor unrest, and this fear has been sharpened by the violence of the 1950s and the criminality of the 1960s. These memories have served to consolidate the image of labor relations as confrontational and threatening. The recent body of labor laws (see section 2.6) and laws pertaining to tenant contracts have further fueled farmers' fears and discouraged them from again relying on resident laborers. Farmers have remained particularly attentive to the possible presence of labor organizers. Yet by becoming totally dependent on a seasonal or occasional labor force, farmers have expanded a market for labor that they cannot totally control in an economy of fluctuating produce prices. This is the central characteristic of the third and last period. It started with a boom—an expansion and an increase in the cost of production—that was followed by a drop in coffee prices.

Farmers have avoided explosive labor relations during the 1990s because of improvements in living standards and because they have shrewdly chosen more effective management strategies. Coffee growers can also count on a powerful ally, the FNCC, to keep in place stringent labor laws (see section 2.5). However, this institution is not always an unquestioning partner of the farmers, and they do not always trust it. It is true that the FNCC has supported farmers when they faced labor confrontations, but it has not always protected their financial interests, thus compounding the impact of labor costs and the problem of labor contracting.

I begin this chapter with a brief review of the early history of coffee farming to outline the range of constraints that farmers have faced. As economic cycles come full circle, coffee farmers may again face the past pressures: shrinking returns, belligerent workers, competition with other sectors for laborers, and costly market regulations.

2.1   The Initial Expansion and Growth of Coffee Agriculture

For more than a century, coffee has played a key role in Colombia's economy. It has stimulated regional activities and has provided the country with a much-needed source of foreign exchange. By 1887 coffee represented 40 percent of the value of Colombia's exports (Palacios 1983: 70). It subsequently continued to gain prominence as an export crop, reaching 80 percent of the value of all exports in 1943 (Jimenez and Sideri 1985: 37). Only in recent years, as other exports grew in importance, has the role of coffee subsided. By 1965 coffee represented 65.5 percent of all exports (Kalmanoff 1968: 31) and in 1987 only 37 percent (Economists' Intelligence Unit 1988)

Coffee was first planted in the region bordering Venezuela, where cacao and tobacco had previously been the two major export crops. By 1870 coffee agriculture had spread south and west over the slopes of the central mountain ranges and into Cundinamarca; shortly thereafter, it spread west to Antioquia and then south through the departments of Caldas, Risaralda, and Quindío (often referred to as Old Caldas). This spectacular colonization changed the geography and economy of the region (Parsons 1968). Investors, speculators, engineers, economists, politicians, and well-established landlords cut down forests and replanted the mountain slopes with coffee trees, thus converting these departments into Colombia's major coffee-producing region by 1925 (Arango 1981: 92, 166; Errazuriz 1986: 45). This new Antioqueño elite began to overshadow the power of the old landlords, representing a new breed of entrepreneurs who were good at managing their farms and investing their profits.

The other well-sung heroes of the Antioqueño colonization were peasants. In 1932, 26.1 percent of coffee was produced on farms with less than three hectares in coffee. Most of these smaller farms were owned by peasants (Machado 1977: 125). However, many of these peasants did not have title to their land and lost their farms when the government put large extensions of public lands on the market (LeGrand 1984).

The conversion to coffee agriculture was as risky as it was dramatic. Farmers required considerable initial capital and a waiting period of several years before profiting from the sale of beans. Landlords and large farmers became indebted to foreign commercial houses and thus were very vulnerable to price fluctuation. Coffee farmers were seriously affected by a downturn in prices from 1897 to 1910. A large share of their debts resulted from payments to laborers, many of whom had to be brought from far away and lodged and fed. These costs became onerous during inflationary periods, when food was very expensive. Landlords also had the headache of attracting laborers during periods when they were scarce as a result of either civil wars or road-building campaigns. In response to these financial stresses and shortages of labor, coffee growers devised modes of production that allowed them to maximize returns and protect themselves from sudden economic shifts. These modes have been described as precapitalist in nature because they entailed sharecropping and/or some form of service tenancy (Arango 1981; Machado 1977; Bergquist 1973; Palacios 1983; Deas 1977, Ortiz 1989). However, large landlords remained vulnerable to market conditions. According to Palacios (1983: 460–64), only peasant producers were positioned to withstand these pressures; as a result, their presence persisted and remained significant through the first eighty years of the history of coffee agriculture in Colombia.

The 1920s marked a brief but significant economic boom, stimulated in part by high coffee prices. Colombian exporters, who had previously controlled the market, actively sought to purchase most of the crop. New monetary policies, however, limited their access to cash. They had become dependent on foreign credit and went bankrupt when the minibonanza ended. North American commercial houses filled in the vacuum and took control over the export of coffee until the 1940s. These commercial enterprises also assumed the final processing of beans, which since 1910 had been carried out in industrial establishments (Palacios 1983: 488–95).

The end of the minibonanza coincided with the depression of the 1930s. Prices began to fall in 1928 and remained below par throughout the next decade (Jimenez and Sideri 1985: 61). When growers encountered exporters' demand for a more standardized and better-graded product (Jimenez 1981: 55), they sought to increase yields by expanding acreage planted with coffee and by minimizing the loss of unharvested beans. At the same time, growers increased crew supervision to maximize quality. This solution implied higher investments in labor at a time when the wages of the seasonal laborers, who had to be brought to help with the harvest, had escalated. Unable to convince the government to bring in cheap immigrant laborers (Jimenez 1995a: 266), growers shifted the new financial burden to both their seasonally hired harvest laborers and their permanent crew of attached laborers or service tenants. However, instead of confronting workers with lower nominal wages, landlords lowered labor costs by enlarging the size of the measuring boxes, by prodding workers to hasten their pace, and by subcontracting some agricultural tasks. Growers also tightened their tenants' labor obligations and reduced the size of the plots given to the *agregados*. This dual strategy gave landlords a greater supply of laborers who did not have to be paid with cash and more room for coffee expansion. Landlords with a large number of *agregados* or service tenants were thus positioned to avoid cash payments to their laborers. The farmers who suffered most were those who relied more heavily on wage laborers (Jimenez 1981).

However, coffee growers could not afford to impose too heavy a demand on their laborers since these tenants also produced the food needed by the hacienda. The landlords also could not totally destroy the incentive built into the system for fear that their service tenants would not comply with labor obligations (Palacios 1983: 354–57).

The fine line between paternalism and exploitation disintegrated when the price of the food crops these tenants produced on their land allotments dropped, and their real wages decreased. Their plight had become too intense; they could no longer tolerate the extra demands made and lower payments received. They responded with strikes and violent action. Two areas intensively affected were southern Cundinamarca and northern Tolima. "By the middle of the decade, mutual aid societies, radical study groups, conspiratorial cells, Liberal dissidents and union activists were beginning to coalesce into a genuine revolutionary movement. Its principal expression was the Socialist Revolutionary Party" (Jimenez 1981: 64). The rapidity with which this movement spread surprised the Socialist Party and alarmed local authorities (Sanchez 1976: 76). Arrests and repression, however, did not stop the organizers. Protesters came to rely on a new ally, the recently formed Communist Party, which offered them logistic support and an ideological framework that helped give focus and meaning to their syndical movement. The central theme of this particular protest revolved around a series of specific contractual demands: permission to plant coffee on tenants' land allotments and replacement of rent in service with rent in cash. In other words, the request was for a market contract with fewer conditions attached to the renting of land.

The most successful confrontations took place between 1918 and 1936 on farms with large tenant populations—generally thirty to fifty resident families—where coffee was the fundamental crop (Bergquist 1986: 339). The syndical movement eventually spread to coffee-processing industries in urban areas (Machado 1977: 268–86). Many of these confrontations involved violent assaults on farm property and persons. The scale and intensity of the protests eventually alarmed the country and opened up a heated national debate over agrarian problems. The Liberal government had to intervene, and Congress passed Law 200, which set some controls on contracts between landlords and tenants. The legislation offered some concessions to tenants and protected landlords by circumscribing tenants' demands (Machado 1977: 287). The passage of this law and others like it (Ortega Torres 1980: 52–59) and the recommendation of the chief of the General Labor Office that landlords should sell some holdings and reinvest the money in processing operations (Jimenez 1995a: 264) helped to co-opt the rural laborers. Law 200 also frightened many landlords, who feared bureaucratic intrusions because many growers held faulty titles to their land (Bergquist 1986: 339). Some landlords responded by evicting their tenants; others, already near bankruptcy, partitioned and sold sections of their estate. The government did not proceed with the feared land reforms; it confiscated and parceled out estates only in cases of extreme confrontation between landlords and laborers and of disputed titles. These moves appeased the demands of many tenants, sharecroppers, and squatters. In most cases, the leaders of the Liberal Party sided with landowners, and repression quietly continued (Sanchez 1976: 124).[1]

2.2 The Expansion of the Wage-Labor Market

Thus, Cundinamarca's large haciendas disappeared. Fifty-nine percent of all coffee was now produced on farms with less than twelve hectares in coffee and relying mostly on family labor (Machado 1977: 124–25). Urrea (1976: 31) estimated that in 1932, 69 percent of those engaged in coffee agriculture were working on their own or their family's farms; only 7.7 percent were occasional wage laborers, and the rest were tenants or attached laborers. In time, acreage in coffee expanded and the market for occasional laborers grew.[2] By 1955 the proportion of occasional laborers had increased to 40 percent (Urrea 1976: 31). Although these estimates are highly speculative and should not be used to argue the precise historical evolution of the market for labor, they serve to illustrate the progressive shift in the organization of coffee farms during the first half of the twentieth century.[3]

Another significant event helped restructure the coffee industry during the 1940s. The FNCC, which came into being in 1927, gained new important functions. The government commissioned the Coffee Federation to regulate the quality of coffee to be exported and to supervise the sale of coffee to foreign exporters (a newly acquired legal right). To perform this role, the FNCC received the financial resources necessary to increase the number of purchasing agencies and storage facilities (Palacios 1983: 517–19). The Inter-American Coffee Agreement of 1940 may have been ill-fated, but the need to empower the Coffee Federation to regulate the market contributed to the restructuring of international commerce. Foreign commercial houses lost ground in their control of local purchases of beans and the export of coffee.

However, political unrest rocked rural society once again, although it was not necessarily sparked by labor struggles.[4] The upheaval had its roots in national party politics and swept through some rural areas like wildfire. Murder, revenge, and armed confrontations between liberals and conservatives led to the abandonment of many farms and to the exodus of both peasants and well-off farmers. It has been calculated that the *violencia,* as Colombians refer to this period, left 101,282 dead and led to the abandonment of 107,720 farms in the central coffee area of Antioquia-Caldas-Tolima (Ocquist 1978: 16, 19, 84). Although all strata of society were equally affected, all coffee regions did not suffer in the same way. In some areas, the peasants became implicated in the guerrilla movement; in others they became the target of extortion and theft (Ocquist 1978: 307). In still other areas *agregados* took advantage of their position and stole from or blackmailed landlords in complicity with guerrillas. Many landlords chose to escape, allowing opportunistic local merchants to seize farms (Ortiz Sarmiento 1985). Since land and harvest frequently changed hands through coercion, it is difficult to determine who profited from the improved international coffee prices that continued through 1958.

Although historians have described the human and political impact of the *violencia,* they can say little about how these events affected the organization of production. It is known that in areas heavily affected by violence, small industries and commerce languished, rural transportation of merchandise became dangerous, and an exodus of laborers occurred. Not surprisingly, in the areas that were more deeply affected by the violence, such as the municipality of El Líbano in Tolima, production decreased by 11 percent between 1942 and 1970 (Errazuriz 1986: 148).[5] In Caldas the shortage of laborers was resolved by reintroducing sharecropping (Arango 1982: 98–9). In other areas, landlords offered higher wages to attract footloose laborers from elsewhere. The FNCC chose to remain on the sidelines: between 1946 and 1955 the Coffee Federation suspended its annual meetings to evaluate national production and to announce policy directions, although it continued to perform its other technical, financial, and commercial functions (Errazuriz 1986: 130).

Regional upheavals, however, did not affect national production, which continued to expand. In fact, national production figures give no hint of regional struggles, changes in ownership, and reorganization of production. The average annual coffee output increased from three million sacks of coffee during the early 1940s to 7.4 million sacks during the early 1960s (Jimenez and Sideri 1985: 82). This robust growth was encouraged by price increases and the eventual peace negotiations between the Liberal and Conservative Parties. Although the central departments of Antioquia, Tolima, Cundinamarca, and the area known as Old Caldas remained the most important coffee-producing centers, a new one was added to the list: the department of Valle. The agrotechnology did not change: the same variety of trees continued to be planted under shade with very little fertilization. Yet despite or perhaps because of the simple technology, the increase in prices allowed healthy rates of returns to farmers' investments in coffee production. According to a survey, the rate of return was 21 percent in Cundinamarca, 48 percent in Caldas, and 70 percent in Tolima (Arango 1982: 47). The more recently planted regions showed the highest rates of return (see fig. 1). Furthermore, coffee continued to represent 80 percent of total exports (Jimenez and Sideri 1985: 113). But it would not do so for long.

Conditions changed by the mid-1960s. Trees that had been planted during the expansion of the early 1950s had grown old; about 60 percent of all coffee was being harvested from coffee groves that were more than fifteen years old. But farmers had little incentive to renovate. Real farmgate prices had plummeted. Furthermore, in some regions there was a resurgence of guerrilla activity that would eventually degenerate into persistent endemic criminality. Though coffee remained an important export, it shrank to about 65.6 percent of all exports (Kalmanoff 1968: 31). The

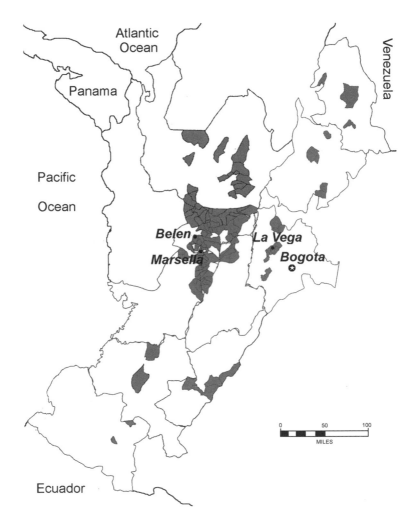

Fig. 1. Regions where coffee is the predominant crop. The shaded areas are the municipalities where by 1985 at least 50 percent of the land in coffee has been planted with the high-yielding varieties; the municipalities with at least 2,500 hectares in coffee, 30 percent of which has been planted with the new varieties; and municipalities with at least 5,000 hectares of traditional coffee groves. The municipalities are not classed by size of farm or coffee grove but overall production, hence they represent the regions with a labor market structure that replicates the characteristics of the one in this study.

real value of the crop decreased by 1.2 percent annually (Kalmanovitz 1982: 106).

Small coffee producers were now the ones to suffer most. During 1955–56 farmers with less than ten hectares in coffee produced 63.2 percent of the coffee (United Nations 1958: 27), but in 1970 such small farmers produced only 52.1 percent (Junguito and Pizano 1991: 87). Only those small farmers who also planted other commercial crops were able to sustain losses in coffee revenue. Peasants had a more difficult time.

The FNCC and the government attempted to ease the situation with price supports and export-retention policies and by searching for new markets in Europe. These measures helped but did not solve the plight of coffee farmers. More drastic policies were necessary, and the FNCC proposed a multipronged strategy. It lobbied for the International Coffee Agreement, which took effect in 1962–63. It was the first significant international agreement that included not only producing countries (as had previous agreements) but also consumer nations. It was renegotiated several times before its final collapse in 1989.

To conform to export quotas while servicing growers' commercial needs, new storage facilities were built. In 1967 the Coffee Federation inaugurated its first large coffee silo in Medellín. At that time, the FNCC had already accumulated 5.3 million bags of coffee (each bag weighing sixty kilograms). Given production estimates for the subsequent year, the FNCC had to be ready to store an annual surplus of 800,000 bags to conform to the new coffee agreement (Kalmanoff 1968: 75–78).

A second halfhearted strategy was to encourage diversification, targeting Caldas, Risaralda, Quindío, part of Tolima, and Valle as the pilot areas. This program sought to reduce the acreage planted in coffee, limit it to the most suitable altitudes, and diversify land use by planting other crops as well. Credit, rural infrastructure, and research on alternative crops were to be the main components of the program. However, the outcome of this policy was the reverse of its initial purported goal, since most of the research effort went to developing a more productive variety of coffee and an improved agrotechnology.

2.3   The Boom Years: Modernization and Expansion

The new agrotechnology recommended by the FNCC opened a new period in coffee agriculture that had a profound impact on the labor market. Colombians refer to it as the period of technification, and it was initially linked to the boom prices of the 1970s (the coffee bonanza). This period was characterized by the introduction of a new variety of coffee trees, *caturra,* that can sustain sun and be planted closer together. These denser groves have nearly four times as many trees as before—an average of 4,515 trees per hectare (Errazuriz 1989b: 11)—and can produce much more coffee if appropriately fertilized. The effect was an astronomical increase in yield per hectare from between five hundred and six hundred kilos to approximately three thousand kilos (see table 1).

Since the support that farmers received from the Coffee Federation (agronomists, credit, marketing agents, and a price-support system for coffee production) was not available for other crops, there was little incentive to consolidate coffee production and grow new crops on newly fallow land, particularly since prices for coffee were then quite high and the marketing of new crops was uncertain. Farmers responded to the encouragement to replant with the new variety not only by renovating existing

TABLE 1.   Coffee Production in Colombia by Type of Agrotechnology (in hectares and thousands of sacks of green coffee)

Year	Total Area in Production	Area in Traditional	Area in New Technology	Total Production
1955–56	686,240	686,240	0	7,100
1960–61	782,900	782,900	0	7,500
1965–66	—	—	0	8,223
1971–72	936,950	921,100	15,850	6,910
1975–76	927,600	806,700	120,900	8,760
1980–81	977,262	637,700	339,562	13,040
1985–86	938,445	544,100	394,345	11,900
1986–87	925,191	521,800	403,391	10,900
1987–88	942,750	499,400	443,350	12,700
1990–91	—	—	—	15,000

Source: The area in production for 1955–56 comes from CEPAL FAO Survey (United Nations 1958: 27); the production estimate for the same year is based on figures cited by Junguito and Pizano (1991: 37). The production estimates for 1960 and 1965 come from Banco Cafetero and are quoted by Urrea (1976: 24) and Palacios (1983: table 78, p. 521), respectively. Errazuriz (1989: annex 1) arrived at estimates for 1971 to 1988, and Junguito and Pizano (1993: 31) arrived at the estimates for 1991.

Note: Data on production are given in terms of number of sixty-kilogram sacks of green coffee. Area in production refers to estimates of area planted with coffee trees that are actually producing; the estimates can vary slightly from author to author. These figures are not comparable to estimates of areas planted in coffee since many of those trees are often too young to be producing or have been renovated.

groves but also by bringing into production areas that were scrub land, pasture, or planted with subsistence crops. Farms that in previous decades had diversified production by planting beans, corn, and sugarcane had now switched to a single crop. In the central coffee area the amount of land planted in coffee increased by 9.8 percent between 1970 and 1980 (Federación Nacional 1985: 6).[6] National output increased from 7.8 million sacks of green coffee[7] in 1970 to 13.04 million in 1980, with 63 percent of the production coming from the new *caturra* groves (Errazuriz 1989b: annex 1). This growth gave the FNCC greater international bargaining power.

The other appeal of this new agrotechnology is that planting trees closer together cuts down the cost of weeding and makes the use of fertilizers more efficient. However, the vegetative cycle of the trees is reduced by 50 percent, forcing farmers to renovate coffee groves much more frequently to justify the required higher rates of investment (Errazuriz 1989b: 12). Another drawback is that exposure to sun increases the risk of attacks by insects, viruses, and fungus. In fact, a fungus (*roya*)[8] has spread through most of these newly planted areas, forcing farmers to spray trees with copper oxychloride. The FNCC has subsidized the application of this chemical by covering the cost of fumigant and labor for all affected farmers, regardless of the size of their holdings.

The impact of this expansion and technological modernization on labor markets has also been staggering (see figs. 2 and 3). Urrea (1976: 31) estimates that the total labor required for coffee agriculture increased by about 28 percent between 1960 and 1970. Errazuriz (1989b: table 14)[9] has estimated that total labor grew at an average annual rate of 5.2 percent during 1975–78. Thirty-one percent of that labor was used to renovate and expand coffee groves. Since these tasks are carried out alongside maintenance tasks (absorbing 18 percent of total labor requirements) during the nonharvest period, laborers were fully employed throughout the year. Many families that had left could now return.

Well-off farmers who were able to renovate their coffee groves profited from the sale of bigger harvests at the high prices that prevailed in the 1970s. Smaller farmers eventually followed, but they had to wait until the FNCC began to help finance expansions with advantageous credit policies (Echavarría, Gaviria, and Téllez 1993; Ocampo 1987).[10] By that time, prices began to drop, and these smaller growers never fully profited from the bonanza. The end result was farms that required more labor during the nonharvest period and more chemical inputs. As prices continued

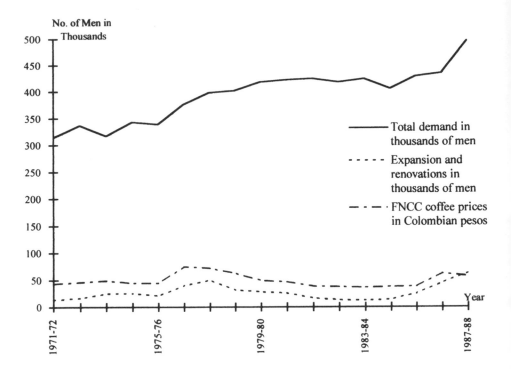

Fig. 2. Labor demand in Colombian coffee agriculture and FNCC coffee prices, 1971–88. The labor demand estimates are based on Errazuriz (1989b: table 14). She calculates that laborers work 260 days per year and that on average they harvest eighty kilograms of berries a day. See chapter 3 for a discussion of labor requirements and Junguito and Pizano (1991: 158–65) for a discussion of other ways of estimating demand. The total demand includes all tasks carried out on the farms. FNCC coffee prices are the amounts paid to farmers. Prices are given in Colombian pesos and have been deflated by the urban cost-of-living index (1978 = 100). Labor demand continued to increase until at least 1992, whereas FNCC coffee prices began to drop after 1987. By 1991 coffee prices were similar to those of 1980 (Errazuriz 1993).

to decline during the early 1980s—they dropped 52 percent between 1976 and 1983—farmers became concerned and began to reevaluate their investment strategies. They began to limit the labor used for weeding and cut down the amount of fertilizer applied.

Price changes also affected decisions about the renovation of coffee groves. *Caturra* trees should be cut down to between thirty and forty centimeters from soil level after the fourth or fifth harvest to encourage more

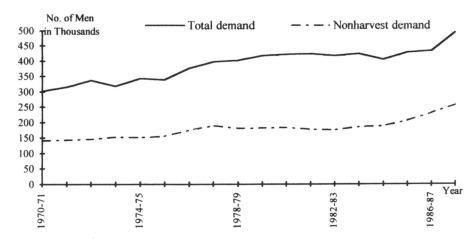

Fig. 3. Labor demand in men/year in coffee agriculture in Colombia, 1970–88. For a discussion of estimates, see figure 2. Nonharvest labor includes maintenance tasks, pest control, expansion, and renovation. Total labor also includes the labor to harvest and process the berries and beans on the farm.

vigorous new growth. These cut trees remain out of production for two years. Older trees should be uprooted and replaced with seedlings from yet a newer variety, *colombia,* that is as productive as *caturra* but is more resistant to plagues. In both cases the coffee groves hardly yield during the first two years. Farmers are thus more likely to take trees out of production to renovate groves when prices are low but will do so only if they expect favorable prices in the future (Ocampo 1987: 22–23). Otherwise, farmers will favor short-term returns and allow their trees to age. Growers also explained that even when conditions are opportune, they cannot afford to renovate more than part of their groves at any one time, with the acreage depending on the size of their holdings. Given these considerations, production trends are determined by the following factors: interest rates, internal coffee prices, changes in cost of production, land distribution, and climatic conditions that directly impact the productivity of trees.

2.4 The End of the Golden Era

The bonanza ended in 1981 when the international price for coffee returned to the same level as 1975. All farmers suffered, but small farmers were the most deeply affected since they had adopted the new technology late and had not fully profited from the high-price period. Medium and large farmers suffered less but were also affected since they were now saddled with newly established *caturra* groves that were more expensive to maintain. When prices were high, this added cost presented no problem. But in 1985 the added costs were burdensome and could not always be passed down to the laborers. Farmers also could not afford to let crops go unharvested, as berries lost meant still lower incomes. All farmers faced this burden after the bonanza of 1978. Many owners of medium and large farms had their difficulties compounded because they had borrowed money to improve their processing facilities to handle the increased volume of coffee berries, a key issue for a successful management of the harvest.

Thus, while growers still adjusted to market fluctuation of beans and input costs, they had lost some room to maneuver. It has been argued (Campillo 1985: 96; Errazuriz 1986: 260) that the economic situation was most difficult for small growers and that it led to the sale and amalgamation of farms. The FNCC has vehemently countered the charge that its new policies were responsible for the bankruptcy of small farmers. Given the available information, it is difficult to confirm whether at the national level fewer small farmers are involved in coffee agriculture.[11] In the municipality of Líbano in Tolima, for example, Errazuriz estimated that there was a sharp decrease in the number of farms below five hectares and a consolidation of land in farms between ten and forty hectares (Errazuriz 1986: 230).[12] However, in Antioquia neither the percentage of farms nor the amount of land held in small farms decreased during the bonanza (Arango, Aubad, and Piedrahita 1983: 16–17).[13] The 1994 census figures might provide the necessary information to determine which farming sector was most deeply affected by the sudden increase and subsequent drop in coffee prices and the adoption of the new technology. The issue here is not whether small farms can be equally productive but whether peasants and small farmers have equal maneuverability and access to credit resources.

The FNCC responded to the plight of farmers, and when in 1986 there was a sudden and unexpected—though brief—recovery of the international price of coffee, the federation pushed up the farm-gate price. Although it was soon reduced, farm-gate coffee prices remained proportionately higher than during the bonanza (Errazuriz 1993: 181; Montenegro 1993: 123). In fact, the FNCC had adopted a price-support policy, which pleased farmers but scandalized many economists. Guillermo Perry (1986) charged that the new policy was tantamount to a stimulus to production, and that the federation could not afford to store so much coffee. His prediction held, renovations continued, though not at a steady annual rate, and national production increased through 1992 (Errazuriz 1993: 182).

The increase in coffee production has been costly for the FNCC. Although the opening of European markets and the signing of special commercial arrangements with countries that are not members of the International Coffee Agreement helped to ease supply pressures (Leibovich and Ocampo 1987: 14), Colombia in the 1980s was producing well above its assigned export quotas. The FNCC had no choice but to store the beans that could not be released for exports. Ocampo (1987: 13) estimates that by 1985 the inventories accumulated were in excess of the annual export quota. The FNCC did not fully acknowledge the financial strain of its policy or its consequences for producers.

When the International Coffee Agreement lapsed in July 1989 and trading countries were unable to arrive at a consensus, prices became totally dependent on the weather and demand in a problematic international market (Junguito and Pizano 1991: 375). The FNCC could neither justify nor afford price supports and began to slowly lower them to match the international trend. By 1992 the Fondo Nacional de Cafeteros, an institution that finances subsidized purchases, was heavily indebted. Coffee taxes and retentions were not enough to shoulder a debt of $500 million. The FNCC had to unravel the safety net that it had offered farmers. It discontinued the sale of fertilizer at subsidized prices and reduced the number of loans for renovation and expansion. The federation also pushed for diversification and even uprooting of trees. By November 1992 the FNCC faced a serious financial crisis.

But it was too late. Early support policies and overoptimistic predictions had encouraged farmers to continue renovating. Most farms were now producing one of the two new varieties, and the trees were still young. National production after the 1991–92 harvest was 37.6 percent higher than after the 1989–90 harvest. Thus, despite the dire economic situation and farmers' attempts to reduce maintenance tasks, the overall demand for labor continues to increase. Although I have no detailed information for the area under study, at the national level wages have remained about the same (Errazuriz 1993: 187). In Antioquia, farmers are coping by shifting types of contracts and cutting down on maintenance tasks (Arango

1993). It thus seems likely that the managerial changes already noticed in 1985 in Risaralda have continued to be implemented. Difficult times eventually came to an end in coffee agriculture. In 1997 the international demand increased and stocks were depleted, and the FNCC relieved eight thousand coffee farmers of their debt burden and adopted a price policy that would pass on to farmers a greater share of the price gains (*El Tiempo,* 1997). The stimulus to significantly change labor-management strategies has once again disappeared. Thus, it seems likely that farmers will continue to adjust to cyclical changes as they have done in the recent past.

2.5   The Coffee Federation (FNCC)

Although the international market and commercial houses have a strong impact on production strategies, the FNCC's impact has been more significant during recent decades. Since the 1940s it has served as the voice of the growers. However, at times its policies have been at variance with their interests, representing instead more complex national economic interests. It is an organization of curious origins.

Palacios (1983: 509–10) captures the FNCC's character by describing it as a private institution that fulfills a public function essential to the nation. When first organized, at the turn of the century, the federation represented the top coffee growers in Tolima and Cundinamarca, but eventually its membership widened to include all kinds of entrepreneurs and small farmers.[14] In 1927 it signed its first contract with the Colombian government whereby it assumed some administrative and industry-research responsibilities in exchange for access to coffee-tax funds. The responsibilities were limited to the management of the agencies that purchase coffee, the control of name brands of beans, and the lobbying for special rates of exchange and for appropriate currency devaluation to ease competition with other producing countries (Palacios 1983: 510–13).

However, the FNCC did not gain real power until 1940, when the Inter-American Coffee Agreement was signed.[15] The government then had to control exports to conform to the quotas set by the agreement. To finance these activities, it created a treasury account (Fondo Nacional Cafetero) funded by a number of taxes. The most important tax is the coffee retention, which was enacted in 1958. In theory, farmers have to give the FNCC (free of charge) a stipulated amount of the coffee they sell. In practice the coffee retention tax is paid by the commercial houses and is reflected in the price they pay farmers. The tax was initially set at 10 percent, but it rose to 39 percent in 1973 (ANIF 1974: 31, 89) and, at times, to 50 percent, as in 1983. The second tax, instituted in 1967, is the ad valorem tax, set at 6.5 percent of the value in foreign exchange of the coffee exported. The FNCC has the power to administer the coffee fund and to handle the administration of the export quotas. The FNCC's regular operating budget is financed by the sale of low-quality *pasilla* coffee, which private exporters are required to contribute (the amount is set at 6 percent of the volume of their exports) and four percentage points of the export tax on coffee (Kalmanoff 1968: 55). These various taxes have engrossed the resources of the Fondo Nacional Cafetero, providing the FNCC with a patrimony equal to more than half the annual income of Colombia's government (Ocampo 1987: 228).

As part of the privilege of administering the resources derived from the taxes levied, the FNCC had to assume the responsibility of issuing certificates of origin for export coffee, handling the export tax, reporting to the International Coffee Organization, and supervising exports to ensure that they conformed to the established quotas. The Coffee Federation was expected to lobby for the maintenance or enlargement of Colombian quotas, to ensure that the international agreements were sustained, and to expand export markets as well as assume responsibility for keeping track of the statistical data on production and export.

This privileged financial and administrative position allowed the FNCC to participate in the creation of the Caja Agraria (Agrarian Bank), an organization that manages the loans destined for coffee growers. It made it possible also for the FNCC to contribute 50 percent of the resources needed to create IDEMA (the national marketing organization) and to finance and control the major commercial bank (Banco Cafetero) that operates in the coffee industry. The FNCC has also invested in a number of profitable commercial ventures: a shipping company (Flota Grancolombiana), a roasting plant in Buenos Aires, and a public-relations firm in New York. Because of its financial power and its semiofficial responsibilities, the FNCC has a presence in the administrative bodies of the national bank, the Caja Agraria, Caja de Crédito Agrícola e Industrial (Agricultural and Industrial Credit Agency), National Economic Council, National Agricultural Council, national railroad, and National Council of Cooperatives. Thus, the FNCC is in an enviable strong position to influence national government policies. Its voice cannot easily be disregarded (Errazuriz 1986: 95). At the same time, the Colombian government depends on the FNCC to reach some policy objectives: amassing enough income to service the International Coffee Agreement, maximizing foreign-exchange earnings, and insulating the economy from short-range fluctuations.[16]

The peculiar status of this private industry federation is clearly reflected in the dual character of its administrative organization. On the one hand, the FNCC has a central body headed by a general manager with considerable managerial autonomy and tenure security (there have been only two managers in the past forty years). It also has a national committee that includes several cabinet ministers (the ministers of finance, agricultural development, and foreign affairs) as well as the manager of the Caja Agraria. On the other hand, the FNCC's policies need the approval of the biennial National Coffee Congress, made up of delegates from the regional coffee committees. These regional councils, in turn, are administered by officers, some of whom are elected by the rank-and-file members. The higher administrative echelons have the dual role of channeling the interest of growers while helping the government enlist their support to advance national socioeconomic needs. This dual role is mediated by a civil-service-type bureaucracy that is well trained and efficient (Kalmanoff 1968: 54–55) but the balance between these two roles is not easy to keep. Regional committees have at times rebelled and have campaigned for congressional candidates who oppose the policies of the FNCC's central committee (Bates 1997). This dual role has also exposed the FNCC to criticism from Colombian economists.

The ambiguity of this role also manifests itself in the procedure used to set the internal price of coffee—that is, the price at which the FNCC commits itself to buy all coffee that meets a certain fixed quality standard. This price differs considerably from the international price and does not necessarily fluctuate at par with it (see fig. 4). In fact, the internal price for "federation type" coffee is not a market price; it is a policy price that takes into account the international price of coffee, the prices of other input factors, taxes levied on exporters, and the exchange rate of the peso. When setting the price of coffee, the FNCC has also considered the need to control production and protect producers from wide price fluctuations. During the years of boom prices, the nominal internal price for coffee has sagged below the international price (the internal price was only 23.7 percent of export price), while after 1987 the internal prices represented a much larger share. The significant point is not the difference between the two prices, since in part the internal price is intended to absorb the cost of processing and commercializing the bean, but the fluctuating ratio

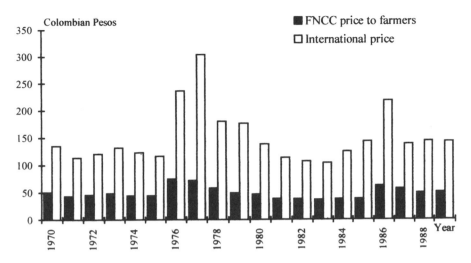

Fig. 4. FNCC price to farmers and coffee export price, 1970–89. The FNCC price to farmers and the international price are per kilograms of dried beans (*pergamino*). The FNCC price has been deflated by the cost-of-living index for urban workers (1978 = 100). The international price has been converted to Colombian pesos and deflated by the same index. The international price and the exchange rate are those quoted by Montenegro (1993: 108) and the FNCC (Federación Nacional 1992).

between the two prices. Figure 4 illustrates this point using real internal and international prices rather than nominal prices.

Growers clearly resent the FNCC's internal price policy. However, when the international price is depressed, the FNCC has incurred losses to support producers' income. Another important FNCC concern has been guarding the industry from production responses that are considered detrimental to the industry in the long run. The internal price is set by a committee that includes not only the FNCC's general manager but also the ministers of finance, agriculture, and development and the manager of the central bank.[17]

Because the FNCC and its auxiliaries—ALMACAFE and coffee cooperatives—are major buyers of the harvest, the official internal price affects the market price of all internal transactions. ALMACAFE owns storage facilities and purchases coffee mostly from the major producers. But the FNCC has helped to organize and subsidize a number of independent local cooperatives that buy coffee beans that do not meet the tighter institutional standards from medium and small producers. These cooperatives assume the cost of further drying and sorting the beans and then resell them either to ALMACAFE or to other exporters. For peasants and small farmers who cannot afford to fully process and upgrade beans, the alternative is to sell to local merchants at a lower price.[18] In other words, although the FNCC has some monopoly power over the market, it does not act as a British-type marketing board that excludes other middlemen. There are a myriad of small-scale middlemen and traders who traffic in coffee. There are also a significant number of private companies that handle the export of coffee. These firms are most active during years of high international prices: during one such period they handled nearly 70 percent of the trade. The FNCC normally handles about 60 percent of exports (most European exports) and takes on this task when private firms withdraw during periods when the international price is low (Campillo 1985: 67; Leibovich and Ocampo 1987: 9–11). The FNCC also has a monopoly over the distribution of coffee for internal consumption, which is an important source of revenue.

Although farmers regard the higher echelons as a distant bureaucracy, they are well aware of their dependence on many of the services the FNCC offers. Its presence in the major producing areas is very real. Municipal committees keep track of all affiliated farmers, the size of their farms, how they use their land, and the conditions of coffee groves. The FNCC is the only institution involved in researching coffee varieties and agronomic practices. It has one major center (CENICAFE) in Chinchiná, Caldas; six major experimental farms; and a laboratory to explore chemical inputs. FNCC agronomists visit farms to answer questions and give guidance. Extension courses are available locally to any small producer. More advanced technical education and training courses for farm managers are offered at the major research centers. The FNCC stored and sold fertilizer at subsidized rates and freely distributed fumigants against rust.[19] It has also organized friendship groups to discuss problems that farmers confront when trying to modernize their farms.[20] The best way to meet small farmers and peasant producers is to walk into the municipal offices of the FNCC on a Saturday morning. Tables are set up, and long lines quickly form. Meetings are arranged, and bulletin boards are covered with information.

Whatever the complaints, and there are many (London 1997), the FNCC is not an elusive bureaucracy. It is probably more accessible and more helpful to larger farmers, but it offers some services to all and provides an infrastructure that can be adapted to organize forums for small farmers. It can also help generate some sense of shared identity and bring together farmers over issues that concern all of them: prices, government policies, and technical problems.

The FNCC has invested a big share of its profits to build regional infrastructure, as required by its contractual agreement with the government. Between 1975 and 1985 the Coffee Federation financed the building of 2,106 aqueducts, brought electricity to 99,301 farms, and built innumerable schools and clinics and many miles of local roads. These activities have helped to redistribute the profits earned from the export of coffee during the years of high prices (Campillo 1985: 90).

The FNCC has not, however, been very accessible to the laborers. This organization has either remained silent or has sided with farmers on labor issues. In its 1984 document on coffee labor markets, "El Empleo y los Salarios en el Sector Cafetero," the FNCC advised farmers to handle shortages of labor by helping workers to settle locally and by readopting the use of share contracts (Federación Nacional 1984a: 21) instead of suggesting higher wages and fringe benefits. At the same time, the FNCC has been unwilling to openly annoy laborers by siding with farmers when, as in 1958, they requested a governmental exemption from family subsidy payments, severance compensation, and workday regulations. The FNCC supported the farmers' request only as a one-year exemption to help them through the post-*violencia* recovery period. Publicly, the FNCC balanced its slight critique of managerial practices by unleashing a lively condemnation of the inadequacies of labor legislation and its abuses. It has also ignored the many newspaper exposés of working conditions on coffee farms.

In 1978 the FNCC participated in a plan designed by the Ministry of Labor and Social Security, with the financial support of the International Labour Office, to aid migrant laborers in coffee regions. The FNCC offered financial aid only to erect small local centers that could serve as way stations for migrants. No lodgings were offered, but these centers provided information about local jobs, access to clinics and showers, and other minor services. The original program had envisaged other services: radio information on labor-market conditions, supervision of available housing on farms, vaccination campaigns, nutrition programs, and training courses in efficient and safe fumigation. Some of these proposed activities required the cooperation of many government agencies. As the supply of laborers increased, these agencies lost interest. By 1985 very few of the centers or their activities remained; the legacy of this movement was minuscule.

One probable reason for the dismantling of much of the program for migrant laborers lies in the fear that it would stimulate and help to coordinate industrial action. This concern manifested itself in the second meeting of the CERSI (Rural Centers for Integrated Services), at which a resolution was passed that explicitly forbade CERSI personnel from trying to mediate labor disputes (Marmora 1980: 30). CERSI's workers were only to direct the concerned parties to the offices of the Ministry of Labor and Social Security and to offer information if laborers requested it (Marmora 1980: 46). The FNCC's silence about this program and about work conditions on many coffee farms makes it impossible to determine the organization's role in curtailing actions that could have empowered laborers to bargain more freely for wage and working conditions.

2.6   Labor Movements and Labor Unions

With the displacement of the attached laborers or service tenants who were at the helm of these early movements, the leagues and syndicates shriveled. Gilhodes (1972) argues that this development resulted from the emergence of an antirevolutionary climate once the former tenants acquired land. They became incorporated into traditional regional life as peasants and lost their identification with landless laborers. Palacios even questions whether the peasant leagues would have spread across all the coffee regions to form a real national social movement (1983: 400). LeGrand also argues that these movements were a popular type of agrarian reform rather than industrial action by a proletariat (LeGrand 1984: 44). She argues that tenants, colonists, and landlords were fighting over rights to public-domain lands rather than about labor relations. "Tenants, rural day laborers, construction workers, plantation hands, all turned their sights towards the land because other economic options were few and because the government's agrarian policy made the reclamation of public lands a distinct possibility" (LeGrand 1984: 46).

However, memories of violence have served as reminders of how bitterly laborers can confront landlords. In some areas like "Red Viotá," the Communist Party remained active and has continued to act as a wedge in labor-relations negotiations on large farms. In other areas, including Sumapaz in Cundinamarca and Villarrica in Tolima, laborers' hostility resurfaced in the form of armed groups during the *violencia* of the 1950s.

Quindío and Caldas experienced similar struggles. However, the brutal confrontations during the *violencia* often lacked a clear trade-union focus or a social platform. They were subsumed under caudillo politics and hence did not generate grassroots organizations or bureaucratic frameworks that could serve to organize labor syndicates.

Nevertheless, wage strikes did erupt, and haciendas were once again invaded during the 1960s. Some of these movements were draped in the banner of the Communist Party or the ANAPO Party and became enmeshed in electoral campaigns, particularly in Montenegro (Quindío) and Viotá (Ruiz Niño 1983: 13). However, the politicization of litigations once again failed to provide laborers with a platform that could help build a strong union movement. Yet out of this history some trade unions did emerge: one of them was the Union of Coffee Laborers, headquartered in Armenia, Quindío (Ruiz Niño 1983: 58). However, there is little information about these unions' presence or activities.

Some attempts to organize the agricultural labor force occurred during the 1970s. The ANUC, a peasant league originally organized under the aegis of the government of Lleras Restrepo in 1968, reconsidered its mission and tried also to attend to the needs of landless laborers. In its 1972 manifesto (ANUC 1975), this organization stated that it represented not only peasants and tenants but also the coffee proletariat in the struggle against rural poverty. However, the ANUC's commitment remained verbal, and its efforts never came to fruition. Zamosc (1986: 243) cites a single attempt in Chinchiná, Caldas, in 1976 when the ANUC tried to organize massive stoppages and encouraged laborers to demand a wage of $200 instead of the prevailing $120. This attempt was thwarted by the landlords' alliance with the local administration: the police arrested all workers who did not have jobs and the governor of Caldas helped to bring workers from elsewhere. Eventually, the laborers and labor organizers quarreled among themselves, and the efforts to organize industrial actions failed (Zamosc 1986: 145). Ruiz Niño, however, suggests that the ANUC intervened positively in Valle and Tolima, but she gives no further details (1983: 55).

Part of the ANUC's problem was identifying the enemy. The owners of large estates and the FNCC were obvious targets. However, the line between them and struggling producers was difficult to define. ANUC considered it unfair, for example, to force confrontations between peasants and "the middle bourgeoisie or the national agrarian bourgeoisie" (ANUC 1975: 82)—that is, farmers with ten to fifty hectares of land, a group that included most of the central area's coffee growers. Whereas this situation presents no problem when conflicts over land are an issue, it becomes a quandary when wage negotiations are at stake. As section 7.3 shows, these "bourgeois growers" often engage in the most exploitative contractual agreements.

It is understandable why the ANUC would consider the FNCC an archenemy. First, the higher administrative echelons are staffed by persons from well-established coffee families. Second, since the 1930s the FNCC has sided with landlords in confrontations over wages. The federation opposed the government's attempt to mediate the labor disorders of the 1930s and proposed the passage of a later law that gave farmers greater protection from tenants' potential demands. It is also clear that while the FNCC provides services to peasants, it is more attentive to their needs in areas of political unrest.

The dearth of unions also results from management strategies and labor laws that hamper union activities. During the harvest, when laborers have some market power, the turnover of personnel on farms is considerable. Laborers move from farm to farm searching for better deals, knowing that their presence is needed only if there are ripe berries to be picked. Furthermore, many harvesters have only a marginal commitment to the job since they have another occupation the rest of the year. The best that a union organizer can hope for is to identify already verbalized complaints and help to spark a brief but effective grassroots stoppage. There have been, in fact, many short-lived and successful stoppages over such issues as piece rates and food and living conditions. Many of these stoppages were settled quickly and went unnoticed. In most cases, they were truly grassroots stoppages, not aided by experienced organizers. Once the disputes were settled, the collective action ended. Although these strikes are short-lived and farm-specific, they do have a significant impact on earnings since laborers will not accept lower piece rates on other farms after they have successfully gained a raise.

It is even more difficult to organize stoppages during the nonharvest period. Farmers still hire laborers for a few days at a time, but the composition of crews shifts constantly. Moreover, during this season there is a shortage of jobs, and farmers do not feel pressed to get work done. They can ignore demands and stoppages and wait for the confrontation to calm down before recruiting a new crew to complete the required task.

Only on farms that have a large number of resident or permanent workers can organizers hope to bring about concerted and sustained action. Even on these farms the organizers face serious obstacles. One of the difficulties is that legislation in effect from 1940 through 1990 protected farmers and handicapped labor leaders. Farmers are allowed to hire laborers for a probation period of sixty days, during which they can be fired without explanation or compensation. Union organizers who took permanent jobs on large farms had to wait a long time before allowing their views to be known. Furthermore, they were not allowed to organize unions in establishments that employed fewer than twenty-five permanent workers, and most farms had a much smaller number of permanent workers. There are other cumbersome limitations to legal industrial action: grievances must first be discussed with farmers and submitted to the Labor Office for mediation; only when this procedure fails is strike action considered admissible and legal. It is thus not surprising that there have been few unions in the coffee region and that they seldom managed to confederate at a regional or national level.

I know of only one recent case of sustained labor protest in Risaralda. It took place on one very large farm in one of the municipalities studied. The incident concerned working conditions for the resident laborers. The organizers followed the required legal procedure and, after some pointed confrontations, submitted their complaint to the Labor Office for mediation. No clear record of the event was available in the Labor Office, and informants either did not know the details or did not want to talk about it. The matter was eventually closed, but workers were fired and the farm retained a bad reputation.

In other agricultural industries, workers have organized unions and sustained strikes. The most violent were the strikes against the United Fruit Company in the "banana zone" between 1924 and 1928 (Urrutía 1969). In recent years, at least 17.8 percent of the banana plantations in Urabá have become unionized, and the unions organized strikes on 14.3 percent of these plantations (Herrera and Botero 1981: 96). However, many union leaders have been murdered, and the area has been caught in a spiral of violence. Sugar plantations also have been unionized. However, in the industrial plantations the management has diffused union power either by creating company unions or by delegating the hiring and supervision of field hands to contractors (Knight 1972: 91–109).

Most of Colombia's labor legislation does not apply to the agricultural sector. Recent labor legislation protects only permanent laborers—

that is, those who are retained on the farm after the sixty-day probation period. The central component of this legislation is the protection against "unjust dismissal." Employers must compensate workers if they are fired without due cause after the trial period. The stipulated severance pay equals forty-five days of wages for each year worked on the farm. Not needing the services of the laborers is not considered just cause. Laborers can challenge the decision and payment received by bringing their cases to the labor court. Employers fault the court for a bias in favor of laborers, whereas the latter insist that the opposite is true. The records in Risaralda are so incomplete that it is impossible to decide which view is correct (see section 7.5). However, there is no question that there were many cases of dismissal without just cause, and that laborers seldom received the compensation owed to them. Furthermore, very few rural laborers qualify as permanent workers. Since the cost of severance pay increases with length of employment, many landlords routinely fire their permanent workers and rehire them a month later, thus avoiding severance wages.

Another important component of the labor legislation is the requirement that workers must be paid at least a minimum wage set by the government. The National Wage Council, which includes representatives of various ministries and the major labor confederations, is responsible for computing and periodically revising the minimum wage. But many years can lapse before this wage is revised. In previous decades the wage varied from region to region and between rural and urban areas. A single standard minimum wage has recently been set, but it is widely disregarded in most rural areas except when the pressure of demand during the harvest forces conformity to the law.

Permanent laborers also have the right to receive a number of fringe benefits:

1. A family allowance that provides benefits for dependent children when the family income falls below a set figure. This benefit is paid directly by the employer.
2. An annual bonus equal to one month's pay, half paid in June and half in December.
3. A benefit to cover nonoccupational illness, employment injury, and maternity leave, financed by a social security tax that all employers must pay and a 2 percent levy on employees. The availability of this benefit, however, hinges on the existence of a regional social security agency.

These fringe benefits cost farmers 26.4 percent of the wage, according to the 1968 Ministry of Labor annual report, but very few workers receive them (International Labour Office 1970: 205). The Ministry of Labor is supposed to send inspectors to check for compliance, but they rarely travel to rural areas. Alternatively, laborers or their representatives could bring complaints to a labor office. However, without union representation, laborers' testimony has little weight. In sum, rural laborers receive very little protection and cannot effectively complain about noncompliance with labor legislation. They have no representatives. Only during the harvest, when they have considerable market power, are they able to bargain for better rates and conditions.

Chapter 3

Risaralda and Cundinamarca

3.1   The Significance of Coffee in the Regional Economies

The virgin mountains of Cundinamarca and Risaralda offered the intrepid
colonizers of the nineteenth century ideal conditions for coffee agriculture.
Since then, both regions have been major contributors of beans for
export.[1] When the FNCC introduced new varieties of coffee together with
credit incentives and other subsidies, Risaralda's farmers enthusiastically
accepted the new technology and proceeded to uproot other crops and
denude the mountain slopes of shade trees. Only in the lowland valleys
unsuitable for coffee do cattle still graze and sugarcane wait to be harvested.[2] Conversely, Cundinamarca's topography and climate have
encouraged diversification. While farmers still plant coffee in what were
once frontier areas, this crop now competes for labor and land with potatoes, sugarcane, and cereals.[3] Furthermore, coffee growers in Cundinamarca have not responded to price incentives with the same swiftness as
their counterparts in Risaralda.[4]

Coffee agriculture provides jobs for 22 percent of the Risaralda's
employed population and has invigorated the commercial life of many of
its municipalities. Although there are other industries, they cluster around
the department's two major cities. But even in these areas, industrial production is limited mostly to food-processing firms; and their output in
1986 represented only 2 percent of national industrial production (in terms
of value added). There has subsequently been continued industrial growth,
but not at the same rate as that of other centers. Conversely, the industrial
production of Cundinamarca's large cities and small manufacturing towns
in 1986 represented 4 percent of the national total. Furthermore, the
region is located near Bogotá, where most industrial production is located.

Although employment opportunities outside the agricultural sector
are limited in both departments, there are significant differences between
them. The men and women of Risaralda who wanted to stay near their
hometown had little choice of employment in 1985–86. They were limited

59

to jobs in construction or the service sector. In our interviews they indicated that in Pereira (Risaralda) they had worked as watchmen, in construction, or as domestics. Some eventually managed to find employment in the commercial sector, either in shops or as vendors in the thriving street bazaar. Cundinamarca's rural dwellers did not have to go far to find employment in commerce or industry (see table 2). They had to travel only to Bogotá, a short bus ride away. Risaralda, however, is surrounded by departments that share a similar economic structure.

Limited opportunities do not necessarily imply greater poverty. During boom periods, coffee can put money into pockets and local government coffers. Local laborers talked about the good years of the 1970s and early 1980s, when they improved their houses or built new ones and bought television sets (see appendix C and fig. 17). The boom years also brought a new life to old towns as local governments and the FNCC built new roads and opened clinics and schools. At the same time, regions so dependent on coffee can suffer when the internal price of the commodity drops, as it did dramatically in 1981 and again in 1992.[5] In rural areas, seasonal unemployment has seriously affected the welfare of working families and has reduced local commercial activity.

The contrast between the departments is immediately apparent when visiting the three municipalities examined in this study. Marsella and

TABLE 2.   Employment by Sectors in Cundinamarca, Risaralda, and the City of Bogotá, 1973

Sector	Risaralda % Employed	Cundinamarca % Employed	Bogotá % Employed
Agriculture	33.6	57.4	1.7
Mining	0.1	1.4	0.4
Industry	15.0	9.4	21.8
Construction	3.3	3.5	7.4
Commerce	13.9	5.7	16.5
Service	20.8	16.9	36.7
Other	2.4	1.5	7.7
No information	9.3	2.7	7.3
Totals	98.4	98.5	99.5

Source: Derived from Departamento Nacional 1986b.

Note: The percentages refer to men and women over ten years of age who were either engaged in work during the week of the census or had been looking for work during that week or the previous week. These figures include people who have been working without remuneration in family enterprises.

Belén are transformed by the harvest from charming, sleepy towns to tense settlements bustling with newcomers. When the harvest ends, commercial activity slows to a crawl, visitors seldom venture into the area, and traders come and go within a day. The lack of good transportation and lodging limits the length of business trips. Visitors to Marsella and Belén who persevere find pleasant walks along traditional streets and enchanting vistas of the countryside. By contrast, it is much easier to arrange for a short stay in the Cundinamarca town of La Vega. Close enough to Bogotá to attract weekend visitors, La Vega has encouraged the building of small hotels and the transformation of many old coffee farms into inns. Although the town is not a bustling resort center and its commercial life is not even as lively as that of Belén, there are many more employment options than in the Risaralda towns. Yet despite all of these differences, those who work on the coffee farms of Cundinamarca do not seem to have experienced life differently from their counterparts in Risaralda.

3.2 Population and Migration

Marsella and Belén became municipalities in 1867 and 1880, respectively. At first they grew at a rapid rate, when the prospect of virgin farmland attracted immigrants from other areas. In time, civil strife and economic recessions brought hunger and desperation. Laborers and sharecroppers went looking for cheap frontier land elsewhere or sought jobs in big cities.

The civil strife known as the *violencia* that whipped through rural Colombia during the 1950s also contributed to the continued exodus of rural dwellers in Risaralda (see section 2.2). Belén suffered from the beginning, and Marsella, though spared, must have felt the tremors of events in Pereira, a city a short distance away (Ortiz Sarmiento 1985: 371). At first, rural dwellers took shelter in the regional towns. Eventually, as their lands were usurped and members of their families were killed, many left the area altogether. No one was spared: landlords, peasants, and laborers suffered equally, sometimes at the hands of neighbors or tenants, sometimes at the hands of strangers. Risaralda, like many other coffee regions, lost much of its population and sense of peace during that period. Calm was not restored even after peace was reestablished by the Frente Nacional. The *violencia* had destroyed the fabric of civil society and social morality. Thefts, holdups, and nonpolitical kidnappings became common during the 1960s, particularly in Belén (Ortiz Sarmiento 1985: 372–75). It is not surprising that well-to-do farmers even now prefer to pay their laborers in town, where there is more protection. As criminality began to subside in the late 1960s and jobs became more plentiful during the boom of the 1970s, Risaralda once again became able to retain its residents and attract the descendants of those who had left (see table 3). Yet suspicion still prevails. Landlords are sensitive to questions about profits and labor relations, offering vague answers. Belén's police station prepared itself for a potential or imagined guerrilla attack during the harvest of 1985 and the police were suspicious of the work and presence of our field staff.

Cundinamarca was not immune to the loss of its rural population. For quite some time patrimonial land was too small to allow all sons to stay in the region. These sons of the peasants who had helped to open the coffee frontier in Antioquia and Old Caldas now had to migrate elsewhere. They migrated to cities and to the Amazonian frontier. Although Cundinamarca was also affected by the rural unrest of the *violencia,* not all municipalities suffered in the same way. La Vega was spared and was only briefly touched by the criminality of the 1960s.

In 1975 the population of the three municipalities could not meet the new demands of the coffee harvest. Farmers had to attract laborers from elsewhere. Since the municipalities of Risaralda are surrounded by others that suffered a similar exodus, farmers had to entice harvesters from more distant regional towns and cities. However, coffee growers in La Vega did not have to travel further than Bogotá to assemble a crew of workers. Nevertheless, the pressure of the harvest is keenly felt by all; it has pushed wages above those of other agricultural industries. Although old residents

TABLE 3.   Population by Department, 1951–85

Department	1951	1964	1973	1985
Risaralda				
Total Population	307,805	437,210	498,609	652,872
% Rural	62.0	47.0	35.0	30.6
Cundinamarca				
Total Population	1,607,910	1,122,213	1,125,642	1,512,928
% Rural	47.2	71.2	63.8	55.4

Source: Data for 1951, 1964, and 1973 were based on Departamento Nacional 1986a. Data for 1985 are the adjusted figures of the 1985 census quoted in Departamento Nacional 1990.
   Note: The census considers as rural all population that resides outside towns and cities with more than 1,500 inhabitants.

have returned and migrants have settled in towns and rural neighbor-hoods, it is unlikely that population will grow fast enough in the near future to satisfy the demand for berry pickers (see table 4). Young men and women are marrying late and are having fewer children (see section 4.2).

3.3   Land and Coffee Agriculture

Coffee agriculture in Colombia has been characterized as a small-farm enterprise. Relative to Guatemala and El Salvador, this characterization is appropriate. While it is true that most of the Colombian coffee groves are small or medium sized, in departments with diversified agriculture these groves may be part of much larger farms. For this reason I give both land and coffee-grove distribution figures for the municipalities in the survey.

In the two Risaralda municipalities studied, most of the land was con-centrated in well-managed farms of between 5.1 and 10 hectares in 1985, and most coffee groves were of similar size (see table 5).[6] Before 1970, when coffee was planted under shade, there was an even greater number of small farms producing coffee. However, some of them went bankrupt when trying to convert to the new varieties. It is quite possible that the cof-fee crisis of 1992 may have forced more small coffee farmers to sell their land.[7]

TABLE 4.   Population in the Three Municipalities of This Study, 1985

Municipalities	1951	1964	1985
Marsella			
Total		20,733	20,985
% Rural		70.3	56.1
Belen			
Total		31,051	24,146
% Rural		80.5	58.1
La Vega			
Total	9,604		9,977
% Rural	89.6		76.1

Source: 1951 figures are based on Departamento Nacional 1951; 1964 figures on Departa-mento Nacional 1964; 1985 figures on Departamento Nacional 1985a.

Note: The census defines as rural the population that lives outside centers with more than 1,500 inhabitants.

At one time Risaralda was self-sufficient in food production, but now only 590 hectares (2.8 percent of the land suitable for coffee) is planted with food crops. Land at higher elevation within the coffee region is reserved for pasture (21.2 percent of agricultural land) since it is too cold for coffee. The lands that are still planted in sugarcane and fruit crops are located in the lower valleys not suitable for coffee (Federación Nacional 1980: 42).[8]

In La Vega, also, most coffee farmers own 5.1 to 10 hectares of land (see table 6), but only about half of the land they own is planted with coffee; 10 percent is planted with other crops, and the rest is in pasture. Table 6 does not include farms that have no coffee trees.

The 1970 coffee census reflected a national pattern of land distribution in coffee that is similar to the one indicated in the tables 5 and 6. The 1970 census, however, records the extension of land in coffee by municipality rather than by grove size or farm size. I can illustrate the representativeness of the three municipalities (see fig. 5) only by comparing it with another major coffee-producing municipality in a neighboring department (Errazuriz 1986).

TABLE 5.   Distribution of Ownership of Land and Coffee Groves by Extension in Hectares in Two Municipalities of Risaralda, 1985–86

	Marsella			Belén		
Extension in Hectares	% of All Land	% Land in Coffee	% of Coffee Groves	% of All Land	% Land in Coffee	% of Coffee Groves
0–2	3.5	4.7	25.9	3.5	5.1	22.9
2.1–5	13.1	15.6	35.4	13.3	16.7	35.9
5.1–10	20.4	21.7	23.2	18.6	21.9	25.2
10.1–15	13.4	14.3	8.0	14.5	15.9	9.5
15.1–20	9.3	9.5	3.0	9.5	9.7	3.0
20.1–30	10.0	9.9	2.1	12.5	12.6	2.3
30.1–50	10.2	9.0	1.3	11.3	8.1	0.7
50.1–100	11.4	9.6	1.0	9.7	9.0	0.5
100+	8.7	5.7	0.1	6.9	0.8	0.0
Total	100	100	100	99.8	99.8	100

Source: Based on data bank on farms obtained from FNCC municipal committees.

Note: Most coffee farmers are members of the FNCC, and information is kept more or less up to date for each member. Only very small farmers are likely to be underrepresented in the FNCC data bank. Since this information is not used for tax purposes and agronomists visit most of these farms, reported farm extensions are likely to be reliable estimates.

The size of a coffee grove reflects, to a certain extent, a farmer's income. However, the age of trees, the density of plantings, and whether the trees are growing under shade or open to the sun also affect yields. Incomes also depend on the internal price of coffee. A well-kept, young, and dense coffee grove of five hectares can bring good returns. By 1980, 30 percent of Risaralda's land in coffee had been converted to the new variety and lacked coverage of shade trees. Because the new coffee groves are denser than the traditional ones, the number of *caturra* trees now growing is higher than the number of the older variety. In both of these Risaralda municipalities, 55.5 percent of the coffee trees were of the high-yielding *caturra* variety that had been planted at an average density of four thousand to five thousand trees per hectare and were producing an average of 170 to 180 arrobas of beans per hectare (Federación Nacional 1983). It is also clear from the coffee census that most farms that have not been converted to the new variety of coffee are nevertheless well maintained.

Smaller coffee groves may bring less revenue, but they are also less problematic to manage, particularly during the harvest. To avoid problems and minimize risk, farmers do not reinvest profits in land purchases after farms have reached a certain size. Expansion and subdivision are ongoing processes recorded both in this study and Errazuriz's (1986) study of Líbano.

Discussions with farmers and managers made it clear that their labor-management strategy relates primarily to the size of the coffee groves, cap-

TABLE 6. Distribution of Ownership of Land and Coffee Groves by Extension in Hectares in La Vega, Cundinamarca, 1985–86

Extension in Hectares	% All Land	% Land in Coffee	% of Coffee Groves
0–2	4.8	8.3	48.6
2.1–5	18.2	25.4	37.9
5.1–10	22.7	25.4	10.7
10.1–15	12.4	10.0	2.0
15.1–20	15.6	13.3	0.2
20.1–30	9.7	7.3	0.4
30.1–50	11.3	5.9	0.0
50.1–100	5.3	4.4	0.2
100+	0	0	0.0
Total	100	100	100

Source: As in table 5.

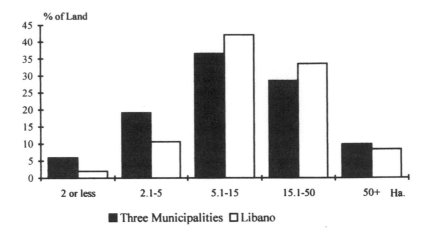

**Fig. 5. Distribution of land by size of coffee grove in hectares in the three munici-
palities of this study and in the municipality of Líbano, Tolima, 1980–85.**   Data on
Líbano is for 1981 and is based on Errazuriz (1986: 231). Data on the three municipalities of this study are based on the 1985 census information gathered by the
FNCC municipal committee. There is no comparable data for this period for similar coffee-producing regions in Colombia. The columns indicate percentage of
land in coffee by size of grove rather than by size of farm.

ital assets, and degree of modernization. Since our findings corroborate
farmers' accounts, I have used these criteria rather than size alone and
have categorized the farms into five types: small farms, medium farms,
medium enterprise farms, large enterprise farms, and large traditional coffee farms.[9] Although I discuss small farmers' strategies, this category was
not included in the farm survey because these growers hire very few harvesters. Peasant farmers are yet another category of farmers, but they no
longer have a significant presence in coffee regions like Risaralda. They
are, however, an important constituency in more marginal coffee-producing areas. I do not discuss their problems in this book.

3.4   The FNCC's Presence in the Municipalities

Risaralda earned a place in the FNCC's National Congress long after
Cundinamarca did so. Risaralda had to wait until it became a separate
department. In 1967 the Departmental Committee opened its office in
Pereira and gained a right to send representatives to the national body.

The number of representatives from each department corresponds to the volume of its coffee production. Wealthy and/or prominent growers express their concerns through these representatives. The only significant institutions representing the medium farmer, whose voice seldom reaches the lofty heights of national committees, are the FNCC's municipal committees, which are concerned with local extension activities rather policy guidelines. Half of the members of these municipal committees are elected by farmers who are members of the FNCC, and the rest are appointed by the Departmental Committee, where local strategies and practices are debated and played out.

Each municipal committee has an office and a budget to carry out extension work, collect information required by the central planners, and purchase coffee. For most farmers these committees are their point of contact with the FNCC. They flock to these offices on Saturdays or when they need to petition for credit, purchase inputs, or request technical advice. These municipal committees have a cadre of agronomists, often trained by the FNCC, who give advice and visit farms to approve credit or check on conditions. Other government agencies like DRI-PAN (integrated rural development and nutrition program) use the facilities of the municipal committees to reach out to farmers with extension courses or information.

The existence of the FNCC and its municipal committees was quite palpable in Risaralda. During the 1970s and early 1980s the federation built 274 schools throughout the department, improved 1,072 kilometers of roads and added another 170 kilometers of roads, brought electricity to 12,866 farms, built hospitals and clinics, and created one vocational school for women and four for men. The FNCC also organized coffee-purchasing cooperatives and subsidized stores that supplied farmers with fertilizer and tools. It organized short extension courses opened to all and friendship groups for owners of small farms with at least two hectares in coffee. Independent of the local committees, these friendship groups would stimulate discussions of technical problems and encourage the modernization of coffee groves.

3.5 The Management of Coffee Farms

Farmers ultimately imprint the management style of their farms. If they live in the area, they are likely to be totally engaged in their farms and to manage them not just according to ledgers and cost analysis but in ways that reflect the farms' actual agronomic condition, the community's labor situation, and their local social network. More disengaged proprietors must rely on indirect indicators and administrators' reports. Both types of farmers might be equally successful, but they are likely to approach the labor process in different ways. It is just as important to know who the farmers are as it is to have information about the size and financial endowment of the enterprises.

No one, of course, can convert a small farm into a large enterprise farm or afford to run a large coffee grove as if it were a small property. Bountiful harvests require more elaborate equipment, larger crews, and many more supervisors; these farms require more stratified systems of command and more elaborate record keeping. In the next section I categorize farms according to ideal types that reflect the harvest's size and scale.

3.5a   The Large Enterprises (Fifty or More Hectares with Caturra Trees)

There are thirteen farms in the three municipalities that fit this category (tables 5 and 6); five of them are in the sample. These farms were larger than fifty hectares and grew *caturra* coffee under sun or slightly shaded by plantains. Coffee production is the major activity of these farms, even in the more diversified municipality of Cundinamarca. However, one of the farms also had a considerable amount of land in pasture.

Some of these enterprises are owned by entrepreneurs who live in Pereira, Cali, Bogotá, or Manizales and are more involved with other investments than with running their coffee farms. They depend on the ability and honesty of the resident administrators, who receive a monthly salary, the legally stipulated fringe benefits, and perhaps a productivity incentive—a bonus pegged to the amount of coffee harvested. These farms are well managed and very productive.

Although many of these owners reside elsewhere, they have well-established roots in the area. Their farms often have been in families for several generations and represent the inheritance of one of the owners' children. Some of the enterprises started as smaller farms and grew through the years by incorporating neighboring farms. Sometimes families have subdivided these properties because their size made management clumsy or because of tensions among co-owners. One such radical change occurred during the fieldwork. A large farm with seventy-six hectares in coffee was jointly owned by twelve brothers between 1985 and 1986. Some of the brothers sold their rights to other brothers. The farm was divided into four independent farms, each with a separate owner. Managerial continuity was maintained in only one of the four sections. Three other brothers hired new administrators, who changed all permanent and resident personnel.

Other owners of large enterprises do not have old and illustrious backgrounds. Don Eduardo was raised in a neighboring coffee region and came to the farm he now co-owns as an administrator. When the owners decided to sell, seven years after he had started to work for them, he found buyers and formed an association with one of them. Now he lives elsewhere and comes to the farm only on occasion. This coffee farm is large enough to require three administrators, but Don Eduardo, his co-owners, and their accountants make all important investment decisions. This farm was also subdivided during the period of fieldwork into two separate properties, retaining their previous administrators.

All of these farms are run by administrators, who must have some basic accounting experience. They keep tally of all expenses and pay the laborers each Saturday. The administrators decide when and where to sell coffee. However, all major financial decisions are made in consultation with the owner, who must also approve any salary and wage increases. Some of the administrators' skills, including the more technical agricultural skills, have been acquired through experience on their parents' farms or through working alongside owners of smaller farms. Most of these administrators are now expected to complement their experience with some formal training at the FNCC's school. Eventually, these administrators purchase their own small farms and shift to running their own enterprises.

Administrators schedule maintenance tasks and decide the size of crews, who will tackle each job, and who will supervise them. They walk the farms' various sections, examine their condition, and decide when each section will be fertilized, weeded, sprayed, and harvested. These are not just technical decisions; they are management decisions as well. If administrators do not space the tasks properly, they might have to pay higher wages or face greater pressures when the berries begin to mature. The administrators must also advise the owners when each section needs to be sprayed, how often it should be done, how much fertilizer to use, and what weeding method should be used. Since these decisions have financial implications, they must be discussed with the owners, but the administrators' voices carry considerable weight since they reflect their and the FNCC agronomists' appreciation of farm conditions.

Administrators hire supervisors and set the rules of discipline for farms. They ultimately must deal with unresolved disputes between laborers and their supervisors or between resident laborers (*agregados*).[10] How administrators relate to personnel depends very much on their personalities and social backgrounds. Some administrators are sons of established coffee farmers, while others made their way up slowly through luck, connections, and/or training. Most come from the same or a neighboring region. They are familiar with laborers' expectations and on occasion will express some concern for their plight, though the administrators ultimately side with the owners. But the administrators identify socially with other local administrators—drinking companions, collaborators, and sometimes competitors. While administrators earn a good income by local standards and are well respected, often they have little political power. Their prestige rests on their ability to run farms that give no trouble and are not the seeds of social unrest or violence.

Administrators rely on supervisors (*patrones de corte*) who may or may not reside on farms with their families. Large farms require at least three supervisors throughout the year and may add a few more during the harvest. Supervisors are selected from among the best and most loyal day-wage laborers. Supervisors who work throughout the year are considered permanent personnel even if they do not live on the farm; they receive a wage and often all legally required fringe benefits. These field supervisors must keep an eye on how work is performed, identify specific field problems, and handle disputes among crew members. Supervisors are often ruthless and not very adept. Good administrators should be able to spot incompetence and bring together a group of field supervisors who reflect the administrators' style of management. They do not often succeed and sometimes prefer to turn a blind eye to the excesses of crew supervisors.

Large enterprise farms located far from towns or dense rural settlements must be prepared to feed their workers and house their harvest crews. Administrators delegate the task of food preparation to the families of *agregados* who are brought in specially for that purpose. The head of the family—usually a man—is engaged as an *alimentador* (food preparer) and receives the fee for hot meals charged to the worker. But *alimentador*'s wife and daughters do the preparation. The *alimentador* himself works either as a laborer or a supervisor and is paid accordingly. He often must also clean the dormitory and the bathrooms. The structures that house male migrant workers in these farms may be adequate, but there is little privacy, and the *agregados* were often too busy to keep their lodgings in good order. Migrants do not favor these remote farms (table 14). Administrators likewise prefer to avoid having to lodge harvesters (see section 5.5).

Roads must be built and maintained in these farms to move the berries from the harvesting sites to the processing stations. Fully mechanized pulping and drying equipment must be installed, and farmers must hire trained personnel with several supervisors to run and keep the machinery clean and functioning. Once the beans are dried, they are either stored on the farm or transported to the place of sale. All large farms must have at least one truck and a driver. Supervisors and truck drivers receive a wage higher than do other personnel.

3.5b   The Medium Enterprise Farm (Approximately Ten to Fifty Hectares, Mostly in Caturra Trees)

There are 151 farms in this size category, thirteen of them in the sample. In all three of the municipalities studied, medium enterprise farms hold most of the land in coffee. Although the owners were very involved in running the farms, most had resident salaried administrators. However, three engaged a son or other kinsman to run the farm on share basis, and three other proprietors hired a resident supervisor to help run the farm. Regardless of who was in charge of the farm on a daily basis, in all cases there were one or two resident *agregados* to help with the supervision of day laborers.

Although owners of medium enterprise farms often reside elsewhere, they are directly involved with the technical aspects of growing coffee and even farm-management problems. Don Roberto, the son of a local coffee grower who became a physician and settled in a big city, regained an interest in the farm after his parents died, and he continues to keep in close touch with his administrator, particularly during the harvest. Besides his professional practice, he owns two cattle farms and another coffee farm. His social contacts are circumscribed by his multiple interests and family commitments. He keeps in touch only with those coffee growers who live in the same city where he resides. Don Rosaldo, conversely, lives close enough to be very involved in the day-to-day running of his farm. As he decidedly affirmed, "Of the 365 days [each year], I am here 340 of them."

He likes to maintain a personal relationship with his resident personnel despite the fact that he has a *mayordomo* (administrator) who helps him run the farm: "It is my occupation to be here rather than walking the streets. Coffee has given me everything. All that I have was given to me by coffee." He inherited the farm from his father and is proud that it remains one of the most productive farms in the district.

Many owners of medium enterprises are local residents. Don Leandro lives on his farm, which he purchased in 1970. He is not a newcomer to coffee agriculture. He spent several years buying and selling farms until he consolidated them into a few larger holdings. Don Ramon is the son of a local farmer who returned to the region after fifteen years' absence and had to relearn the trade. His mentors were the owners of the best-run large farms in the region as well as the FNCC agronomists. Although he resides in one of the regional cities, he spends the harvest time on the farm and comes at least once a month during the rest of the year.

Other owners of medium enterprises have only recently become farmers. They are professionals with no rural roots who became interested in coffee as an investment after the bonanza. Some are technocrats; others are agronomists. They all abide by the advice and guidance of local FNCC personnel and city accountants. These owners may or may not visit their farms regularly, but they do not neglect the business of farming. If they delegate management to resident administrators, the farms will be run like other enterprise farms. If these growers regard their farms as tests of their entrepreneurial ability, they are likely to introduce new business practices and hire administrators or *mayordomos* who have taken courses at one of the FNCC's schools. These owners keep very detailed ledgers of inputs, costs, and yields, and new technology is often tried first on these farms, so they become showplaces for the FNCC. Many of these owners, however, lack the intuitive experience of local farmers who have gone through booms and busts and are not very good at managing personnel. One such newcomer acknowledged his inexperience with laborers and tried to overcome it by using small crews and herbicides.

Women of some means are unlikely to manage farms inherited from fathers or husbands. If they have sons who are interested and available, they will likely invite them to administer the farms on a share basis. Doña Emilia, who lives in the local town, chose to hire an administrator but maintains her involvement with the farm.

Three of these medium enterprises retained a considerable number of resident families. These farms had from twenty-five to thirty hectares in coffee and from eight to eleven resident families each. One of these farms was unique in that the proprietors continued to delegate much of the management responsibility to the *agregados* who had been in residence on the farm for many years. The proprietor retained control of the technical aspects of coffee agriculture and hired an administrator to coordinate transportation and part of the processing of the berries. The drying was completed on another farm owned by the same proprietor. The responsibility of deciding when to harvest and when to bring the laborers was left to each resident family, which was assigned a section of the farmland. These harvesters—the sons and kinsmen of the *agregados*—however, were paid directly by the administrator, who kept the account book of wages. The administrator had to mediate any disputes between resident families and organize maintenance tasks. On other farms *agregados* did not have as much responsibility; they served instead as a readily available labor force that could be used during the maintenance seasons on any of the farms controlled by the proprietor.

Even when there are few resident *agregados,* the administrators of these farms have fewer responsibilities and more limited administrative experience than those on larger farms. Many have taken courses taught by FNCC personnel or at the federation's school in Chinchiná, but most owners retain technical control of agronomic practices and keep the account books.

Nearly half of these enterprises had not yet invested in mechanized processing plants. In some cases, the new coffee groves were still not producing at their peak; in others, the harvest was sufficiently prolonged that they could avoid the investment. Several farmers had other coffee farms, and it is possible that they transported berries there to be processed. Few of these farms had invested in trucks. These owners also tried to cut costs in the lodgings offered to laborers: cots often lacked mattresses and were crowded into small spaces, and bathing facilities were minimal. Only a third of these farms offered adequate facilities by local standards.

3.5c   The Medium Farms (Approximately Five to Fifteen Hectares in Coffee, Not All in Caturra)

Most Risaraldeño coffee growers like to convey an image of small and hardworking vulnerable farmers with less than fifteen hectares in coffee. The FNCC also uses this image in international advertisements for coffee. In our sample, twenty-two farms either had less than ten hectares in coffee or had larger groves with much of the trees still under shade. These farms fit this category because they are not as productive as the medium enterprise farms and are still small enough to be managed by owners with resident helpers. The farmers are closely involved with everyday farm life and participate in the affairs and activities of the FNCC municipal committee and perhaps even in local politics. They may also own a store or bar and hence be familiar figures to farm owners and laborers alike. If they are ambitious and want to become local public figures, they are likely to try to build an image of benevolent paternalism or at least of trustworthiness and civility. For some, this mien comes naturally, but for others it is simply a political strategy. A fair number of them are still struggling with memories of the *violencia* or of subsequent political turmoil, robberies, and abductions. They have become embittered and distrustful and relate to their laborers and their neighbors accordingly.

As is the case for medium enterprises, some of the owners of medium farms are investors and professionals who purchased coffee land during the bonanza and now run their farms from the comforts of big-city residence with the help, in their case, of experienced resident laborers. These owners include enterprising agronomists who either work for the FNCC or have a career elsewhere.

Women who have inherited medium coffee farms are likely to engage their sons, who will eventually take possession of the land, as partners. Doña Rosa's son helped his mother modernize her farm with credit she negotiated. He has an obvious interest in modernizing the coffee farm before her death, when delays in the transfer of the title will handicap his ability to obtain a good loan. In some cases, however, these arrangements are bedeviled by tense relations between parents and children.

These and smaller farms have had a late start in the modernization process. It was not as easy for these farmers to obtain credit, and they had more reasons to fear the risks. In Belén, for example, half of the medium farms had barely started to renovate their coffee groves in 1985–86. In Marsella and La Vega the process had advanced more swiftly; one-third of the medium farms were fully modernized. At present, most of these groves have probably been converted to *caturra* or *colombian,* judging from recent national surveys (Errazuriz 1993). They may also be the ones suffering most from the 1990s fall in the internal price of coffee. In Cundinamarca the situation might not be as dire because 61 percent of these coffee farms also produced meat and milk. These complementary activities allow farmers to balance their financial investments and to keep their labor force working in other activities. However, these Cundinamarca farmers had to grapple with limited financial resources as well as with the double task of having to run a farm and modernize their coffee groves. In Risaralda most of the land is in coffee, so only the technical requirements of these trees and the vagaries of the market mold their style of farm management.

These farms are small enough that the owners, if they reside on the property or have no other occupation, can personally supervise most activities. Trader-farmers who are otherwise engaged run their farms with the help of one or two trusted *agregados.* The organization of these farms is quite informal, and few owners keep careful account books or try to carry out elaborate cost estimates unless required to do so by a loan manager. What they do and how they manage their labor force is shaped by their experience, their perception of social reality, and their social networks. They rely on the technical advice of the FNCC local committee but, for financial reasons, do not follow all of its recommendations. Thus, these farmers cut down on amounts of fertilizer and the number of fumigations against rust.

When these owners cannot afford to supervise all maintenance tasks, they subcontract the task of weeding (see section 7.4). Instead, they use their time to supervise pruning and fertilization When they are ready to renovate their coffee trees, they themselves grow the seedlings—in bags prepared by their laborers—and supervise the transplanting. They have enough coffee to need at least a few harvesters, preferably people known to them, and they offer simple but decent lodgings to their few migrant workers. If the crews are small, they eat on the patio of the proprietor's house. Otherwise, they take their evening meals in the house of their *agregado.* If the farmers hire neighbors, it is not necessary to lodge or feed them. Harvesters prefer to save money by having food brought to them from their own kitchens. These farmers do not have to hire more than twenty harvesters during the peak of the season and most often manage with between four and ten laborers.

These farms are small enough for owners or their administrators to know most if not all of their laborers. Relations are informal and highly personal but not necessarily friendly. Some owners are genuinely concerned about their laborers and are considerate in their treatment; these growers try to pay a "living" wage even when unemployment prevails. But others regard laborers as a class apart, oppositional in nature and with different moral standards. These owners resent having to pay harvesters a good wage while struggling with financial pressures and aspirations. These growers take solace in the awareness that in time the unemployed laborers will plead for a job and can be hired on the farmers' terms. Wages during maintenance season range widely on these farms from miserable to adequate (see section 7.3).

These farmers' considerable financial pressures resulted from the need to renovate and modernize their processing equipment in preparation for the future larger harvests. One-third of these farms had installed some form of mechanical dryer; the rest were still drying their beans in the sun by spreading them either over cement platforms or on protected trays. Very few of these farms had the capital to invest in trucks and had to sell to a middleman who would pick up the harvest or make special arrangements for its delivery.

3.5d   The Large Traditional Farms (Ten Hectares or More in Coffee)

Two farms in our sample fit this category. All of the large traditional farms have enough land in coffee to require considerable labor but are graced by a harvest that does not peak as suddenly or intensively as in modernized farms. These coffee groves also require fewer applications of fertilizer and do not have to be weeded as often, since shade discourages weed growth (see section 3.6). All of these tasks, including harvesting, can be completed with smaller crews over a longer period of time. Because the beans ripen at a slower rate, there are smaller quantities of berries to be processed at any one time. Sun drying is an adequate procedure and avoids an investment in machinery. Many of these farmers also harvest coffee with the help of kin, resident laborers, and other people known to the growers. They can avoid lodging laborers and the problems doing so entails. Trusted *agregados* are all that is needed if owners do not live on the farms.

The appeal of these farms is that they are easier to manage and less costly to maintain. The drawback is that they are not as profitable as modernized coffee groves when the internal price of coffee is high. Although many of these farms may have disappeared by now (Vallejo Mejía 1993: 282), in 1985–86 the FNCC municipal committee listed 414 traditional coffee farms over ten hectares in the three municipalities here considered. Most of these farms were in Belén. It was not clear what prevented these farmers from planting new trees. Some, of course, may have tried and met disaster; others seem to have had multiple properties and were renovating them one at a time. Others were either reluctant to uproot trees that were still producing well or had trouble getting a loan (Paredes Hernandez and Zambrano Ramirez 1987: 223).

Other properties were quite neglected, indicating that either the owners had lost interest in coffee agriculture or the property was being contested. These neglected farms have trouble attracting occasional laborers and have limited labor resources of their own.

3.5e The Small Farms (Less Than Five Hectares in Coffee)

A considerable number of farms and hectares in coffee are owned by farmers and peasants with limited financial resources (tables 5 and 6). None of them were included in our sample. Only 33.4 percent of these farmers had managed, as a result of the FNCC's special credit programs, to start renovating their groves. Not all of the remaining small farmers were willing to transform their farms into sun-drenched rows of *caturra* or *colombian* coffee trees. Some considered the venture too risky and the effort not worthwhile (Federacíon Nacional 1984b: 22–23). Others (particularly in Cundinamarca) preferred to diversify (Paredes Hernandez and Zambrano Ramirez 1987: 23). However, all three municipalities had a number of small farmers who were quite eager to modernize and were waiting for either the appropriate moment or for credit.

Most of these farmers had inherited their land, but others had acquired it through hard work or luck. Don Julio left his father's farm shortly after his marriage and worked as a day laborer and as an *agregado* for a few years. With his savings he purchased a farm that he later exchanged for a heavy truck. After a few years, he sold the truck and returned to farming. His next farm was much larger, and he had trouble repaying his debt. He exchanged this farm for the smaller farm that he now owns. Don Norberto helped his father until he became a full-time contract laborer. He invested his savings in a transport bus, which he sold to buy the farm he now owns. His sons are too young to help him, so he is having a difficult time. Don Oscar purchased his farms from his savings as the administrator of a medium farm and from his profits as an animal trader.

In Cundinamarca it is still customary for farmers with large properties to bequeath some land to each long-standing *agregado* and sharecropper. If the *agregados* are young enough or have sons to help, they could hope to become successful farmers themselves. While the initial lot was likely to be too small to bring much of an income, eventually, either through the purchase of contiguous parcels or through sales and exchanges, these new owners could build viable farms. This transformation from laborer to property owner was easier to achieve before land values skyrocketed. Since land prices have escalated, it is no longer possible for laborers to become farmers.

These small farms are managed by their owners with the help of their sons. The owners sometimes hire a few helpers during the harvest (see section 5.2). Although these farmers pay less than most others, they attract the few hands they need by treating them with respect and feeding them better meals. Those who have attempted renovations do the work themselves, a little at a time. They avoid borrowing because they are afraid of losing the farm to creditors.

Regional professionals also have become interested in coffee, but only as an investment. Until they are ready to modernize, these newcomers engage sharecroppers. Once credit is obtained, the agreement is terminated. From then on, they manage their farms with resident *agregados* to keep an eye on the property. It was impossible to determine how many of the small farms were owned by these investors in 1986. Nevertheless, the small family farm, now probably totally modernized, still has a significant presence. Their old-fashioned cane and mud houses with verandas and gardens were familiar sites during my mountain walks.

3.6   Labor Costs of Production

A coffee grove requires considerable care to produce high yields. Weeds can rob young trees of nutrients and must be eradicated or cut back. The amount of labor to keep trees productive depends on climatic conditions and amount of shade. The new *caturra* trees are planted under sun or, at most, are lightly shaded by well-spaced plantain trees. Regardless of how carefully the grove is weeded, the trees need to be supplied with extra nutrients for optimal growth, particularly if the land has been under cultivation for many years or if trees are very young. Since leaf rust fungus has made its presence felt, farmers have sprayed trees several times a year. The trees also have to be pruned regularly. Pruning and spraying are two of the more sensitive of the upkeep tasks and are performed either by trained personnel or by the farmers themselves.

The harvesting and processing of the berries is also time-consuming. They must be carefully picked, selecting only those that are ripe. Then they have to be processed. The dry beans must be extracted from the berries. In Colombia this extraction is done on the farm using the wet method, which in small farms involves only a vat and a small hand-driven pulping machine. The beans can then be spread out on the yard for drying. Farms that handle large loads must have more elaborate equipment. Once the beans reach an acceptable level of dryness they are transported as parchment coffee to buying centers. The final preparation of the beans—extraction of even more moisture to reach complete dryness and sorting, hulling, and polishing—is done in industrial establishments at major commercial centers. It is now called green coffee and is ready for storage, export, or retail sales.

Large enterprise farms have no choice but to maintain expensive processing equipment. They also need a truck and roads throughout the farm to move large volumes of fresh berries to the processing centers, often located far from where the harvesters are working. Managers must receive a good salary and accountants must be paid. Land, equipment, and administrative personnel represent fixed costs that must be met regardless of how much coffee is produced and what its price is in the market. The variable costs include maintenance and harvest labor and the expense of other required inputs (fertilizers, fungicides). The type and amount of fertilizer used and the number of applications vary according to the financial resources available and the price of coffee (Junguito and Pizano 1991: 111–38). The cost of weeding can be reduced by cutting down on its frequency and by using a machete instead of a hoe. In theory, coffee berries could be allowed to rot on the ground, but farmers cannot afford to lose income from the harvest and consequently always have laborers collect what is on the trees. The FNCC is committed to buying all harvested coffee that meets its quality standards.

Yields decrease as trees age. The older varieties of *arabica* under shade last longer than the more recent *caturra* trees planted under sun. Eventually all coffee groves have to be renovated by uprooting the trees. This renovation can be accomplished by sections, by renovating only the trees that are not producing, or by uprooting all of the trees. The FNCC's recommendation that coffee trees growing under shade be replaced by new varieties under sun implied the cost of removing not only the old coffee trees but also the shade trees. When the vigor of the new varieties begins to decline, it can be stimulated by cutting them back close to the ground. While the rejuvenated growth will yield 20 percent less than new trees, the FNCC recommends the practice since it is much less costly than uprooting and replanting. When prices are high, farmers are often reluctant to cut back trees. But when prices are low and the future is promising, farmers are more likely to cut back larger sections of their coffee groves. All styles of renovations and expansions can then be considered as variable costs, but I discuss them separately in this section because they are not part of the yearly maintenance costs.

Even the simplest renovation requires the establishment of a nursery. The seedlings are grown in small, soil-filled plastic bags and maintained until they have grown enough for transplanting. The ground has to be prepared, and holes must be marked and dug to ready them for the transplanting. Once in the ground, the seedlings have to be watered, fertilized, and carefully weeded until they are well established and producing. The FNCC estimates that this aspect of the process requires 145 man-days per hectare (Errazuriz 1989b: table 7), while renovations through stumping require only an average of seventy-three man-days per hectare (estimate used by Errazuriz 1989b: table 4, based on FNCC calculations).

The amount of labor required for maintenance, harvesting, and processing is considerable even in traditional farms. *Caturra* or other more recent varieties planted under sun require even more labor since they must be fertilized more regularly and yield more berries during the harvest. The modernized farms are thus more costly to maintain. Table 7 describes estimates of average labor inputs on traditional and modernized farms. I have used sources that estimate labor requirements by tasks; there are many other estimates that reflect either different methodologies or farm conditions (Errazuriz 1989b: 50). These estimates do not incorporate the labor required to control the serious fungus infestation of 1985, when whole coffee groves had to be sprayed.

The cost of a harvest can be more or less onerous to farmers depending on how prices and yields affect cash returns. When trees are young, they do not produce as much as during their later peak years; production subsequently decreases again. Yields are also affected by climate and plagues. Table 8 summarizes each of the costs as shares of the total expense of maintaining and harvesting coffee on a model farm in the neighboring department of Caldas; it illustrates fluctuations in returns with shifts in prices and yields and the corresponding harvest and maintenance costs.

Arango vividly illustrates the vicissitudes of coffee agriculture in Antioquia when he lists estimates of net returns to production between 1974 to 1981 (Arango, Aubad, and Piedrahita 1983: 106–10). Table 9 summarizes his findings. It is important to remember that his labor estimates are higher than those of other researchers, so the picture he paints might

TABLE 7. Labor Requirements in Traditional and Modernized Coffee Agriculture, Annual Man-Days per Hectare in Colombia

Operation	Traditional[a] 55.1–60 Arrobas/Ha.[b]	Caturra Plantations (3,000–5,000 trees per ha.)		
		150 Arrobas/Ha.[c]	230 Arrobas/Ha.[d]	200 Arrobas/Ha.[d]
Fertilization[e]	1.9	30.5	45.5	40.0
Weeding[f]	28.2	68.0	48.0	20.0
Insecticides	4.1	2.0	2.0	5.0
Pruning	9.9	NA	NA	NA
Replanting	3.0	NA	NA	NA
Sub-total	47.1 (44.1–46.1%)	100.5 (33.7%)	95.5 (24.0%)	65.0 (27.7%)
Harvest of Plantains	4.0 (3.7–3.9%)			
Harvest of Coffee	41.3–45.4	156.3	240.0	140.0
Processing	8.0–8.7	37.5	57.5	27.0
Transport	1.7	3.0	4.5	3.0
Sub-total	51–55.8 50–52.2%	196.8 66.3%	302.0 76.0%	170.0 72.3%
Total	102.1–106.9	297.3	397.5	235.0
Arrobas Harvested per Man Day	0.54–0.59	0.51	0.58	0.85

[a]The upkeep labor estimates for traditional plantations are based on United Nations 1958. Estimates for the labor required to harvest these plantations are based on the above source estimate of 55.1 arrobas per hectare and Arango's (Arango, Aubad, and Piedrahita 1983: 105) estimate of sixty arrobas per hectare. An arroba equals 125 kilograms of berries.

[b]Based on Arango's estimate of man-days for a plantation with three thousand trees per hectare and yields of 150 arrobas per hectare (Arango, Aubad, and Piedrahita 1983: 88).

[c]Based on Arango's estimates for a plantation in Antioquia, similar to Risaralda, with five thousand trees per hectare and yields of 150 arrobas per hectare (Arango, Aubad and Piedrahita 1983: 88). In Risaralda in 1981 the density of plantations ranged from four thousand to five thousand trees and the yields were about 170 arrobas per hectare.

[d]Based on Urrea's estimates using FNCC figures (Urrea 1976).

[e]In 1985–86 there were fewer fertilizations in Risaralda (Federación Nacional 1980; account book from one farm)

[f]Only 12.5 percent of farmers weed as frequently as is suggested. The account book of a large enterprise farm also reflected this fact.

be bleaker than it really is. Furthermore, in these tables he does not consider that during periods of low prices farmers tend to invest less in fertilizers than they do when prices are high.[11] Nevertheless, the table dramatizes several points: (1) returns are much higher on a modernized farm than on a traditional farm, and by implication, farmers will modernize if they have the resources to do so; (2) windfall profits in 1976–78, coupled with optimistic price projections, encouraged farmers to invest in more

TABLE 8.   Cost Share of Stages of Production as Percentage of Total Costs on a Modernized Farm in Caldas, 1982–86

	1982	1983	1984	1985	1986
General Expenses	24.2%	25.9%	40.2%	35.8%	34.4%
Maintenance	47.5%	42.1%	26.3%	29.7%	39.1%
Harvest	24.1%	32.0%	33.5%	34.5%	26.5%
Yields in Arrobas	229.9	311.7	248.2	237.7	160.6
Returns per					
Arrobas (in pesos)	267.5	584.5	495.5	748.9	1590.9
Coffee Price[a]	37.55	38.50	38.22	38.49	62.61

Source: From account books of a farm in Caldas with fifty-eight hectares in coffee and 6,772 trees per hectare.

[a]The coffee price quoted was the one that the FNCC paid in Caldas in Colombian pesos per kilogram of dry parchment coffee. An arroba is equivalent to 125 kilograms.

TABLE 9.   Returns to Production in Traditional and Modernized Farms in Antioquia, 1974–80

	Traditional	Modernized	
Year	60 Arrobas/Ha.	150 Arrobas/Ha.	230 Arrobas/Ha.
1974	−4.4	2.3	8.8
1975	−2.1	5.0	6.9
1976	27.1	37.1	50.5
1977	17.3	32.9	46.8
1978	5.0	10.9	22.7
1979	−4.1	0.7	9.0
1980	−1.9	1.3	9.4

Source: Based on Arango's calculations (Arango, Aubad, and Piedrahita 1983: 106–10).

Note: The estimates include land rent, taxes, production costs, supervision, and capital investments in coffee plantation. The figures exclude capital investments in buildings and machinery. The returns will be higher for small farmers who administer production and do not consider rent to be an issue. Since Arango's labor-cost estimates tend to be high, returns might be better than he indicates.

renovations, which resulted in a big jump in areas under the new technology from 1975 to 1981 and the slower rate of conversion in the following years (see table 2); (3) the drop in coffee prices encouraged farmers to cut back trees to stimulate future production in expectation of improving prices.

When the FNCC in 1987 revised its price policies by offering higher internal prices and many subsidies, farmers responded by renovating the coffee groves. Credit was perhaps the most important incentive (Junguito and Pizano 1991: 137; Echavarría, Gaviria, and Téllez 1993: 138). When the FNCC terminated some of the subsidies, farmers faced serious difficulties. Their plight was heightened by labor costs that had been pushed up by high demand during the harvest. Fearing the loss of their farms, farmers have once again sought to cut down maintenance costs by curtailing the number of times they fertilize and lowering wages during the maintenance season. Thus, the complex interplay of policies, market forces, financial pressures, and laborers' power contributes to labor-management strategies.

Chapter 4

Laborers and their Families

Small hamlets with carefully tended gardens, schools, and perhaps stores dot the mountains of Risaralda, often nestled in a crevice or a turn of the road.[1] Most of the inhabitants of these hamlets are landless laborers living in houses built by them or their parents using traditional designs and techniques. The effect is pleasing to the eye. The well-balanced shapes supported by delicate cane frames, covered with mud, and with brightly painted doors have made this region architecturally famous. These rural neighborhoods are alive with visitors late in the afternoon. Doors remain unlocked, and people feel safe. Some of the larger hamlets have schools and stores, making them as attractive to live in as towns. One can sense stability and communality, and older people talk of how they are looked after and cared for by neighbors. Each of these hamlets has a core of residents, often related, who either were born there or have lived there for many years.[2] Although many laborers live in these hamlets, others have settled in the towns or wherever they have been able to build, buy, or rent houses.

4.1 Home Ownership

Owning a home is not a preposterous proposition for the coffee laborers of Risaralda (see table 10). Many of them build their own houses on land owned by their parents, given in exchange for services rendered or even as a gift. Landlords and aspiring politicians who want to generate a following of loyal workers or voters are quite willing to part with a small piece of land on the edge of a road. Patronage as a political tool is well entrenched in rural Colombia. As one worker related,

> They gave me the land [four months ago], and I started to build. Asking, because I had to ask. One gave me the boards, another the nails, the other the cane, another the cardboard, and so it went. And I went to the mayor of Marsella and told him that I was very poor and I am

about to build but the wood is [far away] . . . and they brought me the wood in the truck of the municipality.

SENA and Acción Comunal (local action groups) have helped local residents with grants of land, gifts of materials, and loans to build slightly more substantial houses. These organizations have also helped to create new neighborhoods. These rural projects are tied to the aspirations of local politicians, who are nurturing the votes of recipients. As one woman explained, "No vote, no land, and since my husband refuses to vote, we have to rent."

But even with gifts and the cooperation of government agencies, the building of a house can be protracted. It takes a long time on a laborer's income to put aside money for a roof, water pipes, sanitary facilities, and electricity. One informant vividly explained the problems of trying to build a house: "I am not capable of finishing it; I started five years ago and cannot finish. I have a little room there; the other [room] is occupied, true, but we could not sleep there because the winter would kill us." Most of the houses in rural neighborhoods or towns have running water, electricity; and sanitary facilities.

Recent changes in building styles to unattractive cement-block structures are more costly. Owners of such houses build them even more slowly than do owners of traditional houses. Furthermore, these new style houses

TABLE 10.   Permanent Residence of Married
Harvesters in Risaralda and Cundinamarca ($N = 253$)

Type of Tenure	Married Harvesters
Own	55.73%
Rent	26.88%
On Loan	17.39%
Total	100%

Source: Field survey data for both departments.
Note: The figures are based on all married harvesters who were surveyed in both departments, since most resided permanently in one of the departments. Harvesters who lived on farms were excluded from the count as were those who gave no information. There was no significant difference in rate of ownership by department.

can be built only when both spouses work. As the wife of a laborer explained,

> When I have the opportunity, I go out to work so as to be able to finish the house. And wages are not enough! . . . We started the house, and first we would build a room, and then the other, and so on. . . . With every harvest we buy materials. . . . [We have been building] for about seven years and have not finished yet.

Not all laborers have either the expertise or inclination to build a house; many instead try to purchase dwellings. Among the forty-seven laborers visited during the summer of 1986,[3] twenty-six owned the houses they inhabited. Seventeen of these owners had built their houses. Nine others had purchased houses: three had done so with money from inheritances; three had used cash received as severance pay when their contracts as permanent farm laborers ended; two received loans from the Instituto de Crédito Agrario (Agrarian Credit Bank); and one had received a loan from SENA.[4]

Other workers borrowed houses from kinsmen, friends, or even landlords. Houses that were once the residence of *agregados* are loaned to reputable families in distress. The only direct benefit the landlords expect is that since many of these houses are located on small coffee plantations separated from the main house, the presence of the family will discourage theft of beans.

As a last resort families will try to rent houses in town, the only place where rental property is available.[5] Town residence may also be a matter of preference: it offers ready access to secondary schools, alternative employment, and other amenities. A short walk puts any town dweller within access to large and small coffee plantations where they may find employment.

Rurality and urbanism are not two distinct categories. They are dimensions that shape, without entirely determining, the strategies chosen by laboring families. Housing availability, number of sons contributing to household budget, preferences, and ability to finance further schooling for children all play a part.

> I would like to live here near a town so that the family can study, though they do not like to study. Look, I have a daughter who is twelve years old, and she is crazy for me to take her out of school. . . .

In town one has more facilities, it is easier to make money—fixing clothing, taking the lunch to laborers, caring for children. Well, life is more favorable.

But for some people there is a delicate balance of preferences that leads to difficulty in making up their minds, and they move back and forth between settings:

It is better [to live in town]. I can work in family houses . . . as a domestic. Ah, [but] my husband would say that it was better on a farm [as *agregados*], that we could make more on a farm, with animals and everything. And we would go again [to a farm] until [finally] we stayed here [in town].

Another woman who had lived in many urban areas, including the city of Medellín, explained,

I prefer to live on a farm because I can help myself. I don't have to buy onions or cilantro, lettuce, peas, or potatoes. And I raise my chickens. I said to [my husband], let us go back [as *agregados*] to a farm, where we can have animals and everything.

The surveyed harvesters have also moved from towns to rural areas, and vice versa. There were 126 families in Risaralda (32 percent of the surveyed harvesters) who had moved from one municipality to another or from one setting to another. Twenty-two of these migrating families had shifted residence from a town or city to the countryside and twenty had done the reverse. In Cundinamarca twenty-eight families had shifted residence (25 percent of surveyed harvesters' families): six had moved from a town or city to the countryside and an equal number had done the reverse.

The desire to settle in a rural area betrays laborers' dreams of owning their own farms. Until recently, land prices remained reasonable, and this dream was not totally out of reach for rural wage laborers. Of the forty-two small farmers I visited and interviewed during the summer of 1986, five had managed to buy their one-to-five-hectare farms some ten years earlier from earnings as wage laborers, and two others had bought farms with their earnings as a chauffeur and a muleteer, respectively. Those who acquired their farms more recently had purchased aging coffee groves that they had sharecropped or managed for several years. But by 1986, none of the landless families that I interviewed believed that the dream was still possible. Land prices had skyrocketed. Unrealistic as owning a farm may have been, these laborers smiled wistfully when I asked about the prospect of doing so. It is, after all, a dream rooted in childhood. Some of the so-called rural proletarians had been raised on farms owned by their parents and wanted to own land themselves. Thus, the distinction between farmer and landless laborer is as fluid as that between rural and town resident. A landless laborer may have started his life as a son of a farmer, lived in various towns and rural areas, and, with some luck, may have purchased a small farm of his own. A family of farmers does not necessarily reproduce another family of farmers, and the same is true of a family of laborers. These shifts do not bring about a drastic reorganization of the family. The definition of roles and obligations remain much the same and conform to Gutierrez de Pineda's description of the Antioqueño family (Gutierrez de Pineda 1976).

4.2   Getting Married

When a young man feels ready and is able to assume an obligation, he marries. Traditionally, the ideal moment of marriage is when a young man is between the ages of nineteen and twenty-six; his bride should be in her late teens. However, some rural women have, for some time, preferred to wait until they were twenty (Gutierrez de Pineda, 1976: 188), and many more women have recently chosen to remain single (Puyana 1985: 192). Among the families I visited, a number of women between the ages of seventeen and twenty were still living at home. The 1985 census corroborates our observation: on average, women now have their first baby at the age of twenty and probably have not been married for long (Departamento Nacional 1986a: 802).

Marriage implies a dramatic change in lifestyle for young men. They must forfeit their previous carefree lives and the prospect of occasional travel. Instead, they assume the responsibility of finding more permanent sources of income and a home for the future family. Marriage itself is considered the acquisition of an "obligation," and each child is considered another such obligation. Not all young men come to terms with such dramatic changes in lifestyle. Several women I talked to described their families' many moves as a result of their husbands' boredom and desire for a change of scenery.

Regardless of the lifestyle fancied by the husband, soon after marriage the young couple begin to raise a family. It is a stressful period, and some young men and women prefer to live with each other (*se arriman o viven arrimados*) for a while before deciding on marriage and family. In some highland areas this period is described as a period of getting used to each other and is de rigeur before entering into a marriage arrangement. Such is not the case in Risaralda, but these free unions are a clear and open option that may or may not end in marriage.[6] To ease the inevitable financial stress, the husband or companion is likely to work for the woman's father.

The number of children is not entirely left to providence. A little over half of the rural families (56.5 percent) interviewed by Gutierrez de Pineda discussed the number of children they wanted and handled the matter through sexual abstention (1976: 119). Traditionally, couples expressed a wish to have two sons and two daughters (Gutierrez de Pineda 1976: 173). However, families with more than four children were rather common. The total number of children was related to the order in which sons and daughters were born. Couples continued to have children until they had enough sons to balance the financial demands of raising their daughters. If a balance was not achieved, some of the daughters would be sent to work as domestics in towns. Very few of these girls would earn enough to send regular remittances to their parents.

In recent years, the Colombian government has embarked on a planned-parenthood campaign that has resulted in a dramatic decrease in the birthrate and the size of families (Bonilla 1985; Gomez and Morant 1987). Large families with between eleven and sixteen children are now rare (see table 11). In 1985 the mean number of children per woman in Risaralda was 3.02 and in Cundinamarca was 3.75 (Departamento Nacional 1986b). Households are also smaller. The harvesters surveyed in Risaralda and Cundinamarca came from households with 5.3 individuals (standard deviation 2.82). It was not clear how the reduction in family size was achieved. Some women I talked to mentioned the use of birth-control measures. It was not easy to determine if men participated in such decisions. Many women, with the advice and support of doctors, decided to terminate their fertility.[7]

4.3   The Growing Family

Small children roam around houses and neighborhoods enjoying themselves with little thought of school or work. Parents hope that the young children will attend school and mind their lessons, but few daughters and even fewer sons go to school regularly, and parents often complain about their children's disinterest in graduating from primary school.[8]

Although many young sons fail to attend school, they do not at this early age engage in productive activities. Only a 15.9 percent of boys younger than ten helped in the coffee harvest or earned a bit of cash by taking lunches to laborers in the field (see fig. 6). Most boys simply stayed home. At age eleven boys are more likely to start working: about half of the ten-to-fourteen-year-old boys worked with their parents in the harvest, and 18 percent of them tried to find year-round employment.

Parental expectations increase by the time sons reach fourteen, and at age sixteen they are expected to look for jobs. However, only during the harvest can they be sure of employment. Later in the season, when work slacks, they are the first laborers to be let go, and younger boys may not earn a full wage. Parents of adolescents find it difficult when their sons are sitting at home. A father is likely to consider accepting either a work contract that allows him to bring a son as a helper or a job as *agregado* on a farm where his sons may also find employment. As a despairing mother

TABLE 11.   Fertility Rates in Rural and Urban Sectors of Colombia

Period		Total	Urban	Rural
1960–64	(1)	7.0	6.1	7.9
1965–66	(1)	6.5	5.2	7.7
1967–68	(1)	6.0	4.6	7.4
1973	(2)	4.7	3.6	6.7
1976	(3)	4.2	3.3	6.1
1978	(4)	3.8	3.1	5.4
1980	(4)	3.6	3.0	5.1
1985	(5)	3.0	2.6	4.2

Source: From Gomez and Morant 1987. Their information for each period was based on the sources listed below.
  (1) Elkins, H. *Encuesta Nacional de Fecundidad.* 1973. ASCOFAME.
  (2) DANE La Fecundidad en Colombia. 1978. *Boletín Mensual de Estadística,* no. 325, 1978.
  (3) DANE-CCRP. *Encuesta Nacional de Fecundidad.* Colombia, 1976.
  (4) MINISALUD-CCRP. *Segunda Encuesta Nacional de Prevalencia de Anticonceptivos.* Colombia, 1980.
  (5) CEDE *Informe de Avances de Evaluación de la Cobertura del Censo.* Bogota, April 1987.

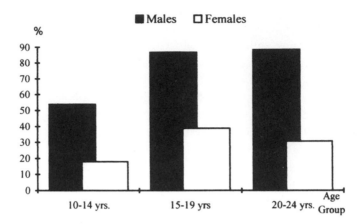

Fig. 6.   Percentages of young males and females in each age group who worked during the 1985–86 harvest in Risaralda and Cundinamarca municipalities. These data include not only the informants but also other members of their families.

put it, "What we suffer to have the house well supplied [with men]! If one of them works, the others are sitting because it is hard [for all of them] to find work. We are more than crazy to go to a farm!"

Working sons do help with family expenses, but there is no hard-and-fast rule to determine the share of their contribution. However, young children hear their mothers talk about how their older brothers helped on their parents' farms or worked for wages to help support their families. In this way, boys learn what is eventually expected of them: "Ah! I say to my son, that one. Look, you are now big. Go and work around and help your father." Sons are later likely to hear their parents complain about food shortages and lack of money. But these are vague and unformed messages, to be interpreted by sons as they wish and circumstances allow.

When sons are young, their mothers are likely to handle their earnings and use them to buy shoes, clothing, and school supplies, leaving the children with only enough for sweets. As the sons get older, they receive the money themselves and are likely to pass it to their fathers or to purchase and contribute food and household goods. The mother of an eleven-year-old who worked with her harvesting coffee explained, "He does the food shopping . . . and then if I realize that the groceries are going to be short, I add some [money of my own]."

Older sons receive their own paychecks and decide for themselves how much to contribute to the family's grocery shopping. Although parents expect help, they are sensitive to their sons' growing social and personal needs.

Of course, they are not bad sons. When they work they give a little help; they give for their own food. You see? But they also need their money. How can one take all of it? One cannot! Then when [the sons] are working with [their fathers], they buy their own food or they pay me for the food, as any other laborer would [that I have to feed]. That is all the help they give. They need the money to dress and for whatever.

Need, affection, and personality play significant roles in easing or blocking the flow of exchanges between sons and their families. A caring old father was given money for marketing: "They give him the money. They leave little for themselves. But sometimes they themselves figure out what is needed [and bring the groceries home]." A twenty-seven-year-old son recalled, "Since I was the oldest, I had to give half, and the other [half was] for clothing and to have fun." At the same time, this son was unwilling to alter his lifestyle to be available to his parents at all times. Although he had gone away several times, only occasionally did he send money to his parents.

TABLE 12.   Permanent Occupation of Young Males and Females in Harvesting Families in the Three Municipalities of This Study

	Women by Age Group			Men by Age Group		
Occupation	10–14 (N = 89)	15–19 (N = 103)	20–25 (N = 88)	10–14 (N = 115)	15–19 (N = 223)	20–24 (N = 112)
Home	30.34%	58.26%	67.05%	9.57%	3.59%	1.79%
Student	66.29%	15.53%	4.54%	57.39%	14.80%	1.79%
Work	3.37%	26.21%	28.41%	33.04%	81.61%	96.42%
Total	100%	100%	100%	100%	100%	100%

Source: Field survey data.

Note: Since there were no significant differences among the municipalities, the three sampled populations were incorporated in this table. Only the male and female members of local resident harvesting families are included in the count. Hence, these employment figures differ significantly from other census information for the same municipalities.

Tension, disappointment, and ambition can get in the way of filial responsibility and weaken the bond between sons and parents. Not all sons are willing to give up dreams of travel and adventure, and many find it difficult to get along with their fathers. They may choose to roam for a few years, coming home only occasionally. Among the sixteen families interviewed who had sons old enough to travel, seven had at least one son temporarily away; most commonly, between one to three sons were away, and one or two remained at home.[9] In some cases, the sons' absence left families in poverty.

Eventually, the sons' travel results in employment elsewhere. There is then little contact between sons and parents. Many could not even say where their sons were; none of these adult children sent regular remittances. However, some sons do come back periodically, laden with gifts. In one case, grown sons returned every three to four months: "They are very good, very noble sons," said the mother proudly as she showed me the refrigerator they had bought her with the proceeds from their employment. Another mother was visited by her sons who lived in Medellín and went to stay with them for extended periods of time. These were opportunities for the sons to buy her clothing and give her money. But in most cases, visits are rare, and remittances are not regular.

Daughters are much more housebound than sons. Only rarely are they allowed to work away from home, and they do so only in jobs that are considered appropriate for women, a category that does not include working on a coffee farm (material work). Women are considered too delicate. Those who have harvested and then stopped explained that this work was bad for their health, that it caused headaches and rheumatism. Some would not even harvest coffee in their own backyards for fear that young men would look down on them. Young unmarried women who must harvest coffee (because of either family poverty or the desire for pocket money) must be accompanied by their mothers, fathers, or brothers.

In general, men feel threatened by working daughters because of the implication that they are unable to meet their obligations. Still, many men consider unmarried daughters a major burden and resent them. Fortunately, some occupations are considered not to challenge women's frailty or femininity (see section 5.7b and 6.1b). Domestic work, employment as salesgirls or vendors, sewing, hairdressing, and secretarial work are the favored occupations and are considered appropriate for permanent employment. However, these occupations require some training, which is not always feasible in poor households. Furthermore, even when families can afford training, the demand for secretaries, hairdressers, and seamstresses is small, and few women find employment. There is a significant demand for domestic servants, but that occupation has little prestige, and local salaries are too low to entice many young women. Only by going to big cities can women earn enough money to make it worth their while.[10] However, not many mothers are willing to let their daughters emigrate while they are still young:

> She had an offer of work in Bogotá, but [it was] too far . . . and then it was no good because I could not keep an eye on her. And she likes to work and everything. . . . But I have a cowardly heart. I cried very much and told her: Margarita, do not go, better to go hungry. Yes, we are in need, but I would not know how she is.

To be at home is the wish or the fate of the majority of adolescent girls. Their restlessness curbed, they learn to limit their horizons and aspirations to domestic activities and not to venture beyond their neighborhood to visit friends. The traditional larger family must have provided some relief for young girls on isolated farms. In town, life is less lonely, and social contacts are more frequent and easier. One young town woman said that she does not get bored at home: she simply has to create the appropriate climate in which there are things to do. Hence, she does not find the need to go to work and does not think it proper.

After marriage, or upon entering a relationship, men expect their women to stay home. Women even lose the company and support of their mothers and sisters unless the couple lives near her parents. It is initially a very lonely existence. A twenty-year-old woman who was living with her companion far away from any hamlet tearfully said that she could not take this existence much longer. She was alone all day, with her man coming to eat something in the evening and then going out again, hardly stopping by during weekends. She had nothing to do. She said, "I would be better off if I had children," but she did not yet want to be tied down. In time women get used to this isolation and hardly venture beyond their garden unless they live in a hamlet and have family or friends close by.

> I seldom go out—once in a while to town. . . . I am thinking while I am visiting that there is a dress to make, something to do. . . . A little walk and I go and come back.

I hardly go out just to go out. Sometimes to the doctor or for a meeting in the school. Nothing else. I hardly go out.

In Risaralda, women do not even go out to market, although they are responsible for preparing food.[11] Said one woman, "What an embarrassment if I had to go and buy a pound of rice. If ever I had to, I would make sure that it is carefully wrapped [to disguise it]." The weekly shopping for food is done by husbands or adult sons so that women do not advertise that they are without protection or companionship and the men convey that they are capable of assuming obligations. Women are also ashamed of having to bargain or buy on credit.

There is nothing better than for men to market. Ah, because we go to buy groceries and there is not enough money. Then the man looks for a way, for a store, or finds a loan of money, or searches, or whatever. Of that I have no idea. I never wanted to go to market.

Some women in Risaralda were aware that women in other parts of Colombia were very much engaged in handling the weekly budget but on the whole found this situation amusing, just as these women were amused by my desire to buy my own food. Many women considered themselves incapable of managing the budget or even of knowing how to shop.

[To buy] something, I have to ask him because I do not know how much it costs. I tell him [what to buy] . . . and I have to ask him how much it is. . . . I would like to shop, but sometimes I like to make lists of groceries, and it adds up [to too much]. . . . I would like to have everything.

The image of women as greedy for luxuries and incompetent at managing a budget or dealing with financial problems totally subverts the autonomy of laborers' wives, rendering them helpless and subject to the vagaries of irresponsible or egotistical husbands. "He brings the marketing, and whatever he brings . . . I ask no questions," was one woman's half-formed response to a question about how much of her husband's income flowed into a household's weekly budget. The husband's authority is morally justified: said one woman, "The man is the head, so says the Bible."

Thus, young women face marriage with strong feelings of inadequacy, with little worldly experience, and probably with considerable apprehension about their dependence on their future spouses, from whom they will need permission to work and to plan a family. For the most part, they were, until very recent years, young adolescents marrying men in their middle twenties, which must not have been easy.

> Came the moment and . . . must have been a fit that I had to get married. And that's my story. No more pleasure, as they say. We are so poor. At least he turned out to be a good husband because he is hardworking.

Wives' experiences are even more depressing when men cannot come to grips with their new responsibilities—when they drink, abuse their wives, and are insensitive to their families' needs. Young women must find their own way around the failings of their men and poverty. The latter may be a burden shared, discussed, and jointly resolved, but the former rarely is, and women must solve it on their own.

Many wives do eventually assert themselves and convince their husbands to let them work or otherwise find ways to contribute to the family income. Others manipulate or confront their husbands to protect themselves and their children from abusive behavior.

> I go [to work], and he gets mad because I am over there. He says that women are for the kitchen. I like it because our daughter takes charge of the kitchen, and I go to grab some money to help because we do not have enough for food. That is why I say it is better to be on a farm [as *agregados*] because there are animals, and if one struggles it always brings some cents.

These women find strength not in cultural dicta but in their own childhood experiences. In general, women who worked after marriage had mothers who helped in the farm or worked as domestics. Their mothers and, to some extent, their fathers helped these women differentiate ideal from real circumstances. With that knowledge, one woman advised her husband of her expectations in no uncertain terms:

> I follow him because I could see that he has judgment and because I always had to. But [it is important] that both behave responsibly . . . because [for one] to work so that the other spends it, no. I have told him that I follow him because I can see he has judgment.

If women work on the same farms as their husbands, it is quite likely that he will receive the wages for both. However, if she works elsewhere, she will receive her weekly payment and is free to administer it as she wants. She is unlikely to use it to buy food unless her husband drinks or is ill. Typically, she saves her earnings to buy clothing and cover school expenses and some luxury items, leaving the food buying to husbands and sons.

In recent years young unmarried and recently married women with no children have been able to renegotiate their roles. Those who live in towns may look for appropriate employment to have some financial autonomy and to contribute toward household comforts. Daughters or wives of coffee laborers occasionally can earn money by making clothing, by caring for children, or from other small entrepreneurial activities. One woman worked as a domestic for many years. Her earnings allowed the husband to build a house that brought some measure of prestige to the family. Another couple jointly planned an elaborate strategy that included her working as a domestic for a number of years. With their joint income, they built a nice house in town with a little store attached to it. They then decided to start a family, since the wife could now stay home and tend the store. But these women are still in the minority and have the good fortune to have supportive and considerate husbands willing to endure the mockery of other men.

4.4   Older Parents

Household size shrinks as sons and daughters grow, marry, and move out. Older fathers, however, continue to feel burdened as their earning capacity begins to wane. Farmers are reluctant to offer them employment in weeding and fertilizing between harvests. Furthermore, older men are less likely to bag heavy sacks of coffee berries as they once did. They find it hard to sustain medical expenses and periods of unemployment. Their plight is eased if an unmarried son stays at home and helps with daily expenses. However, sons grow restless and show no qualms about leaving old parents on their own. Indeed, there is no expectation that a child should remain unmarried to care for old parents or that they should be absorbed within a married daughter's household. Only one of the 128 households we visited included an old mother. It is more likely for young grandsons or granddaughters to live with their grandparents to help with cooking and errands (see table 13).

I found that men continue to work for as long as they can. According to the 1973 population and household census of the two municipalities of this study, 67.4 percent of the men seventy years or older were still employed, at least seasonally (Departamento Nacional de Estadistica 1973). Older couples can expect only occasional gifts of money or clothing and, when daughters live nearby, trays of prepared food in the event of illness or unemployment.

4.5   Female-Headed Households

There is a small but significant number of households in which women are the acknowledged heads. These women were abandoned or widowed or are prostitutes with children. Some of the abandoned women never married. The increasing frequency of consensual unions without marriage may in time lead to an increase in the number of female-headed households.

There were twenty-seven such households among the harvesters surveyed in Risaralda. For the most part, the mothers stayed at home while her sons and perhaps her daughters went off to work. Some of the sons earned a living in coffee agriculture, and others worked in the service sector or construction. Daughters were likely to be domestics, but one worked harvesting coffee. In the twelve poorest (and generally smallest)

TABLE 13.   Composition of Rural Households and the Households of Harvesters

Household Composition	% of Rural Households[a]	% of Harvester's Households[b]
Single Adult	4.30	9.24
Couple	4.40	12.45
Couple and Other	3.10	1.60
Parents and Child(ren)	57.20	54.22
Parents, Child(ren) and Other	13.30	0
Single Parent and Child	6.50	13.65
Single Parents, Child(ren), and Other	5.30	4.02
Single Adult and Other	5.50	4.82

[a]The percentages are derived from SER Survey of Rural Households in Coffee Municipalities in 1985 (Velez, Becerra, Gomez, et al. 1986). This survey also included farming families that are more likely to retain sons and daughters or incorporate other kinsmen who may help with farm labor or aged parents who may in fact own the farm.

[b]The figures for harvesting households are based on our sample of 247 local harvesters in Risaralda. This population is comparable to the population considered in the SER survey.

female-headed households, the mothers worked as domestics or harvesting coffee most of the year.

4.6   Summary

Coffee laborers come from families not unlike the families of local small farmers and poorer town dwellers. Most of these families have longstanding roots in the area, though some had to leave when jobs became scarce. The recent expansion of coffee farms has made their return possible, perhaps not to the area where they were born but at least to the same department. However, if the returnees are unable to find available houses or to build their own dwellings, they may have to once again search for work elsewhere. Renting is only feasible if there are many young sons who contribute their wages. The availability of housing and cost of rental are key factors determining the location and characteristics of labor supply, as Griffith (1995: 268) has pointed out for commercial agriculture in the United States.

Many of the families interviewed during the summer of 1986 welcomed the opportunity to resettle in Risaralda, since coffee labor represents their cultural tradition and way of life: their parents grew coffee, or these workers tended it as wage laborers. Thus, coffee laborers are a distinct segment of the agricultural labor force. However, not all children want to follow in their parents' footsteps. Circumstances, education, growing aspirations, and family tensions have encouraged sons to search for other occupations or to emigrate. The local supply of future laborers thus will reflect not only birthrates and wages but a complex set of familial, cultural, and social dynamics.

Laboring families do not automatically clone themselves. Some authoritarian fathers do not become cruel tyrants. However, young men may learn brutality in the workplace and use it to manage their own children. The abused children of this region often run away and carry that experience to their future workplace. Thus, home and farm are intertwined in the social reproduction of the labor force; the nature of social relations in both settings is as important as cultural rules in shaping attitudes, ability to work with others, and technical experience.

The wanderings of young laborers have served to connect each family to a number of other municipalities. Fathers and sons often return to these places for a few weeks or a month after the harvest in their own neighborhood has ended. However, these seasonal migrations are circumscribed by the obligation to provide for their families and to do the weekly grocery shopping. Fathers must return every so often or leave a son at home to assume this responsibility. Heads of households in Cundinamarca are less likely to be so constrained in their movements since women are freer to shop and engage in activities outside the home.

Recent changes in demographics—smaller families, delayed marriages, and increased longevity—are likely to significantly affect the local supply of laborers and the welfare of working families. Parents may have fewer mouths to feed but will also have fewer contributors to the household income. Children will feel the burden of supporting parents, who are likely to live longer than previous generations. Unless real wages increase proportionately, many more sons will be tempted to emigrate to avoid contributing more of their income for a longer period of time. Both developments will constrain the supply of laborers and might force farmers to search further afield and explore new supply strategies.

The coffee labor force is likely to become progressively more male in character if incomes improve, since women are reluctant and find it less necessary to do that work. Poverty sent women to harvest berries and still forces some to do so. But increased educational opportunities have opened new horizons. More years in school has not always translated into employment in appropriate occupations away from coffee groves, but education has made women more reluctant to accept labor as harvesters. If farmers want to continue to tap this labor supply, they will have to find new ways to attract it. Interestingly, some have done so by organizing all female crews of harvesters.

Roles and lines of authority within the family are clearly defined. Yet this role ascription pattern has generated neither coordination nor a well-balanced single-purpose partnership between spouses. Indeed, goals are often in conflict, with a husband wanting to roam or drink and a wife wanting new clothing and a comfortable, stable setting. In more traditional unions, the husband's goals take preeminence, but the wife may subvert them if she feels they run counter to her interests and those of her children. While cultural values sanction the authority of husbands, the submission of wives, and the obligation of each in the creation of a family, these mores do not beget joint familial aspirations other than the fundamentals of Christian ethics that sanctify birth, private property, honesty, charity, and love. Furthermore, family members do not sit together to plan who will work for wages, how much each will contribute, who should migrate, and what should be their income goals. Thus, the model of a household proposed by the new household economics fails here because it assumes a single utility function and perfect coordination among members. A more complex simulation model of the household needs to be constructed, as Hart (1992) has suggested. Such a model should identify the significant roles and consider the rights and obligations implied for each. It should also outline patterns of communication and the ability to negotiate role performance. Being able to arrive at a solution that satisfies various members of the household also depends on the degree of autonomy that each one is allowed. In Risaralda, sons have much more autonomy than daughters and wives. But husbands control communications. The sons' freedom lies in their ability to go away and find their own places in society. Daughters have that option only if they marry or become domestics in an urban household. Given this scenario, the household as the unit of analysis does not seem useful for examining the participation in the labor market in coffee agriculture. Instead, I focus on individual actors and recognize differences in social aspirations and responsibilities.

Chapter 5

The Harvest

Agricultural economists often analyze the labor market only during the harvest, neglecting the season that follows. Such an approach is warranted when planting and maintenance jobs are highly mechanized, but such is not the case with coffee. In this study, I highlight two seasonal markets, harvest and maintenance. Although some men work during both the harvest and the maintenance season, the experience of the harvest is very different from farm work the rest of the year. Farmers also consider the harvest a season that requires special attention. The social and technical pressures inherent in the harvest, as chapters 5 and 6 will show, affect the recruitment and management process and lead to very different types of contracts than exist during the rest of the year. The farmer's foremost concern is the timely collection of berries and insuring that harvesters do not damage trees. The laborers are concerned about working conditions and pay and are aware that during the harvest they have enough power to negotiate.

The harvest intensifies the demand for labor beyond the capacity of the local population. Nevertheless, coffee farmers have chosen not to manipulate supply except through information flows and wage enticements (see section 8.3a). The growers rely on these methods to lure laborers who have finished harvesting in neighboring areas. The harvest market thus is geographically wider than the maintenance season labor market. It is not, however, delimited by geomorphic features. The boundaries are socially defined by kinship and friendship links reinforced generation after generation. Thus communities become interdependent with other communities, sometimes sending and sometimes receiving harvesters.

The market power of laborers during this season does not necessarily threaten the financial viability of all farmers. Some farmers are relatively wealthy and have easy access to bank loans. Others, however, have trouble meeting paydays, particularly early in the season. Many of these financially strained farmers also have lower-yielding coffee groves that are less attractive to laborers. Although the demand sector is far from homogeneous, all farmers have to compete during a short window of time for the same pool of workers and have to offer similar contracts and pay rates during the harvest.

Although contracts may be similar, the management of the labor force varies considerably from farm to farm. A small farmer who has only two to three workers on any one day can be much more informal and relaxed than the manager of a large farm who has to handle crews of about one hundred laborers. These differences impinge on harvesters' perception of the attractiveness of particular farms, which, in turn, molds the reaction of farmers. In this interplay, management style clearly affects the quality of performance and the reliability of harvesters. This interactional reality reiterates that it is inappropriate to analyze wages without also considering how the labor process is managed. In this chapter I describe the harvest strategies akin to each farm type and the reasons for adopting them.

Differences in the condition of the coffee groves or in the work experience do not severely affect the distribution of harvesters according to age or home residence. Except for the very small farms that hire mostly kin and friends and the few that make an effort to attract women, on most other farms young and old, migrant and local work together on the same crews. The harvest labor market is not segmented by type of enterprise.

By subsuming a discussion of demand and supply under the rubric of the strategies used to attract and manage laborers or to find jobs, I stress the role of actors in structuring the market for harvest labor. Actors choose among the various equally feasible management options open to them. Each of these strategies, although they do not segment the market, affect the work environment, the efficiency of labor, and the boundaries of the market (see chapter 7).

5.1   The Management of the Harvest

The cycle of warmer and cooler seasons characteristic of Colombia's coffee regions affects the ripening rates of the berries throughout the year. A period of protracted warm weather hastens the process. The berries ripen one by one, and slowly the clusters are transformed from a mass of green to mottled bunches and finally to bright red spots on trees. The berries eventually become black and fall to the ground. Heavy or constant rains are said to soften the stems that attach the berries to the branch, causing them to fall even before they turn black. Blackened berries or those that are allowed to rot on the ground yield lower-quality coffee that sells for a

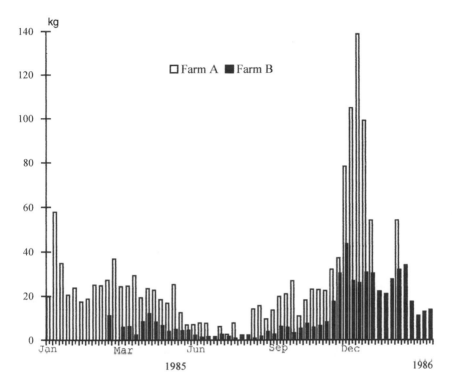

Fig. 7. Amount of coffee harvested on two enterprise farms in Risaralda. Both farms are located at about the same altitude, though in different municipalities. Each column represents the weight in coffee berries harvested each week. No information was available for the first months of 1985 for farm B.

much lower price than do berries that are picked when red. Farmers fear this unnecessary loss of revenue and diligently organize the harvest to make sure that berries are bagged before they fall or turn black. One by one they are picked as they turn red, the harvester moving from branch to branch and from tree to tree. When all of the trees have been gone over once, harvesters must start over again to select berries that have ripened since the harvest began. Harvesting is thus a continuous yearlong process, tedious and slow when only a few of the berries in each cluster can be picked, then faster and more rewarding as what remains of the cluster turns bright red, and then slow once again when only smaller clusters more hidden from the sun are finally ready for picking. According to a thirteen-year record in the municipality of Chinchiná, which borders Marsella, 73.5 percent of all berries are harvested between September and December; this is the period known as the harvest (see fig. 7). The midharvest, which takes place from March to April, only accounts for 6 percent of berries harvested annually. The pattern is similar in Cundinamarca, except that the peak months differ.

In Risaralda and its neighboring departments the months of July and August are hot enough to accelerate the ripening process. In Cundinamarca the ripening process starts in January. If the sun continues to shine in September and the temperature remains at normal levels, then the trees will change in color by late October in Risaralda and by March in Cundinamarca. Farmers must then prepare to work quickly to gather berries before they fall to the ground. But sudden cooler spells, not unlikely in this area of Colombia, will slow down an already started ripening process, and the preparations for large-scale harvesting of berries must be set aside. Farmers must wait and see. They must keep watch over the coffee trees and on the sky. Heavy rains do not affect the ripening process but give greater urgency to the picking of ripened berries. October, November, and December are rainy months, sometimes with heavy downpours threatening not only the quality of the harvest but the ability of the workers to pick swiftly. The ground becomes slippery with mud. Plastic-covered figures move slowly among the trees, sometimes hooking themselves to trunks to avoid sliding down dangerous slopes. Bad moods prevail, and harvesters are reluctant to come if weather conditions slow their work.

Farmers face the period when most berries are harvested with a certain amount of trepidation. While they usually start with a crew of laborers who were hired to weed and fertilize, they must make sure that if rains threaten they will have access to enough laborers to avoid loss of revenue. Nineteen-eighty-five was a particularly unnerving year for farmers. Sudden cooler weather slowed a ripening process that had been in full swing. Preparations for massive hiring had to be delayed. Then a brief spell of warmer sunny weather helped to complete the ripening process. Crews were readied once again, only to have harvesting plans canceled when heavy rains began. Farmers worry at such times that laborers, who have come expressly to harvest, will tire of waiting and return home. On this particular occasion the supply of harvesters was assured by the eruption of a nearby volcano that destroyed many coffee groves in a neighboring municipality, sending a number of worried and unemployed laborers in search of jobs.

Uncertainty is both a reality and a state of mind during the harvest season; farmers cope with it in various ways. Some try to judge the number of laborers they will need under different harvesting conditions and recruit accordingly. This is easier for farmers with coffee groves located in the colder, higher slopes, where weather fluctuations are not as great and are easier to guess. The difficulty with this strategy is that farmers may have to pay higher rates once competition for workers increases. A second strategy is to hire as many workers as possible to complete the harvest in the shortest period of time. This last approach, however, implies that farmers have no cash-flow problems and are willing to rely on a proportionately high percentage of nonresident laborers who must be housed and fed and who are considered by many farmers to be less desirable.

On occasion, farmers are caught short of laborers and must take time off from supervising the harvest to bring workers from elsewhere. At such times, neighbors may get together and share in the cost and trouble of transporting laborers. These farmers prefer to take the chance of occasional labor shortages and the bother of a trip than to rely on labor contractors. They are convinced, and their experience seems to confirm, that eventually enough laborers will come to the farm to ask for jobs. At most the owner, administrator, or field supervisor will go down to the municipal township to recruit workers. If these farmers prefer to use local harvesters, they rely on personal networks of permanent laborers and field supervisors.

Competition for laborers among growers is kept at a manageable level because temperature varies with altitude. Berries start ripening more quickly in coffee groves at lower altitudes, where most laborers will work first. As the ripening process moves up the slopes, so do the harvesters. These altitude variations serve to limit the total number of men needed in each region at any one time. Furthermore, in the neighboring municipalities of the department of Caldas, the harvest starts a little bit earlier, and in the department of Valle, the harvest begins a bit later. Local harvesters are thus joined by others who have finished working in their hometowns. Even within the same farm, some areas will ripen before others, allowing farmers to use smaller crews for a longer period of time than if the ripening process was more uniform.

Nevertheless, the competition for labor is keen and highly skewed, since not all farmers find it equally easy to attract harvesters. Because they are paid by the amount harvested, laborers favor the higher-yielding *caturra* trees, which produce enough berries to quickly fill workers' sacks.

Rains dampen trees, and harvesters who must work in densely planted areas are permanently wet. Thus, most workers prefer farms with *caturra* trees that are neither too close to each other to hamper movement and add to discomfort nor too far apart to slow progress. Coffee groves on steep slopes are uncomfortable, dangerous, and hard to harvest. Hence, the owners of these groves must pay more to attract workers.

Local residents prefer to work close to where they live (see table 14). Since the harvesting day is long and tiring, a long trek home is to be avoided if possible. Farmers near the municipal township are in a privileged position to attract local residents as well as those who arrive there from other municipalities. Many in this group of harvesters prefer to be close to the amenities of town life and to work on farms with smaller labor crews and more personalized treatment.

The most difficult farms to manage well are the traditional coffee groves that are not well kept and are far from access roads. These landlords found themselves having to pay three to five pesos more per kilo of berries to compensate laborers for the extra time required to pick the

TABLE 14.   Work Site Preferences of Male and Female Harvesters in Risaralda and Cundinamarca

Preference	% Harvesters	
	Locals ($N = 295$)	Migrants ($N = 197$)
Farm Size		
Small	29	38
Medium	22	18
Large	23	20
Location		
Near Town	69	49
Far From Town	9	22
Modernized Coffee Grove	88	81
Density of Coffee Grove		
Medium Density	63	66
High Density	5	5

Source: This table includes all the men and women in the survey.

Note: The vertical line within each category should add to 100 percent. When it does not, it means that the remaining harvesters are indifferent in their preferences. For example, 26 percent of local harvesters are indifferent to the size of farms; the rest are almost equally divided in their preference by size. *Near* for local harvesters means near their homes. In the case of migrants, it means near town. *Density* refers to how close the trees are planted to each other.

berries of lower-yielding trees. They often also had to travel elsewhere to get harvesters. In general, the owners of traditional coffee farms have to pay more during the harvest if they use the piece-rate method than the owners of productive *caturra* farms. Not surprisingly, the owners of unkept farms complain that

> The laborer looks for the best coffee, and then they leave you. Then there is problem with everything: the food, the sleep, the pay. Everything becomes difficult. They come and harvest only the good trees, leaving the bad ones untouched.

The strategy used by some of these farmers, who do not want to invest any more money in coffee, is to hire as many laborers as they can when berries are ready for picking, letting the workers go while waiting for more berries to ripen, and then rehiring the laborers. It is a wasteful and difficult system to manage. It angers the resident laborers who sell lunches to harvesters because it makes it harder for them to keep food-preparation costs down, and it causes bottlenecks in the processing of berries.

Successful managers coordinate tasks to assure themselves steady and reliable supplies of workers and to keep resident laboring families content. Managers also must attend to cash problems and make sure that they can sell beans at a rate that will match their need for laborers or that they will be able to borrow money. The harvest is a costly season, even on modernized farms, and can consume 28 percent of a farm's revenue (see section 3.6). Hence it is important to manage the harvest carefully and avoid unnecessary labor expenses.

To harvest berries as they ripen, farmers or managers must walk the rows of trees and mark off the areas and the order in which they should be harvested. With the crew supervisors, the farmers will mark with flags the rows within each area that are to be harvested each day and assign them to different crews. The workers in a crew will move together down a row, each working on a different tree. Once all the ripe berries are picked from a tree, workers move on to the next available tree. The harvester puts the berries in a small bag; when full, it is emptied into a sack set somewhere near the row. Workers have their own sacks and must carry them at the end of the day to the weighing station, where the laborers wait their turn to have the berries weighed and the amounts earned recorded in a ledger. The sacks are examined at the weighing station to see if they include green berries or leaves. If so, the worker is either warned or immediately dismissed. The field supervisors are responsible for making sure that trees are not damaged by careless, fast harvesting and that workers stay in their assigned rows. The supervisors must also handle disputes and fights among laborers that arise out of accusations of theft, intrusion into assigned areas, or personal issues. To deal with theft of berries among laborers, farmers or managers have guards watch the half-filled sacks, and the harvesters are expected to pay the guard's wages. Firings often result from damage to trees or from failure to resolve personal quarrels. Laborers will approach managers and crew supervisors with complaints about food, lodging, and general working conditions. Tempers flare when workers are unable to sleep and when tiredness is exacerbated by inedible food. These problems are much more acute on larger farms. On smaller farms, the picking of berries is likely to be organized in a more informal manner, and conflicts are less evident.

Once harvested, the berries have to be soaked to soften the pulp that surrounds the kernel. After a few hours, they are washed, and the remaining pulp is scraped away mechanically using very simple hand-operated mills or larger, electrically driven machines. After a final washing the beans must be immediately set to dry. The drying process should begin no more than twenty hours after the berries are picked and usually starts within ten hours. Smaller amounts of berries do not require elaborate equipment: running water, a few tubs, and a grinder similar to those traditionally used in European kitchens to grind meat are all that is needed; likewise, drying the beans can be accomplished with a minimum of fuss. The beans are spread in the yard on wooden trays or a cement floor. It takes from several days to a week, depending on weather conditions, for the beans to be sufficiently dry to fetch a reasonable price. The greater the degree of dryness, the higher the price paid for the bean. Only private buyers purchase half-dried beans and will use wetness to gain extra leverage in the bargaining process. Whenever possible, farmers try to avoid having to sell wet coffee. They try to improve their own drying facilities to handle the flow of harvested beans. With credit from the FNCC, many farmers with smaller groves have built ingenious drying devices consisting of trays that slide under a protective roof. When the sun shines, the trays are pulled out; they are quickly pushed under the roof when rains begin. By setting a number of trays under each roof, bottlenecks can be avoided on medium farms. Larger farms require industrial dryers driven by electricity, a much more expensive venture that also requires electrification. Farmers must build what best suits the volume of their harvests and preferred hiring strategies. Once the capacities of the drying facilities are set, farmers cannot drastically alter their hiring strategies. Thus, good managers must balance the size of the crew with the facilities available for drying. If too many laborers are hired, unprocessed berries may accumulate and rot. Processing bottlenecks must be avoided at all costs. This is a problem in Colombia, where the initial processing stages are carried out on the farms. In other mild-coffee producing countries, like Costa Rica, the processing of the berries is done away from the farm, in commercial plants or cooperatives. At one time, the FNCC attempted to institute a drying cooperative not too far from the area of our study, but the venture ended in failure and it was abandoned (Errazuriz 1986: 315).

In sum, the size of the labor crew and the ratio of harvesters to hectare of coffee depend on a number of factors: the type of coffee plants grown, the condition of the groves, the distance to population centers, the processing facilities, and the cash resources available. In the following section I describe how each type of farm manages the harvest.

5.2   The Harvest on a Small Farm

A harvest of about five thousand kilograms of dry coffee beans can be handled by three to four individuals.[1] This amount of coffee can be produced on a two-hectare farm that is densely planted with *caturra* trees or on a traditional four-hectare farm. Hence, most small farmers can handle the harvest on their own, as long as they have two or three adult sons willing to help.[2]

Not all farming families have two adult sons still at home. Young families try to make do by hiring just one harvester for a few days to keep up with the ripening process and the accumulation of berries. In rare cases, wives help wash, dry, and sort coffee beans, since these operations can be carried out near the house.[3] These women were brought up to work alongside their parents and are willing to continue their involvement in farm activity. Indeed, one wife was assigned a set of trees near the house; she was able to keep and manage the money from the sale of the beans and used most of it for household expenses.

As sons reach age ten, farmers begin to teach them to harvest and to help on the farm. By the time they are twelve to fourteen, they work alongside their father. If they are diligent, they are able to bag almost as much as any adult. When they are a bit older they can handle the portage of heavy loads and the washing and processing of the beans. At this point they become full-fledged laborers on the family farm. However, they are never full partners in the enterprise. Young sons continue to be clothed and fed by their parents and have no claim to a full share of the proceeds. If they want to spend money on entertainment or save money for their eventual marriage, they must work for wages elsewhere. They do not shirk their commitment to the household but balance it with days worked elsewhere. Since the berries do not ripen all at once and the harvest is small, it is possible to help parents full time for a few weeks and then to go elsewhere for a while.

When the farm is producing enough coffee to require a constant crew of harvesters, fathers are then likely to recompense their sons with money wages.

> They do not charge me, but then they are adults; one is always aware that they need [money], and of course this is not the time one gives them much, but when there is a way one gives them [something] to compensate for what laborers earn. Of course, they do not work expecting compensation. If one wants, one can give them something. They do not claim it.

This farmer paid his son just a bit below the ongoing wage; another paid the son a quarter of the prevailing wage; and yet another paid his sons only if they were employed at the time he needed them.

Older parents with less energy are likely to engage their sons' help by promising a share of the revenue. One system used is to separate a lot for the son to harvest, paying him an agreed-on percentage of the sale of those beans. More frequently, older parents with five or more hectares divide their farms into sections, giving a section to each son interested in this arrangement. The sons assume full responsibility for production, processing of the coffee, and the upkeep of their parcels. In return, they receive half of the revenue from the sale of the beans harvested. If the parent is a widowed mother, one of the sons may exploit the whole farm under a share agreement. In this way old or widowed farmers solve the harvest labor problem and help their sons get started.

Farmers without sons at home must hire outside help. At one time, labor exchanges helped small farmers cope with a sudden need for laborers, but the regional growth of a wage-labor market has blocked labor exchanges. When hiring wage laborers, farmers prefer to approach friends or neighbors first. If they can afford it, they will pay the ongoing wage, but friends might be willing to work for a discounted rate for a few days. Only one farmer mentioned taking turns with his brother and working on each other's farms.

5.3   The Harvest on a Medium Farm

In farms where the harvest is above 625 kilograms of dried beans (the yield from five to seven hectares of coffee), wage labor has to be employed even when sons help full time. If the owners live on the farm, they will handle the processing of the berries and supervise the harvest labor. If they have other occupations or live elsewhere, they will either rely on trusted resident laborers or, more rarely, engage someone on a share agreement to manage the harvest.

On these medium-size farms, the harvest is managed with a labor force of five to six harvesters, some of whom may be family members. Most medium growers prefer to hire kinsmen, friends, and neighbors; if unable to do so, farmers will approach other local residents. In this way they can avoid having to incorporate strangers into their households. Small crews are not difficult to supervise and not very problematic to feed. Wives can prepare the food, though they enlist daughters if they are old enough to help. The harvest mood on these farms is relaxed and informal. They are not only much favored by male harvesters but are seen as appropriate work places for neighboring women who need to make some money (see table 14).

Some of these farmers are short of cash by November and are not always able to get an advance on their harvest. They have no choice but to work initially by themselves, perhaps with the help of their sons. After they sell between thirty-five and sixty-two kilograms of dried beans (by 1985 costs and prices), which may take from two to three weeks, they are in a position to hire some laborers. Even then, it is important to keep wages low during the first few weeks.[4] Other medium farmers can afford to hire harvesters at the beginning of the season.

5.4   The Harvest on a Medium Enterprise Farm

Eventually all of these farms require a labor force of twenty to thirty harvesters during the peak period (see appendix A). These farms combine to create most of the demand for laborers. Hence, their management strategies will determine which type of labor contract will prevail in the local labor market.

These farms are large enough to require resident supervisors even when the owner lives there. Supervisors are likely to be trusted employees who have lived on the farms as *agregados* for a number of years. At least a second married resident laborer is required to oversee the housing for migrants, and his wife and daughters prepare the lunches and snacks required by the harvesters. If the owners do not live on the farm or are involved in other activities, they also hire administrators. Thus the management of these medium enterprise farms is somewhat more hierarchical than that of smaller farms. It is certainly more impersonal. Yet because the crews are still of reasonable size, the setting remains relatively comfortable and attractive to harvesters. Smaller crews make not only for more relaxed working conditions but also for less theft and shorter waiting periods at the weighing stations at the end of the day. However, these farms are already too impersonal for women to work there, the crews too mixed for them to venture there on their own. The few women who were harvesting in 1985 on such farms were spouses or daughters of resident laborers.

Supervisors find it easier to manage the laborers at the beginning of the season, when crews are small and consist mostly of local residents. Eventually, migrants have to be hired to meet peak requirements. It is then that supervisors begin to experience "bad moments" and often respond by becoming authoritarian and ruthless. Impersonal and hostile management relations feed budding tensions, and complaints, such as "very boring place," "one is resigned," "one gets the food," "I am going because of the bad mood of the people." Some harvesters nevertheless decide to stay on. The owners themselves grow more bitter when they cannot manage personnel. Their bitterness spills into attitudes about their labor force:

> Today's laborers are people of bad blood. They work hating the owner, not only in the countryside but also in town. This is the aftermath of the syndicate movement that distances the worker from the patron. Let us blame not the government but the idiosyncrasy of the laborer and of the Mafia that tears down everything.

This perception reinforces the negative regional stereotype of migrants. They are seen as shiftless, unreliable people who move from place to place, region to region. They are accused of bringing drugs and causing problems, being greedy with money, being irresponsible in their work, and spending their money on liquor and women.

When owners of medium enterprise farms were asked to talk about recruitment problems, some of them hesitated and gave contradictory information during the course of the interview. One claimed, "I have practically no problem getting laborers." Another began by admitting difficulties and ended by saying that in some regions the process is complicated but in the last three years he had no problems. Still others managed to convey more directly and vividly the chaotic nature and uncertainty that surrounds the recruitment process. Most troublesome is that farmers can never be sure that laborers contracted in the town square will show up at the farm on the appointed day. Then the farmer or his manager has to deal with a frustrated *agregado* who has purchased and prepared food that he will not be able to sell.

> You should have seen the town last Sunday. The people gathered with their bags in the square without knowing where to go. There is more than enough of that everywhere. And what happens is that people do strange things. They are here on this farm, and [when] someone else comes commenting that on another farm they pay better, they go there. And the people go mad. This is why I like to work with people I know, who work the whole week.

Although many managers of medium enterprise farms recruit mostly local men (see table 15), others rely on a fair number of outsiders and must be prepared to offer lodging and food. The lodgings may consist of rooms with between four and twelve bunk beds or larger spaces with more beds. In either case, the facilities are likely to be more orderly and the food of better quality than on the very large enterprise farms. Confusion and fights are kept to the minimum during work and in the evening. Hence, migrants do not avoid the medium enterprise farms, though the workers also do not favor these establishments. As one migrant explained, "Socially I do not like to deal with strangers because of their vices, [but] on these farms there is less anxiety and danger."

Another important consideration is the need to upgrade the processing equipment to avoid having to lay off crews when unprocessed berries accumulate. This decision is particularly hard because only at times do they harvest enough to require higher drying capacity; their existing equipment usually suffices. They have to be careful not to overinvest and be short of capital to pay wages or to upgrade coffee groves. As it is, most of these farms dry their coffee under the sun, using complex facilities only to wash it and protect it from the rain.

It is not easy to manage these medium enterprises, and few people have the financial experience or the personality to adroitly supervise their personnel and to keep a close check on the account books. Many of these farmers become ruthless and opt to increase supervision and the number of rules. However, there is a significant group of owners and managers of medium enterprises who have better rapport with their workers and manage to retain steady harvesting crews. These growers are more likely to maintain very productive coffee trees.

5.5   The Harvest on a Large Enterprise Farm

Although these farms have a significant presence, they capture a smaller share of the labor market than do the medium enterprise farms (see appendix A). However, these large growers set the prevailing piece rate. Other farmers say that they have to follow the rate offered by large well-maintained enterprises, and these growers acknowledge receiving telephone calls asking how much they are going to pay. The managers of the large enterprise farms use high pay to attract a steady supply of workers who would otherwise prefer to work on smaller farms.

The harvest is regarded with dread by the managers of these farms. Size compounds problems and makes it hard to coordinate operations smoothly. To achieve efficiency, these farmers must be sure not only of a steady flow of laborers but also of appropriate equipment to move the berries from the harvesting sites to the processing plants and to dry the beans fast enough to make room for fresh berries. Storage facilities are advisable when operations are this large, thereby allowing farmers to sell beans when it is most suitable.

Since farms are extensive and many harvesting sites are very distant from weighing stations and processing plants, roads must be opened and kept up, truck drivers hired, and equipment kept in running order. In the past animals were used, but now land is too expensive and coffee too rewarding to leave some areas in pasture. One very large farm had devised an ingenious system of ducts that carried the berries directly to the processing plant. Such systems are warranted only on large and highly efficient farms.

Only electrically powered processing facilities can handle the volume of these large farms during peak season. These facilities are housed in a separate building that may also serve as a dormitory or dining room. The processing equipment consists of a set of washing and soaking tanks connected to machines that hull the beans. Rows of rotating drums with circulating hot air serve as dryers. None of these plants feature cutting-edge technology. A number of hands are still required to move the beans from one operation to another, but two to four laborers usually suffice. These workers must be trusted individuals and are usually selected from among permanent farm residents not only because of their familiarity with the equipment but also because of fear of theft.

Fear of theft prevails throughout all stages of the harvest. Laborers fear that coworkers will steal berries, and owners fear that field hand supervisors and weighing superintendents will keep some beans for themselves to sell undercover. Hence, farmers value administrators or supervisors who keep an eye on personnel. It is thus not unusual for these very large farms to have one or two administrators and a number of well-paid trusted men to help coordinate, supervise, and regulate tasks.

One job that must be carefully handled is the sectioning of the coffee grove into lots, establishing the order in which they will be harvested, planning the timetable when the workers must return for reharvesting, and the assignment of rows of trees to members of a labor crew. If this procedure is not well planned, many berries will fall to the ground before the crews arrive to harvest or time may be wasted going over trees that have not yet reached an optimum stage. Only an experienced administrator can map out what is to be done each week. The secondary task of supervising the quality of labor and mediating disputes between harvesters falls entirely on the crew supervisors. For each crew of twenty harvesters, there is usually one supervisor, who earns a fixed wage. These supervisors are usually farm residents who not only receive commissions but are assured of employment throughout the year. Some supervisors make extra money by feeding laborers.

Farms that require 150 to 240 men at any one time cannot hope to rely entirely on locals. Large sleeping quarters and bathroom facilities are built and must be kept clean. Most of these housekeeping jobs are assigned to the permanent personnel who can hardly cope with the extra work. Consequently, lodgings, for the most part, are dirty, inconvenient, and unsanitary. Farms with decent lodgings are rare and usually cater to a small proportion of the population of harvesters. Large, dark rooms with tiers of cots covered by old mattresses or straw mats are typical. Clothing and personal possessions must be kept on top of bunks or hang from a few pegs. Ventilation leaves much to be desired, and sleeping quarters are permeated by the fumes of fermenting coffee berries. Bathrooms and washing facilities are often coupled, making it difficult for tired workers to maintain cleanliness. It is not surprising that disgruntled workers often fight and steal from each other and that smoking of marijuana and *basuco* (a half-processed cocaine paste) is rampant on large farms during the harvesting season.

The need to maintain constant large crews and the impossibility of selective recruitment contribute to the chaos and tension at harvest. Field supervisors find it often difficult to assert themselves and to keep arguments from developing into fights. Administrators resent the lack of care in the preparation of food and the stream of complaints they must handle.

> It is difficult to find field supervisors who are capable of handling the personnel. The greatest problem is the lack of education and work conscience. The management of laborers is marked by the conflict between owner and worker. That conflict leads the workers to damage the character of the supervisors who are good. People do not love large enterprises. And during the harvest one must demonstrate that one's will prevails.

> The most difficult thing is to manage people. When one is harassed by the amount of coffee to harvest, then is when the problems start. The workers complain about the food, the lodgings, . . . and one has to grant requests because what one wants is that they pick the coffee.

Not surprisingly, negative images of laborers are often voiced by the owners and administrators of these large enterprises:

> [The workers] do not care two hoots about the owner. Today they say, "He is very rich. Let us take him for a ride." One gives them bathrooms and they break them, they clog the pipes, make the worst messes. . . . There is malice in them. They even steal from each other.

The only farms that manage some semblance of order and are reputed for decent treatment are those that are close to settlements so that local harvesters can return home to eat and sleep. It is thus understandable that many large growers have encouraged the development of local settlements and, to that end, have provided some land and construction material. Two large farms near one of the municipal towns in Risaralda assured themselves of large crews of local residents by paying special attention to the needs and requirements of women. These farmers have organized all-female crews and provided loaders to carry heavy sacks to the weighing stations. Most of these women come from one neighborhood and harvest year after year on the same farm. When the season starts, the administrator sends word, and the regular seasonal female laborers begin to arrive. He is pleased with this arrangement and explained that the women were more careful, easier to manage, and good pickers. Whatever the reasons for his innovative strategy, he was aided by the fact that women in this municipality seem to be more ready to participate in the harvest than women in other areas. Yet another solution adopted to cope with the harvest's disorder is to delegate the responsibility of hiring, lodging, feeding, supervising, and readying the berries for processing to a large number of *agregados* living on the farm. Two large farms in one of the municipalities used this harvest-management system.

Not surprisingly, coffee farms do not grow beyond a certain size. On the contrary, owners often sell some land when management becomes cumbersome and investment uncertain. Indeed, two of the large farms in the survey were divided during the year of our study, and one sold a considerable parcel of land.

5.6   The Harvest on a Traditional Farm

In 1985, there were still some farmers who had not renovated their coffee groves and found it difficult to compete for laborers with the *caturra* farmers. Most of these traditional coffee groves were small (see section 3.5d), and were owned by farmers who had multiple properties. Owners who lived elsewhere entered into a share contract with either a relative or an *agregado*. Once the farm was renovated, the contract would be ended and the relative or *agregado* would remain as an administrator. The owners of smaller traditional coffee groves avoided labor shortages by hiring neighbors to whom they offered the use of their processing facilities. The few large coffee groves that had not yet been planted with the new variety of coffee were also in a very bad state, with impassable roads and very old trees. These farms were not necessarily run by absentee owners; in some cases, the owner was very old; in others the inheritors were awaiting the settlement of their estate.

5.7   The Harvesters

The harvest requires considerable personnel.[5] Even if women were more willing and interested in harvesting coffee, the local population would not suffice.[6] At the time of our survey, 63 percent of all harvesters in Risaralda were local residents.[7] Only 40 percent of harvesters resided in the municipality selected in Cundinamarca. This municipality also had a number of other crops requiring the attention of wage laborers, so the local population had a greater choice of employment opportunities.

Although local and migrant harvesters are not very different in their backgrounds and experience, they approach the harvest in very different ways. For local residents in Risaralda, the harvest is the only well-remunerated employment available. If they want to stay with their families, they have no choice but to pick coffee. If they are good at it, they will save some money. Migrants are men who have completed the coffee harvest in their area of residence and then venture elsewhere, either because they want to travel or because they need more money than they can get at their regular occupations. Thus, when migrants and locals offer their services, they are motivated by different concerns and are likely to behave differently when negotiating their contracts or withdrawing their services. To fully understand the dynamics of the supply sector, each group has to be considered separately. In the following sections I discuss how local men, migrant men, local women, and ambulant workers behave during the harvest period: their preferences, concerns and priorities, and observations about available harvesting opportunities.

5.7a   The Local Male Harvesters

Local harvesters represent 55.13 percent of the male labor force and 58.58 percent of all laborers during the harvest. Most local harvesters are landless agricultural laborers who have been working in coffee year round, moving from farm to farm in search of full-time employment. Some (21.6 percent) have a regular permanent job on the farms where they were interviewed. Most local laborers have been harvesting coffee since they were young (only 7 percent started in another agricultural activity). Farmers value these workers because they are readily available to harvest berries as they begin to ripen.[8] They are soon joined by local peasant coffee farmers or their sons (7.8 of local harvesters)[9] and men who are engaged in other occupations (5.25 percent). Teachers, salesmen, and men in service occupations, mining, and construction find it financially rewarding to harvest coffee (see table 15). Local construction, in fact, ceases during the harvest and school vacations are timed to allow students to pick coffee. Restaurants, bars, stores, and street vendors, however, are very busy, and these workers are unlikely to give up their occupation to harvest coffee. When the harvest and the associated commercial activities end, these latter individuals may go elsewhere to harvest. The presence in the coffee harvest of twenty-eight local men with nonagricultural occupations is not impressive, but it is significant. In these three municipalities there are no large cities and the opportunities for urban employment are very limited (see section 8.1a).[10]

Local harvesters find work by approaching nearby farms or by standing in the town square where they will encounter farmers looking for laborers. Some hear of harvest jobs that are about to start through friends and some are contracted by field supervisors who know them (see table 16). Local harvesters often return to the same farms, but they do not necessarily wait for familiar opportunities. They harvest where they can and when they need a job and, unless the conditions are unattractive, remain on the same farms until their daily income drops below what they can expect to earn elsewhere. They move from farm to farm, perhaps returning eventually to where they first started harvesting. They often work in two or three places within a walking radius of their homes. They do not move as frequently or as unexpectedly as farmer's complaints imply.

Most local harvesters prefer to live at home and chose a job site according to this preference (see table 17). Staying at home is not only more pleasant than life in the barracks, but also allows workers to save

TABLE 15.   Major Occupations of All Male Harvesters, Risaralda and Cundinamarca ($N = 419$)

	Nonagriculture	Agriculture	Student	Other[a]	Totals
Locals	5.25%	44.63%	4.32%	1.29%	55.49%
	(28)	(190)	(10)	(3)	(231)
Migrants	9.55%	29.12%	0.53	4.25%	43.45%
	(48)	(131)	(1)	(8)	(188)

Source: Field survey of all harvesters.

Note: These figures record the answers to a question about the most important occupation held during the twelve months prior to the harvest. Five people did not answer the question. The figures include harvesters on all farms.

[a]Included here are the occupations that were hard to categorize (fishing, mining, and so forth).

money. By working on farms that are close enough for a young child to walk to, laborers can have meals brought from home and thus avoid the food charge. The location of homes thus limits the earning opportunities of laborers. Some hamlets were located far from coffee groves, and their residents suffered not only during harvest but also throughout the year. These realities are also taken into consideration when trying to buy, build, or rent a house (see section 4.1 for a discussion of other considerations). Some local families borrow houses until they find neighborhoods where they can find employment during most of the year. Other families (43 percent of the harvesters surveyed) choose to settle in the local towns and work in the surrounding farms.[11]

5.7b Women Harvesters

At the turn of the century, many large farms used to have numerous (about twenty) *agregados,* and it is quite probable that this mode of labor organization, which involved whole families, encouraged greater female participation (see section 2.1). It is also possible that landlords forced

TABLE 16. How Harvesters Learned of Their Jobs on Farms Where They Were Interviewed, Risaralda and Cundinamarca ($N = 393$)

Reason Given	Local (%)	Migrant (%)
Worked There Before	21	13
Approached Farm	21	28
Approached by Farmers	13	27
Friend Brought Him	17	6
Went to Town Square	24	25
Kin of Farmer	4	
Total	100	99

Note: The percentages represent responses to a question about how the harvesters obtained their present jobs. This table does not imply that this is the way these workers obtain all harvesting jobs through the season. They may have worked at first on a farm known to them, and when that job was finished, they may have obtained the second job in the manner indicated in the table. The table excludes the men who are permanent residents on the farm.

agregados directly or indirectly to commit the help of their family members. However, on the one farm we surveyed that used this traditional form of management only six of the thirty-two harvesters were women; each received a separate wage.

Women are equally reluctant to enter the coffee grove in their own farms, preferring to contribute to finances by raising animals or cooking for laborers. On only two out of forty-three small farms that I visited in Risaralda did wives or daughters acknowledge helping with agricultural tasks. Three other farms were headed by widows who fully participated in most farm tasks. In another case, the wife harvested part of the coffee only to protect herself and her children from an irascible husband who drank most of the proceeds from the farm. It is now unusual in Risaralda to find women harvesting coffee as wage laborers. We encountered only thirty-eight local independent women harvesters (11.11 percent of the harvesters) and four others (1.17 percent) who had come from elsewhere.

It is somewhat more common for women to accompany their husbands or fathers to the harvest and help them bag coffee, perhaps for a few hours or a few days (see section 7.2). In these cases, the men receive the pay and decide what to do with the money. Of course, women are not likely to help unless their fathers or husbands are generous. Most farmers allow for helpers and rely on the male laborers to assume responsibility for disciplining helpers and loading the heavy bags. Women helpers come and go as they wish; they integrate harvesting with their other obligations. For the most part, their participation remains unrecognized in surveys and the census. On one of the farms in the sample, five harvesters brought their wives to help them, and another man brought two daughters. Thus, out of

TABLE 17. Residence of All Male Harvesters, Risaralda and Cundinamarca, 1985 ($N = 418$)

Harvesters	At Home (%)	Rent (%)	On Farm (%)	Total (%)
Locals	76.19	2.16[b]	21.65[c]	100
Migrants	2.14[a]	6.42	91.44	100

Note: This table includes all migrant men for whom information on residence was available.

[a]Migrants in the process of moving who have acquired or borrowed homes.

[b]Single men who rent rooms during the harvest.

[c]*Agregados* and others who are permanent residents on farms.

a total of seventy-five harvesters, six were accompanied by women on the day of the survey. No other farm kept similar records.[12]

There is some incentive for wives to help their husbands, particularly when there are a large number of children and the men are reliable spouses (see appendix C). But there is little incentive for daughters to work when no direct rewards are realized. Only parental authority, moral obligation, hunger, and parental generosity may induce these girls to accompany their fathers to work. These girls have also more to fear than their mother, since public shame and ridicule for working on the land may thwart their chances of a good marriage. Unaccompanied women must be careful to select appropriate farms because working on the harvest can taint their character and call into question their virginity. (Prostitution is rampant in coffee areas, and prostitutes are known to work as harvesters.) Neighboring farms with small crews of familiar faces are preferred. As a manager of one of the large farms explained, there are too many men and too much noise for women to come to the groves. This farm attracted only six women in a crew of 231 men; they were hired only if accompanied by a male family member.

To attract women, large farms must cater to these workers' concerns: not to be associated with men during work, rest, or meals and to have someone carry the heavy bags of berries from the groves to where they are weighed. In only one of the two Risaralda municipalities did farmers provide facilities attractive to women harvesters. Three large farms close to the town (two of them in our sample) arranged for the transport of bags. The women brought their own food and were assigned lots far from the men and close to the town. The female workers received the same pay during the height of the harvest and were not necessarily placed in lower-yielding sections of the farm. The women seemed satisfied with those working conditions; when asked to evaluate the farm and to state reasons for wanting to stay, they voiced similar responses to those of male harvesters. When I asked the manager his reason for reintroducing all-female crews, he responded that women were more docile and more careful with the trees. The fact that sometime ago there had been some serious labor disturbances on that farm must have been on his mind when he talked about docility. During the height of the harvest season, this farm employs about ninety women and about ten men as harvesters. The women are recruited from the very beginning. The size of these crews increases as the harvest proceeds. Many of them continue to work even after the harvest (see section 6.2b).

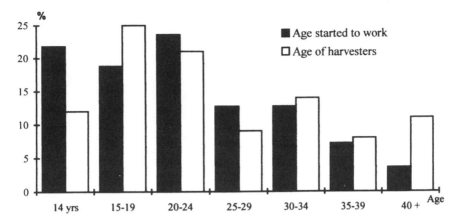

Fig. 8.   Age distribution of women harvesters in Risaralda and age when they first harvested coffee.   The started-to-work column represents the percentage of the women surveyed who started to harvest at that particular age or in that age group ($N = 57$). The harvesters' group includes the female members of informants' households who were picking coffee at the time of the survey ($N = 119$).

Another important consideration for women is proximity to where they live so that they are available to their families in case of emergencies. If they have small children, they only consider going off to work if they have an older daughter who can and wants to stay home to supervise the younger children.

Women who harvest on their own or as helpers start to work when they are ten years old or later and may continue to do so after marriage, but only until the first child is born (see sections 4.2 and 4.3). Mothers may resume (or start) work after one of their daughters is old enough to care for the younger children. As sons become old enough to help with wages, women begin to withdraw from the harvest.[13] Figure 8 shows the age distribution of women harvesters.

In Cundinamarca women are somewhat freer to work and move outside of their homes. They and their male partners also do not share the same disdain for physical work voiced by the women and men of Risaralda. Many more Cundinamarca women were harvesting at the time of our survey (16.6 percent of the forty-two local harvesters surveyed).

A higher participation of women as seasonal harvesters would relieve farmers living close to settlement areas from the uncertainties of supply but would not help those with coffee groves that are too small to organize separate female crews or are removed from sites of dense habitation. These farms will have to continue to rely on male harvesters willing to sleep in barracks.

These limitations explain in part the uneven rate of participation of women in the harvest throughout the central coffee region. There are pockets where their presence is noticeable and others where no one mentions their role in the harvest. Around Manizales in Caldas, Calderon de Cuellar (1976: 63) recorded a very low participation (1.55 percent of the harvesting labor force). However, on one of the large farms of Tolima, at times women numbered 50 percent of the harvesters; their presence dropped to 20 percent at other times (Ruiz Niño 1972: 266). In Risaralda, the uneven participation of women can be seen in the occupational survey of the families of harvesters. In one of the municipalities studied, only 5.15 percent of the women were said to be gainfully employed in agriculture in 1985. In the other municipality, 12.89 percent were similarly employed.

The attraction of nice clothing and appropriate entertainment may tempt more young women in the future to go to work before they marry and thus may eventually alter the idealized perception of how women should behave. But such a transformation will take time, and in years to come women may continue to favor alternative employment, to avoid walking the thin line that shields them from disgrace. It is unlikely that more married women will enter the labor force while their children are small, but the possibility of building and furnishing nearby permanent residences may lure some older women to the harvest to transform their simple dwellings into fashionable town-style abodes. Waxed floors, crocheted decorations, and nicely tended veranda gardens currently bring more prestige to a housewife than does a sofa in front of a television set.

5.7c   Nonresident Laborers

News about the harvest spreads through neighboring departments via the radio and telephone conversations among relatives and friends.[14] By the time the harvest is in full swing, the local town squares are teeming with recent arrivals. About half of these laborers have come to the area in the past and are familiar with the setting. Thirteen percent of nonresident harvesters returned to farms on which they had previously worked. Thirty-four percent, mostly young men, are exploring new sites.

Though cost of travel is a factor, more important to laborers is famil-

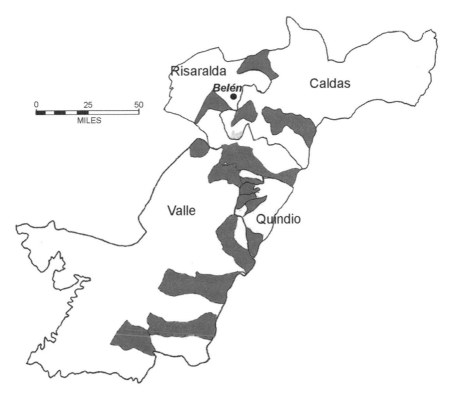

Fig. 9.   Municipality of origin of migrant harvesters in Belén

iarity with the setting and connections that may help them find jobs quickly and cheaply. Although we did not record the actual distances that migrants had traveled, we are able to identify the municipalities they came from (see figures 9 and 10). For the 196 male harvesters in both municipalities, regional contiguity seemed irrelevant. The majority (70.4 percent) of the male harvesters in both departments came from municipalities that were not adjacent but were predominantly coffee-producing regions (see figures 9 and 10). Only 9.7 percent came from adjacent coffee municipalities, and 1.5 percent came from adjacent municipalities where coffee agriculture did not predominate. A fair number (13.8 percent) came from distant municipalities not known for coffee production.[15] Harvest timing differences cannot fully account for the predominance of laborers who came from further away since altitude has a greater effect on the ripening process and those differences are noticeable within short distances.

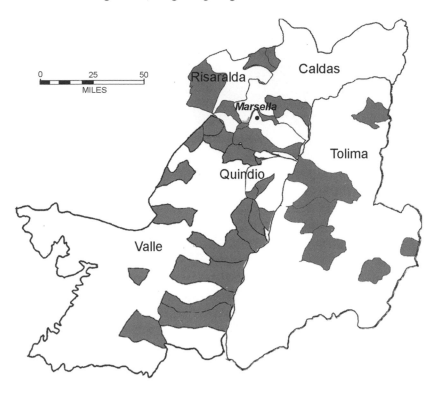

Fig. 10.   Municipality of origin of migrant harvesters in Marsella

The arrival of nonresident laborers calms the anxiety of farmers with less productive or more awkward coffee groves who have trouble attracting local laborers. They welcome a town center teeming with job seekers because they know some will have to come to these less appealing farms. For most other farmers, too many people hanging around leads to tensions, fights, and thefts. However, it is unlikely that in normal circumstances unemployed men from other municipalities will stay around for long. If arriving laborers find themselves having to wait too long for a job, they will return home.

Searching for an appropriate farm is more crucial for nonresident harvesters than for local ones, since they have to cover traveling and food expenses and should have something to show at the end of their stay. At the same time, they are handicapped by unfamiliarity with local coffee farms and the timing of demand in each farm. They must also consider living conditions, since they will certainly have to sleep in rooms or barracks, some of which are uncomfortable and unhealthy. The older men, who may come accompanied by younger sons, are particularly mindful of living conditions, preferring the smaller to medium-size farms where they are more likely to share rooms with two to five other laborers rather than fifty to a hundred others. The selection of a farm for its size, however, does not guarantee that food and lodgings will be tolerable. Harvesters complained just as much about lack of cleanliness, flea infestation, and absence of mattresses and light on some of the smaller enterprise farms as on the large ones. Many laborers strongly object to the confusion, noise, and insecurity of the large barracks, where the smell of fermenting coffee pulp outside their windows mixes with the smell of marijuana and *basuco.* The younger harvesters (twenty to twenty-five years old) are often more resilient and take the tension and discomfort of the barracks more in stride; they talk of companionship and friendships forged in barracks and smaller dormitories.

Thus, nonresident harvesters move from farm to farm more frequently than do locals, finally settling at a farm in full production at which they can bag enough coffee and tolerate living conditions. Nonresident harvesters' only advantage over local residents in the search for a good farm is that location does not matter very much; hence, a wider range of farms can be considered. A friend or a relative can also help shorten a job search or time their arrival appropriately. The migrants first approach farms at which they previously worked; 20 percent of all male nonresident harvesters had come to their farms because they were familiar with the farms or were acquainted with the owners/administrators. Twenty-six percent of laborers had found the farm where they were working through friends. The remainder (54 percent) reported that they got their present jobs either by approaching the farms on their own or by standing in the central square.[16]

It is not possible for these nonresident harvesters to work on only one farm. They must move around not only to search for a worthwhile work situation but also to look for another farm when there are no berries ready to be picked where they are. It is not their nature to move from place to place, as portrayed by farmers: it is their fate. They are quite happy to remain harvesting on an appropriate farm for as long as possible. When asked why they were planning to leave, 72 percent of local harvesters and 61 percent of nonresident harvesters said that they expected that there would be no more berries to pick at their current farms.[17]

Costly travel, uncomfortable lodgings, and often unrewarding returns do little to attract the more settled, older population. To make the trip worthwhile, a married man must not only cover food and travel expenses but must also earn enough to send home for groceries and to save for other purchases at his return. A fast and diligent harvester on a good coffee farm will certainly profit from his weeks away from home. But only about 34 percent of the male population was fast enough to earn a good income.

Not surprisingly, only a small proportion of migrant men are married, and very few local married men go elsewhere to harvest (see table 18). Reluctance to make full use of this opportunity rests also on the cultural perception of marital obligations. As mentioned earlier, married men must not only pay for their families' food but also procure it for them. A man's absence from home will weigh heavily on others who rely on him for protection and sustenance. Those who go away may do so because they have sons old enough to do the shopping, have family close at hand to help with those tasks, or are married to relatively independent women. Out of the thirty-two migrants whom I identified as married men, twenty-eight had harvested away from their hometowns at least two years in a row. These men had resolved the practical problems associated with their obligations and could engage in repeat migrations. Thus, married men ignore harvesting opportunities in neighboring municipalities and departments, selecting only those where they have connections or that take place at a time when jobs are scarce at their places of residence. These men do not travel to maximize incomes but to escape hunger. Push factors prod the more cautious men. Only the men who feel comfortable about leaving families behind are enticed by the pull of higher earnings.

The situation is quite different for younger, unmarried men. They

TABLE 18.   Marital Status of All Male Harvesters, Risaralda and Cundinamarca

	Single[a] (%)	Married (%)	Widowed or Separated (%)	Total
Locals	64	32	4	100% (N = 228)
Migrants	80	16	4	100% (N = 196)

Source: Field survey of all harvesters.
[a]May include men living with women but without children.

have no obligations and are no longer under strict parental control. They may come and go as they wish. Parental expectations are minimal. Some help when their fathers are ill or out of work; others offer occasional presents of clothing to their mothers and perhaps their sisters (see section 4.3). None of these obligations conflict with seasonal departures.

Whether married or unattached, the migrant harvesters (44.87 percent of all male harvesters) have learned their trade early in life, having been raised in areas where coffee agriculture prevails. Most of them come from families who have long resided in their home areas (60 percent in Risaralda and 74 percent in Cundinamarca). About half of them (51.93 percent) reside in towns, and some have other occupations (see chapter 6).[18] The most frequent occupations are construction, services, vending, mining, and crafts. These occupations have strong seasonal cycles, periods of unemployment, and low wages. The coffee harvest provides these town dwellers with some financial relief and allows them to retain their preferred nonagricultural occupations.

5.7d Ambulant Harvesters

In his article about ambulant harvesters, Ramirez (1983) suggests that the coordinated seasonality of coffee and cotton has allowed some people to specialize as harvesters of various crops. Thus, from September to December these people work in coffee in areas like Caldas and Risaralda; from December to February they work in cotton agriculture in the department of Cesar; from March to May they return to harvest coffee in Cundinamarca; and from June to September they move down to Tolima to harvest cotton. According to Ramirez, the intensification of production in coffee areas was a boon to the careers of the ambulant harvesters, or *andariegos.* The survival of these wandering people depends on the staggering of the various harvests and on wages that are high enough to cover costs of travel. These traveling migrants should not be confused with the nonresident harvesters discussed in the previous section or with many migrant farm workers in the United States.[19] They themselves use the label *andariego* and recognize the unsettled character of their lives. They are single men without homes.

One of the *andariegos* interviewed traveled from Risaralda to the northern coast, returned to neighboring Tolima, and then went back to Risaralda and Valle, his original place of residence. He combined cotton and coffee harvesting and found that his income from these two crops, though not entirely satisfactory, was better than if he stayed in one place. He is a good harvester, managing to earn about 1,250 pesos a day. However, out of that sum he had to pay two hundred pesos per day for food and save enough for the bus ticket to the coast (eight thousand pesos).

Ramirez (1983) has suggested that the wanderings of *andariegos* are rooted in the social conditions that propel young men to move out of their homes. Indeed, many young men joined migrant streams after running away from abusive or alcoholic fathers. Others did so when they became homeless and lost their families due to the *violencia* of the 1950s or the criminality of the 1960s. It is possible to trace the residence of many of them to the regions where *violencia* was rampant. Risaralda was one such region. However, by their own accounts, these men migrate to see the world or because they are restless. If their words are to be believed, this strategy is not always born of financial necessity or desperation.

Although moved by some inner spirit, they do not seem to be at peace with the conditions imposed by their wanderings. They complain about living conditions and treatment. One *andariego* was very troubled by bathing facilities, the superabundance of plantains in the local diet, and the treatment by the police. Their reputation, linked to a horrendous historical period and to a counterculture of rootlessness, leaves them open to abuses that they counter in a similar style. Eventually their wandering spirit seems to wane, or women catch their fancy and they settle down to married life. Many more settled informants recalled an earlier period of their lives when they were *andariegos,* though they might have been using the term more loosely.

Ramirez (1983) has argued that *andariegos,* though vivid figures in many Colombians' imaginations, are a dying phenomenon in rural Colombia. A comparison of Urrea's findings for 1975 with our survey ten years later confirms his observation for coffee agriculture. Whereas Urrea (1976) found that 30.86 percent of the total labor force in the region that includes Risaralda were *andariegos* (individuals who said that they had no fixed residence during the past six months), we only found 8.8 percent who answered this question in the same manner.

Although cotton was mentioned by many *andariegos* as the crop worked after coffee, the importance of that crop as a source of revenue has decreased considerably. Only two local harvesters and eight nonresident harvesters mentioned that they would harvest cotton after coffee. Twenty of them had done so in the past two years. This trend is also confirmed by Deygout's (1980) findings that only about 10 percent of the cotton harvesters were *andariegos* in 1980. Mechanization of this crop is probably responsible for this change. No other crop seems to have taken the place of cotton in the cycle of migratory harvesting. Some ambulant laborers mention going to harvest one or more of the following crops: soya, sorghum, sugarcane, rice, tobacco, cacao, and even coca. The combination of crops seems to be idiosyncratic. No one sequence predominates over others.

The pool of laborers that farmers can tap for the harvest without using contractors is firmly centered in the region where their farms are located. Coffee growers have neither tried nor been able to mobilize a significant number of men working in other crops, even in regions like Cundinamarca with a more diversified agricultural sector. It is not uncommon to encounter a highly specialized agricultural labor market even in the United States, with harvesters following a crop from locality to locality. Several factors contribute to crop-specialized labor crews: a year-round demand for labor, conflicting seasonal demands with other crops in the region, and earnings closely tied to experience. Until there is sufficiently detailed comparable material, common-sense particularistic explanations and the responses of the laborers will have to suffice. Coffee laborers say simply that they work only in coffee because that is all they know. My interpretation is that few of them, even young men, are willing to venture beyond the coffee area and experiences that are familiar to them except through personal or impersonal networks. Thus, another factor can be added to those listed earlier: the use of contractors to mediate the flow of labor. Industries that rely on contractors for the harvest will draw from a wider and more diversified pool of laborers. The unwillingness of the farmers in this study to use such agents forces reliance on a pool of laborers where the young predominate, and these workers are unlikely to come unless farmers can match earning expectations.

Chapter 6

In Search of Work

The market is not simply structured by the level of the demand for workers and their availability. A shortage of hands does not always lead to higher wages—laborers must be aware of the existence of other job openings and of other farmers willing to pay higher wages. If laborers are not aware of these phenomena, they are likely to accept first offers that may be much lower than what other laborers receive. Limited information leads to a wide dispersion of wages in the market. Thus, it is important to consider information flows in any market analysis.

Economists have integrated the relevance of information when modeling job-search strategies. They point out that gathering information requires time and effort (a cost) that is only warranted if job seekers think that it will get them better-paying jobs. "Rational" job seekers are expected to keep looking for job openings until the cost of finding a better one is balanced out by how much better the next offer is likely to be. Economists assume not only that people search for jobs rationally but also that they do so randomly. The models that have emerged since this approach became popular are quite elaborate. They incorporate not only the obvious costs of looking for a job (transport, food, newspapers, and so forth) but also the harder-to-measure social costs. These models also differentiate between the rationality of unemployed and employed job seekers.

Sociologists have criticized these efforts for their failure to realize that job seekers are members of a society that provides them with institutional settings that can facilitate or hinder the flow of information and mold job-search strategies. Granovetter uses a different phrase to describe the process of finding employment: the means of connecting a person to a job (1995: 145). In a 1974 survey, he found that many individuals had not actively searched for jobs. Rather, they heard about openings through a network of connections and in the course of activities that had nothing to do with searching for jobs. Thus, Granovetter includes existing overlapping social networks among the elements that structure the market (1995:

148). These networks define flows of information about jobs and about workers (Griffith and Kissam 1995). They also define the boundaries of local markets.

In chapter 5, I described how social preferences and social norms affected the choice of farm on which each category of harvester was willing to work. Women, local men, old migrants, and young migrants responded differently to farm conditions. Another important finding was that only 45 percent of the local men and 54 percent of migrant men found their present jobs through active searches. Others had worked farms before, were taken there by a friend, or were contacted through shared social links. In other words, nearly half of all harvesters were connected to their jobs through social networks. They did not look around first to find out who paid more or calculate how much the search was costing them in foregone revenue. They did not "rationally" decide where to work. They went where they were taken or to farms with which that they were familiar. However, networks do not entirely structure this market. Laborers stay on farms only if they do not hear about better farms or better rates somewhere else. Furthermore, since the farms where these laborers usually work may not be hiring when they need a job, harvesters have to alternate between letting the network find jobs and active searching either in the town square or by visiting farms. This process expands the networks. Thus, networks themselves are built through both social relations and job-search activities. As Granovetter (1985) explains, the economy is embedded in society. At the same time, economic activity helps build social relations.

I also pointed out that farmers use a mix of strategies to recruit a crew of harvesters. The growers wait for familiar laborers to come on their own, mobilize the networks of permanent farm laborers, and actively search for unfamiliar people in the town square. Mobilizations through networks often assure a more reliable and loyal crew of workers who will arrive at the appointed time. It is the preferred mode in smaller farms. But even these farmers do not attempt to screen all workers they recruit. On the larger farms, screening is a luxury. Farmers and administrators instead control performance through supervision and firings.

During the harvest, farmers are concerned about the uncertainty of supply, the pressures to get a job done, and the complexity of the task. Laborers are concerned about finding a profitable coffee grove and a farm appropriate to their gender, age, and marital status. Supply conditions in the local market and in other related localized markets also affect laborers' choices of job-search strategy. If there is a slow flow of harvesters from elsewhere, farmers are likely to offer very competitive wages from the start. Laborers can then avoid the cost and discomfort of a job search and approach only familiar farms, thereby avoiding the negative aspects of searches. Supply conditions thus also affect the adoption of specific job-search patterns.

After the harvest, market conditions change. There is an oversupply of laborers, the nature of tasks to be performed changes, and demand becomes intermittent. In this chapter I describe the search strategies of laborers during the off-season in Risaralda.[1] When information is available, I also discuss how workers and farmers find each other after the harvest, when opportunities and pressures have changed dramatically. Laborers become more actively engaged in gathering information about when each farm in their area is likely to start maintenance tasks, or they begin to consider alternative job possibilities. Right after the harvest, some laborers can still afford to rely on networks and wait until farmers who know them well send word that the workers are needed. However, as the season progresses, most workers can no longer afford to search rationally. The distress of uncertain prospects is now too painful, and a job in hand is the only feasible goal. Farmers, conversely, face very different circumstances and manipulate them to their advantage. The growers do not look for workers but instead wait for them to come. As chapters 6 and 7 show, this position gives farmers an added advantage and allows them to reduce wage costs.

The study of occupational trajectories and search patterns provides a more complete view of the local market structure. It is important to remember, however, that searches are modified according to demand-supply uncertainties, time pressure to complete the task, cash resources, and farmers' management strategies.

6.1   Looking for Jobs after the Harvest

As Christmas approaches in Risaralda, the main harvest slowly comes to an end. With fewer berries ripening at any one time, the passes along each row of trees are faster, and harvesters emerge with disappointingly light loads. The workers no longer realize the high incomes of previous weeks, and many begin to return to old jobs. It is time for migrants to plan their return home in time to celebrate the holidays: only 22 percent of the migrants in Risaralda decided to stay and look for another local farm where they could continue to harvest coffee. It is also the time for students to go back to school. Thus, only local men and women remain to finish the harvest.

By January 1985 harvest incomes had decreased drastically, and farmers had begun to pay daily wages instead of by piece rate. The growers also had begun to organize maintenance tasks to offer weekly employment to efficient and reliable workers. Male laborers would not be willing to work only half days harvesting the few remaining berries. These workers had to begin to look for longer-term employment and to plan for leaner months. However, women, who had fewer employment options, lingered on the large farms, with all-women crews harvesting berries on a piece-rate basis. Those young men who resented drudgery and loss of leisure were inclined to take time off from work and lazily plan what to do.

This is the time when coffee groves are weeded twice, fertilized, and pruned. It is also the time when fungicides are sprayed to contain the damage of rust. Figures 11 and 12 illustrate variations in labor input throughout the maintenance season.

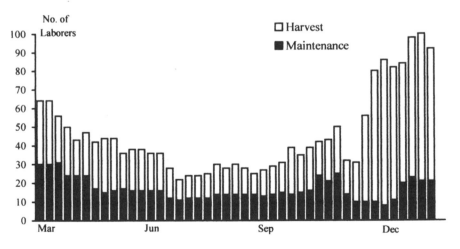

Fig. 11.   Number of laborers hired for maintenance tasks and for harvesting on an enterprise farm in Marsella, 1985.   Each bar represents a separate week. This is a large enterprise farm in Marsella that hires nearby residents for most of the year. It is farm B in figure 7. The graph is based on entries on account books listing laborers hired by the week.

Even if expansions and renovations are taken into account—during the season of 1985–86 this demand was small—the demand would fail to fully absorb all the men willing to work in agriculture. I have calculated that to maintain all of the coffee trees growing in the two municipalities of Risaralda, farmers need only 5,144 men working full time during the thirty-eight weeks of the maintenance season. In addition, 839 men are needed in tomato production and other agricultural activities that depend on wage labor (see appendix A). The total demand of 5,983 is undoubtedly lower than the number of men likely to be seeking agricultural jobs (see table 19).[2] If the supply estimates are correct, farmers can afford to avoid hiring workers considered irresponsible or incompetent. When speed and efficiency are at issue, as in midseason weeding and harvesting, farmers are happy to enlist the help of younger men. Hence, any willing twenty-year-

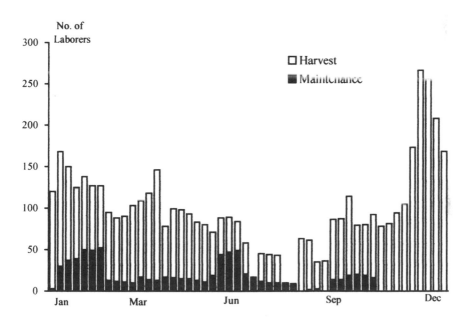

Fig. 12.   Number of laborers hired for maintenance tasks and for harvesting on a large enterprise farm in Belén, 1985.   Each bar represents the average number of men hired each particular week. This farm is one of the largest enterprise farms that hires many women harvesters. No renovations were carried out during 1985, so the labor demand during maintenance was lower in 1985 than for other years. This farm is farm A in figure 7.

old or younger man can find employment when maintenance tasks start and for the secondary harvest. Farmers favor married men for fertilizing or spraying since they are considered more reliable and are certainly more experienced. But the farmers' preferences do not altogether determine who works on a farm and who stays at home. There are also the search goals and strategies of laborers, and the laborers' stories must be juxtaposed with the seasonal market changes and farmers' behavior.

6.1a   Young, Unmarried, Male Laborers

With money in their pockets, younger unmarried men are not eager to wield machetes and take on the more arduous job of weeding—not quite yet, unless their families rely on their financial help. Many take a rest and

TABLE 19.   Supply of Male Laborers during the Maintenance Season in Risaralda, by Age Group, 1985

Age Group	Total Number	Subtotals by Age Categories
15–19	1,022	
		1,022
20–24	1,181	
25–29	813	
		1,994
30–34	939	
35–39	691	
40–44	530	
45–49	425	
		2,585
50–59	634	
60+	438	
		1,077
Total	6,678	6,678

Source: The figures are based on the preliminary results of the 1985 census (Departamento Nacional 1985a).

Note: This table includes only the males who said that they were laborers in response to the question of what job they had held the previous week, regardless of whether they were remunerated. Also included are men who are looking for employment as laborers but not those who have been unemployed for a long time.

delay searching for jobs or search only on the few farms near their homes until family needs become pressing. About a third of the sons in the families interviewed had been out of work off and on since the harvest and were not eagerly looking for jobs. As one of them plainly put it, "And then I just loitered about." His mother corrected him, saying more delicately that he was "resting."

The more adventurous men use this time to visit family or friends who live elsewhere or to travel to regions unknown to them. With money for bus fare and food, they can go off to places where kin will offer free lodgings or travel with friends in search for farms in need of laborers. They can subsidize their stay by working as laborers or, if they time their travels correctly, make some extra money as coffee harvesters. They can go to Quindio, a neighboring department, where the harvest is still in progress, or delay the trip and go to Valle later on in the year to catch the high harvest period there. Of the 113 single men between fifteen and thirty-five years old who were interviewed in our survey in Risaralda, sixteen said that as soon as there was no more coffee to pick at the farms where they were working, they would probably travel elsewhere to continue harvesting. The oldest among them had previously been to Quindio and Valle and were likely to go there again. In fact, twenty-three of these young harvesters had gone away at least once in the past two years, not only to Quindio and northern Valle but also to Caldas, Tolima, and Antioquia, all located within the central coffee region. These men tend to wait, however, until they reach age nineteen to travel on their own to follow the coffee harvest in another municipality (see table 20).

From their comments, local young men clearly travel elsewhere more out of adventure than need. Their wanderlust is easily satisfied within the familiar radius of the central coffee zone, and they return home after a few weeks or a couple of months away, some never to go away again. Young men with unhappy childhoods or greater impatience and inquisitiveness may continue to roam for many years, hardly staying in one area for any length of time. With companions, often met during travel, these men follow one harvest after another. These are the "wandering men" or *andariegos* described in Colombian literature (see section 5.7d).

Some young men prefer to use their energies and resources exploring different employment opportunities or searching for alternative occupations (see table 21). They say that they are either bored with country living or find it too hard and financially unrewarding. The easiest local alternative is to work in construction or road building, which pay well for men who are in good health and are strong. Street vending, an apprenticeship in a small carpenter's workshop, or helping in a store are some other local opportunities open to young men.

The more ambitious young men dream of jobs in bigger cities as messengers, mechanics, or industrial laborers. These dreams are hard to realize for those who do not have relatives in cities to provide free lodging and connections. Many of these men believed that to be hired they would need an army registration card. While it is possible to get an army registration card, unless they bribe a relevant official they are likely to be drafted as soon as they register. The practice is so common that the acquisition of an army registration card is often discussed in terms of the price of the signature. It can also take years to acquire this card. The young men we spoke to said they would have to spend their savings from a harvest season—about ten thousand to fifteen thousand pesos—to acquire this card. The price is higher if the family is known to have some money. Opinions differ as to the employment opportunities for which the registration card is required. All agreed that a card was necessary to apply for a permanent job in the municipality, and many insisted that they would be asked to show it if they solicited a job in settings such as a sugar mill in La Virginia or a factory in Pereira. Some feared that they would be asked for the army registration if they were stopped by the local police in a strange town. For that reason, mothers expressed a reluctance to let their younger sons go away.

Only fourteen of the men younger than age thirty-five had found local

TABLE 20.   Occupations That Local Single Males in Risaralda Expected to Hold after Harvest ($N = 113$)

Age Group	Local Coffee Farm	Harvest Elsewhere	Town/Urban Occupation[a]	NA or NI[b]
14–19	19	6	12	14
20–30	21	8	14	3
30+[c]	10	2	3	1
Total	50	16	29	18
	(44.24%)	(14.16%)	(25.66%)	(15.93%)

Source: Field survey.

[a]For an itemization of these occupations, see table 21.

[b]In this column under not applicable (NA) are included the young men who said they would go back to school as well as those who were of school age. Others did not give information (NI) about job prospects or job searches.

[c]May include some widowers.

employment in construction or the service sector and were returning to it right after harvest; fifteen others said they would try to search for nonagricultural work in the coming year. In other words, 12.38 percent of the young harvesters did not have to look because they already had town jobs. Another 13.27 percent planned to try to find such employment either locally or further away, despite the many obstacles and limited availability of town jobs. An equally ambitious group of young men, 14.16 percent of the total, were going to explore options elsewhere by working on another coffee or cotton harvest. A small group were very young (6.19 percent) and were returning to school. The plurality (44.24 percent) were planning to stay in the coffee sector the rest of the year. Whether these workers stay, go, or find other employment, they will probably always retain a link with coffee agriculture. As long as they stay in Risaralda, they will always participate in the harvest. Even if they move, they may return annually to visit family and again earn good money in the harvest.

TABLE 21. Jobs Held and Job Searches in the Nonagricultural Sector by Local Harvesters in Risaralda between Fifteen and Thirty-five Years of Age (*N* = 113)

Occupation	Previous Employment[a]	Employment Search[b]
Construction	6	3
Mining/Craft[c]	1	0
Commerce/Service	7	4
Transport	0	1
Messenger	0	2
Mechanic/Apprentice	0	3
Other	0	2
Total	14	15
	(12.38%)	(13.27%)

Source: Field survey.

Note: This table includes only those younger men who said they would look for occupations other than agriculture after the harvest.

[a]This column indicates the most important occupation held by the young men during the previous year.

[b]Records the number of men seeking jobs that differed from those held the previous year.

[c]Mining in this area refers to panning gold in local streams.

In sum, less than half of the young unmarried harvesters compete with their older married counterparts for employment right after the harvest ends. Some young men actively looked for and found jobs. Whether they accepted what came first or searched to find what they wanted is not known. Since their families did not expect them to contribute a fixed amount to household needs, many did not feel compelled to search actively for jobs or to take on what they considered to be unpleasant jobs on unpleasant farms. Late in the season I asked some unemployed young single men about their plans to look for employment on local farms; they responded with vague and evasive answers. Parents often talked about wanting to help their sons find employment and would approach the farmers for whom they worked to request jobs for their sons. In fact, some fathers ask for job contracts rather than day jobs to keep their younger sons fully employed (see chapter 7).

6.1b   Women Harvesters

Most of the women in our original sample who were harvesting as independent workers were either spouses of resident laborers or friends or neighbors of the farmers. After the harvest, these women stayed home or went back to school. A few returned to jobs as domestics or continued to earn money washing and mending clothing. Only 15 percent of the women from harvesting families worked year round. Unlike young men, most women who wanted permanent employment preferred not to be known as agricultural laborers.

However, many women who worked at the large farm that had reintroduced all-female crews remained there to work throughout the year (see table 22). Although there is one major harvest and sometimes one minor harvest, berries do ripen throughout the year (see fig. 7). While most of these berries are picked by the resident laborers or by labor crews hired for maintenance tasks, on this exceptional farm the job was assigned exclusively to women, and the farm retained about thirty women harvesters throughout the year for that purpose. This system has financial advantages for the owner. Women continue to be paid by the weight of berries picked, even though the postharvest proceeds are very low. Indeed, day earnings sometimes fell below the regular day wages paid at that particular farm. Men would not accept such contractual arrangements, but women did because they were desperate enough to welcome any income and had few other opportunities that paid better.

TABLE 22.   Harvest and Postharvest Employment, by Age Group, of Female Family Members of Harvesters in Risaralda ($N = 417$)

Age Group	Working in 1985 Harvest	Permanent Occupation[a]				Total in Group
		Harvesting	Other[b]	Student	Home	
10–14	15.58%[c]		3.9%	66.23%	29.87%	77
	(12)		(3)	(51)	(23)	
15–19	24.1%	4.82%	19.28%	15.66%	60.24%	83
	(20)	(4)	(16)	(13)	(50)	
20–24	27.4%	4.11%	26.03	5.48%	64.38%	73
	(20)	(3)	(19)	(4)	(47)	
25–29	28.13%		6.25%	3.13%	90.62%	32
	(9)		(2)	(1)	(29)	
30–34	48.28%		17.24%		82.76%	29
	(14)		(5)		(24)	
35–39	12.82%	2.56%	2.56%	2.56%	92.32%	39
	(5)	(1)	(1)	(1)	(36)	
40–44	18.52%	3.70%	3.70%		92.60	27
	(5)	(1)	(1)		(25)	
45–49	6.25%		12.50%		87.50%	32
	(2)		(4)		(28)	
50–59	7.14%		7.14%		92.86%	14
	(1)		(1)		(13)	
60+	9.09%		27.27%		72.73%	11
	(1)		(3)		(8)	
Total Number of Women in Occupation	89	9	55	70	283	

Source: Harvesters in field survey except those on the one farm that had all-women crews. Inclusion of this farm would have resulted in an overestimation of the participation of women in the labor force.

[a]These columns list the responses to the question of what the most permanent occupation for each female member of the household was during 1985. Some of these women may also be included in the column labeled "Working in 1985 Harvest." It also includes female harvesters interviewed.

[b]The most common occupations were: salesgirl, domestic, seller of lottery tickets in the street, food vendor, and laundress or seamstress. Very few women were secretaries or teachers.

[c]Refers to the percentage of all women occupied in that activity within that particular age group. The total number of women in that age group is listed in that last column.

That this manager could retain women as agricultural laborers throughout the year may also have resulted from the special relations that he had established with a particular town neighborhood. Most residents of this area are the third-generation descendants of three settlers who had enough land to allow their children and grandchildren to build houses on their property. Children run from house to house; adolescents shift their sleeping quarters among relatives to suit their needs and ease family tensions. This camaraderie, support, and kinship make it easier for these women to endure possible ridicule from other town dwellers. Their grandmothers, who were highly respected in the town, and mothers had worked on this particular farm. Hence, the third generation had no difficulty accepting employment as harvesters either for a short season or for the full year.

The only realistic postharvest alternatives available to other local women from laboring families is work as servants in the town or washing or mending clothing. Living in town, as many do, women may be able to find employment in stores or earn some money selling lottery tickets in the street. Some older women have become food vendors and retain that occupation throughout the year. Table 22 indicates the rate and degree of participation of women—sisters, daughters, mothers, and spouses of harvesters in the survey—in paid employment during and after the harvest. Table 23 indicates the range of occupations chosen by women who are employed.

According to census figures in the municipalities of this study, women's participation in the labor market has grown from 12 percent in 1973 to 22.2 percent in 1985 (Departamento Nacional 1973, 1985a). This growth parallels that observed in the rest of rural Colombia: according to Urrea (1986: 16), this participation has increased from 17.5 percent in 1973 to 21.3 percent in 1985. Although in Risaralda women with little education were still reluctant to work for wages on a regular basis in 1985, a change was noticeable among better-educated women. Three other factors have been noted to draw more local women to steady employment: towns now offer more and varied employment opportunities, more young girls are attending school, and these schools are no longer fostering subservient domestic roles for women (Saxena 1995).

6.1c   Married Men

Burdened with the obligation of supporting wives and children, married men—40.6 percent of Risaralda's local harvest labor force—are more concerned with regularizing their income than with exploring other options. They do not talk about changing occupations or traveling to cities to see what they can find. After the harvest, 73 percent of the married laborers in our Risaralda sample (in contrast to 44 percent of the young men) said they would look for jobs on local farms; 13 percent (compared to 27 percent of the younger men) said they would return to occupations or jobs that they had held previous to the harvest. Only 10.26 percent of the married men said that they would look for another occupation or travel to another harvest.

Coffee trees demand considerable care throughout the year. Large enterprises can afford to retain permanent crews and occasionally hire extra helpers (see figures 11 and 12). However, most other farmers hire few men for only short periods to weed, fertilize, or renovate. Good managers

TABLE 23.   Most Frequent Remunerated Occupations of Women in the Labor Force in Risaralda

Occupation	Census Survey		Harvesters' Families (1985)[c]
	1973[a]	1985[b]	
Professionals[d]	14.13%		5.08%
Administration[e]	4.58%		1.69%
Commerce	6.07%		18.64%
Services	10.45%		3.39%
Domestics	30.85%		44.06%
Agricultural laborers	8.16%	6.76%	18.64%
Nonagricultural laborers	1.19%		3.39%
Other	12.93%		
No Information	11.64%		5.11%
Total	100%		100%

[a]These figures are taken from Departamento Nacional 1973. They include all women in the municipalities.

[b]This figure was taken from Departamento Nacional 1985a, the census of the two municipalities studied. The only occupational category that corresponded to the 1973 census was that of agricultural laborers. Hence, other categories were excluded. The numbers are also lower than for the 1973 census because the census was taken a month before the harvest started in 1985.

[c]Data are based on field survey of harvesters and hence include mostly the women of the families of agricultural laborers. To avoid a bias, also excluded are the families of harvesters who worked on the farm with all-women crews.

[d]Most women in this category are teachers, and some are nurses.

[e]Most of these women are secretaries.

will time these tasks according to agronomic requirements and to minimize competition with other growers. They also take into account the seasonality of income and ability to raise the money to pay the wages. The
labor market is tight only right after the harvest, when many farmers are
pressed to carry out jobs that have been delayed. Once these tasks are
completed, the demand for labor decreases and is more evenly spaced
throughout the year.

Thus, most laborers have to shift from farm to farm during the maintenance season, hoping to put together a palette of farms that are good
places to work and that will provide employment throughout the hard
months. Many workers thus achieve nearly full employment throughout
the year. They blame the unemployed for their plight: "A good worker
always finds a job," is a common statement. "Those who are out of work
[are so] because they are lazy or do not have the stamina." Although 97
percent of the laborers of all ages that I visited in their homes during the
summer of 1986 indicated that they had worked at least part of every
month during the past year, some acknowledged that they had faced periods of unemployment between jobs. If the periods are short, laborers will
remember the month as one when they were employed. When the periods
of unemployment are longer or more frequent, they are not forgotten.

Laborers must then take into account pay and work conditions as well
as estimate how long the job will last. Laborers do not shrink from accepting a well-paid job that may last for only one week if they know that other
nearby farms will be hiring after that. But later in the maintenance season
workers often prefer longer-lasting jobs even if they offer lower pay.
Clever or more desperate laborers approach other farmers when it seems
as if contracts are about to end to avoid the inevitable days of search with
no pay. However, it is not always possible to guess correctly because farmers share very little information when they hire laborers.

> One has to be very awake, with eyes wide open, to always have work.
> I am a person who when I begin to feel they are going to tell me there
> is no more work, I begin to talk to one and then the other, and so with
> everyone. I ask my workmates, "Man, where do you think I can find
> work?" They tell me, "Perhaps so and so has work."

The wife of a laborer explained of her husband, "Last week and the week
before he was working on [a particular farm, and] he had been working
there for several weeks, but when they took out some personnel he went to

[a different farm] and they gave him work for the week." She added, "This week, he found work [at a third place,] and we do not know how he will do there." Except on the large enterprise farms, laborers are certain only that they are unlikely to be hired for more than two months at a time.

> Seven weeks is the maximum. After that they tell you there is no more work. Or the owner or manager will tell you, "Man you have to go elsewhere for about two to three weeks before we can give you work again."

The seven-week limit alludes to a loophole in labor laws that allow farmers to avoid all fringe benefits and severance payments when they hire temporary laborers. But farmers will rehire laborers, particularly known, trusted, good workers. Patronage thus does not ensure permanent employment, but it does keep future options open.

> We do well and we work well. So we return, we go elsewhere, then we return, and if one is a good worker they give you a job.

Still workers must find something else to tide them over until they are needed. Alertness and readiness to move as soon as one knows of another job are perceived by farmers not as astuteness but as unreliability. They bitterly complain that laborers come and go as they please. Irresponsibility and disloyalty are common complaints voiced by farmers, who seem to forget how desperate the situation can be for laborers and how farmers themselves contribute to this desperate state of affairs.

Distance is another important consideration. Although there is a relatively good local bus system, all laborers walk to their jobs to save money on fares. Postharvest wages are low, and even a small deduction can seriously limit workers' ability to support their families. Another avoided expense is the cost of a meal purchased at a farm. Colombian laborers are used to a hot meal at noon and a snack in the afternoon. If they work very near their houses, they can return home for lunch; if they work further away, they will ask one of their children to bring them lunch. However, parents do not ask very young children to venture out on their own or ask ten-year-old sons to travel for more than half an hour. Given that in 1986 the cost of food at a farm was two hundred pesos a day and the highest daily wage was seven hundred pesos, it was just as profitable and much more comfortable to accept a nearby job for six hundred pesos as a job further away for a higher amount. Also, it is more likely that nearby jobs would be at farms where laborers are known and valued; therefore, they can hope that owners will be flexible and try to keep the laborers employed until they can find other jobs. According to laborers, some farmers are accommodating, perhaps because they want to assure themselves the availability of good workers during more pressing agricultural periods.

The hope of good wages when jobs are plentiful early in the season entices workers to continue their searches. A good wage is a culturally constructed concept of the amount of money necessary to satisfy family obligations, adjusted to what is conceived as possible in the market (see section 7.2). Yet the expectation of such a wage plays a limited role during postharvest job searches. Laborers rarely know what they will be paid unless they have recently worked at a particular farm and the farmer maintains the same wage throughout the season (section 7.3). Laborers are reluctant to ask about pay scales and length of contract during the maintenance season, and few farmers offer any information on the subject. Even when laborers are informed, they are often too desperate to reject offers if they are married and have children to support.

Wages, distance, knowledge of labor needs, acquaintance, and past experience with particular farmers all play a role in determining where laborers search and which offers they will accept. Laborers with larger families bear greater burdens and weigh wages and contract length differently than those with few or no children. The number of working sons is not likely to affect their choices. Male heads of household regard themselves responsible for their families. Sons' help is welcomed but not required, and the amount contributed by each son relates to his willingness and his father's earning ability. Sons of men who waste their earnings on drink or who pass up too many employment opportunities may pass some money to their mothers, but they are likely to leave the household or withdraw their contribution if the father places too much reliance on their wage packet.

A careful evaluation of the aforementioned elements affecting search decisions and acceptance of contract conditions can help to predict laborers' strategies. Right after the harvest, distance, wage, and permanence are the three most important elements that determine where laborers look for jobs. At first, they may either approach farmers who the workers know pay well or go directly to farms where the workers are known. They may also wait to hear from friends and relatives about the availability of jobs on farms that hire for longer periods of time. Since work is then plentiful, these laborers know that within a few days they will receive various offers. The length of the search varies according to how much money has been saved from the harvest and the number of dependents. But even at this time, money and length of the initial contract are not the only important criteria. Laborers want to establish links with the few farmers who are likely to call them back later in the season.

As the postharvest season progresses, laborers must search further afield, often walking for an hour or more to their place of employment. Length of contract and adequacy of wage subside in importance as the period of hunger approaches. Just a few days of work are then welcomed.

> One has to respond each week with food for the family. Well, one begins to worry, becomes muddled, and begins to think, "What will I do after the last day?" Then one begins walking during the week to this farm and the other farm. Until suddenly, one has luck and one finds work for two or three days. Someone tells you, "Man, I am going to give you two to three days of work although I have nothing to do, just to tide you over."

Nine of the twenty-two married laborers I visited in one of the municipalities of Risaralda acknowledged facing periods of unemployment that became longer as the maintenance season progressed.

> At first I found work nearby, all around here, but recently it has been very hard. There was a week that I had no work, and I did not know what to do with the family, so on a Sunday I went down below [to the town square], and Monday I went there, and I found the job that I have. It is the job that [pays] three hundred pesos [half the prevailing day wage].

When one listens carefully to these accounts of a search for jobs, another distressing reality emerges: a day without a job can be a day of hunger. With harvest savings gone and little possibility of buying on credit, laborers are desperate. They walk longer distances to work, may even go away for a short period, and accept wages that are too low to feed their families. Those who are unwilling to stoop to miserable incomes or who entirely lack offers must scrounge to feed their families. Neighbors and families will help with whatever they have. Farmers allow unemployed laborers to cut plantain stems to eat. Pawnshops abound and accept any recently purchased household appliances. The exchange will bring enough money to buy food for a couple of weeks. Regardless of how resourceful and hardworking these laborers are, July and August are uncertain and bleak. All dread this season, which locals call the period of cold or hunger.

Laborers explore other local job opportunities at this time. They may be able to work clearing pasture, caring for cattle, or in tomato or corn fields, but since Risaralda is primarily a coffee municipality, such opportunities are scarce. Few workers are able to branch out into such nonagricultural rural jobs as cutting trees for sale, carpentry, fishing, and charcoal production. In the summer of 1986, however, many laborers could survive building roads or digging new sewers in town. All such work is scheduled to take place after the harvest, and contractors are supposed to hire only local laborers. It is hard work, paid by the meter, and suitable only for the younger, stronger, married men. Local jobs in construction, commerce, or the service sector are harder to get and usually go to the same people who year after year work in these occupations after the harvest.

When the situation becomes so desperate, some married laborers also begin to think about traveling to another municipality where the main harvest has already started (see table 24).

> If they now tell me [at the farm] that there is no more work, I will have to go to Palestina [in Caldas] since coffee in warmer parts comes earlier than in these parts. So one looks when they take you out and begins to think that the only opportunity for work is [in Palestina], so let us go there to see if the coffee is coming and they will give us work.

TABLE 24.   Participation of Local Married Men in Other Coffee Harvests, Risaralda

Participation in Other Harvests	Since 1985 Harvest	In 1985 before the Harvest	During 1984	In the Past Two Years
Yes	2.5%	7.5%	7.5%	27%
No	97.5%	87.5%	70.0%	46%
NA	0	5.00%	22.5%	27%
Total	100%	100%	100%	100%
	(40)	(40)	(40)	(40)

Source: The first three columns are based on open-ended interviews with laborers during the summer of 1986. The last column is based on our survey of harvesters in 1985.

Palestina, the municipality these laborers were considering, is not too far from where they were then working. Although most people would prefer to go by bus, they were planning to walk to save money. Both men were born in Palestina and could cut costs by staying with friends or relatives. Knowing the place, they could quickly survey the state of the harvest and decide whether to stay there or return to seek yet another job. None of these searches can take very long because families must be fed and savings have long evaporated. The few other married men who had gone elsewhere to harvest had also gone to familiar places.

Following the harvest may be financially rewarding, but it is only so for those men who can harvest fast enough to earn more than nine hundred pesos a day (1985 costs and wages)—that is, those who can harvest at least ninety kilograms a day. When asked how much coffee they thought they could harvest at the height of the season, 32 percent of the harvesters in the survey mentioned figures below ninety kilos. Married men prefer not to leave their families alone for long unless kinsmen or friendly neighbors will offer protection. Many men hesitate to put their wives in the difficult position of having to raise the money for food and do the weekly grocery shopping. It would be equally worrisome to leave the house unattended. A family in tow would be a costly venture and restrict movement. Since women are not expected to enter the coffee groves and no special lodgings are available for men and their families, the family presence would be a heavy financial burden. Rooms in town would have to be rented, a difficult and expensive proposition. It is thus not surprising that few married men go away despite hardship at home.

Most married men with many dependents appear more inclined to explore the availability of permanent positions as *agregados* on one of the local farms (see sections 3.5a and b). About half of the families I talked to during the summer of 1986 had, at some time or other, accepted positions as *agregados*. Some of them were hoping to again move to a farm, but doing so is not as easy as it once was.

> We have talked to many owners to see if they would give us a placement. And my son who is interested, he tries to find a position. And several of our friends around there are helping us.

It can take several months or even a year before an appropriate offer comes up, and after a few months the arrangement may turn out to be disappointing or unsustainable (see section 7.5). Relations between farmers and laborers are fraught with tensions that can be resolved only by moving on. Yet some seem willing to keep trying, while others give up after the first unpleasant experience. Still other laborers with large families find the relation too demeaning to accept (table 6.8).

Most *agregados* last at best three years on a farm. They then either leave of their own accord or are fired. A lucky few receive some fringe benefits and severance pay when they leave the farm. For reasons I discuss in chapter 7, these extra benefits are unlikely to play a role in the search for a job as an *agregado*. In conversations with laboring families, I clarified some important issues. The first consideration is that they will receive housing, which is of interest to those families that have not yet built or bought houses. The second consideration is that the farmer is likely to hire the young sons of the *agregado* before hiring outside occasional laborers. As one spouse explained, "Look, [our sons] are crazy for him to find a farm so that they will have work every day, every day, so they do not have to go elsewhere. They do not want to stay in homes that they are no good to them." Positions as resident laborers may also be welcomed by families with many daughters, who can help prepare food to sell to day laborers. Some families find the arrangement profitable, and some daughters welcome the opportunity to contribute to family expenses, but the women of other families prefer not to engage in this activity. Not surprisingly, most families seeking such contracts were recent arrivals to Risaralda. They were looking for a place to live and had not yet established the networks necessary to assure themselves an income during the cold or hungry season. A position as *agregado* cushioned the initial lean years until the family got established. It is not that these laborers had a greater preference for security but that their situation was more fragile.

6.2   Job Searching and the Labor Market

The search ends when laborers agree to accept job offers. According to economic models, such acceptances occur when the remuneration offered is higher than the value of remaining unemployed. In other words, laborers are expected to accept jobs when they meet aspiration wages, when better prospects seem unlikely, or when continuing to search seems too costly. When coffee berries begin to ripen, laborers know that the number of jobs available will rapidly escalate and the search will be cheap and short. Social networks structure about half of the harvest searches and are instrumental in delimiting supply sources. Most laborers (young men and migrants) gear their searches, within or outside their networks, to realize their preferences. Farmers must respond to these expectations and allow wages to rise during the harvest. This inflationary tendency is likely to be most strongly felt in the farm sector that depends on young and migrant workers—usually larger farms. Married men, who represent a smaller proportion of the harvest labor force, favor farms that offer the prospect of employment during the maintenance season. They are willing to consider a farm that pays a bit less but will offer work most of the year.

But as the market changes with the end of the harvest, job search strategies also change. Some laborers then have to struggle with difficult decisions: whether a refusal will bring more distress than the acceptance of a low-paying job. For young men who have no responsibility for the welfare of parents and siblings, the choice is rather straightforward. These men are not tempted by low wages. Young men value money to dress well, drink, and provide entertainment, but they also value the freedom to search for more comfortable or socially prestigious occupations and to see the world beyond their communities. These men measure job offers against preferences and wage expectations. Search models that include social costs and culturally molded preferences are very useful in explaining what jobs young men are likely to take, for how long they will search, and when they are likely to prefer unemployment. (See Devine and Kiefer 1991 for a review of these models.)

However, most of the agricultural laborers during maintenance season are likely to be married men.[3] For them, the monetary payment has a different value than it does for their young, unmarried sons. Older men use money to quell hunger and pay for necessities. At the beginning of the season, like their sons, wage and preferences are more relevant than are other considerations. These men search through contacts and approach places where they have previously worked. The length of their search depends in part on their savings and the number of dependents. It also depends on the breadth of their contacts. Married laborers who have broad contact networks are often willing to wait a bit longer for a farm that will offer employment for a longer period of time and better conditions. Networks are important not only because they transmit information about jobs but also because they convey ability and honesty to potential employers. As the season progresses and the chance of long periods of unemployment increases, even a low-paying job is tolerable. Search models of married men must then include the following elements: number of dependents, laborers' aspiration and reservation wages, laborers' cash savings, the extent of laborers' networks, the cost of the search, the regional rate of unemployment, and the number of days that laborers have been without work.

The maintenance-season market thus sustains a wide range of wages, many of which are far from suitable. This market is structured by employment uncertainty, social networks, and, as chapter 7 shows, by the unwillingness of many farmers to offer information about jobs.

Chapter 7

Wages and Contracts

Search models have been coupled with microeconomic models that consider commodity prices, costs, and labor productivity to explain the format of the contract and the remuneration to the laborer. Regardless of how complex and sophisticated these models become, they cannot achieve their avowed end if local conditions do not meet the assumptions of a market exchange. One of the fundamental assumptions is that laborers have the right to alienate their labor and the right to claim remuneration. In Risaralda not all people who pick berries are free to sell their labor for remuneration. Daughters and boys usually "give" the berries they pick to the head of the household, who then receives all the family's wages for berries bagged. Husbands often block their wives' attempts to participate in the harvest as independent wage workers, encouraging the women only to collaborate. In this way, husbands retain full control of family income. These familial transfers represent nonmarket exchanges that come close to the model of gift exchange (C. A. Gregory 1982: 12). Laborers receive familial "gifts" of labor; then, using this "gift," they negotiates their contracts with farmers. Although the actual proportion of labor that was exchanged outside of the market could not be determined, the relevance of this flow should not be underestimated (see sections 5.7b and 7.2). Piece-rate payments can incorporate the effort of others, which may explain the popularity of this form of payments in local markets where laborers have a right to claim gifts of labor from family members.

Another assumed characteristic of a market contract is that the exchange is open, and compliance with the terms of the agreement is insured either by legal or customary sanctions (Durkheim 1957; Weber 1978; Woodiwiss 1987). Durkheim also argued that full protection to negotiate implies the right of one of the agents in the contract to break the agreement if conditions are not met (Lukes and Scull 1983: 224). In rural Risaralda only harvest contracts are openly negotiated in a consistent manner. During maintenance season the prospect of persistent unemployment effectively bars laborers from quitting when they realize that farmers have failed to comply with minimum-wage legislation or promised payments. Supply conditions create power imbalances that affect bargaining equity (Akerloff 1982: 489; Weber 1978). Landlords also use their powerful political connections to obstruct investigations or to ensure that the regional labor office rules in their favor, thereby leaving laborers without institutional protection.

There is another essential condition that must be met if "rational" market models are to apply: both agents must be assured the right to bargain. Bargaining can occur only if the terms of the agreement are openly discussed and explicitly negotiated. This is the case during the harvest season. After the harvest farmers do not always fully specify what they will pay or other terms of agreements. This situation is not unique to coffee agriculture in Colombia. Robertson (1987) has pointed out that many of the African sharecroppers he interviewed acknowledged that they were unaware of some of the contractual conditions; they claimed they would not have made the agreements if they had been aware of all of the terms. Although it is rare, even in bureaucratic market societies, for parties to a contract to be fully informed of contractual terms, only in the literature on implicit contracts is this reality acknowledged (Hart and Hölmstrom 1987). I argue that this issue should be explored in all discussions of labor markets and should be included as part of search models. Whenever possible, field-workers should try to record details of the hiring process and note how often contracts are not fully explicit. What each party receives and how each party is protected depend on the explicitness of contract negotiations. The laborer's welfare is likely to deteriorate further if contractual terms are undisclosed and are coupled with a power imbalance. When laborers have little market power and little political protection, undisclosed contracts will leave them worse off than will explicit contracts, which can at least be evaluated if not negotiated. The wage received is then likely to differ from the wage predicted by a market model.

For collaborative agreements to occur, both parties must share moral values and a vision of social equality. Alternatively, each party has to painstakingly build faith in and mutual dependence on the other. In Risaralda, landlords are often inconsiderate; they view laborers as irresponsible individuals of an inferior class and forfeit the chance to build a clientele of committed occasional laborers by failing to allow them to explicitly bargain for wages and fringe benefits.

When contracts are explicit—mostly during the harvest—laborers bargain for security, working conditions, and appropriate pay, whereas farmers bargain for lower costs, timely availability, compliance, and high performance. Economists argue that self-interest is enough to enforce compliance when contracts are explicit, when employers meet laborers' expectations and workers voluntarily accept jobs. This argument, however, can only apply when demand conditions do not have sharp seasonal variations. In Risaralda, harvesters know that regardless of how efficiently they work, many of them will not be retained after the berries are picked. Farmers thus insure quality labor only through supervision and by firing workers who repeatedly flaunt the rules. Surveillance, however, leads to confrontations and discourages collaborative behavior. Only small farmers avoid the problem because they draw their laborers mostly from the social networks that they have painstakingly built (see Granovetter 1995 for other examples). Each type of contract is thus associated with a set of managerial strategies, and the effectiveness of and preference for each type must be discussed within that context. These strategies, in turn, must be evaluated in terms of the social and political consequences of the practices and farmers' concerns about them. Bardhan (1984) has argued that it is in the interest of many farmers to move away from contracts defined in purely economically rational terms to more personalized, complex, contractual relations that may not only stimulate supply but also foster deference, compliance, and commitment.

In this chapter I consider a number of other issues beyond the negotiated wage and financial fringe benefits and discuss the contingencies of each type of contract and the farmers who favor them. Readers can relate contracts to management strategies and sanctions by referring to the cited sections of chapters 5 and 6. When relevant, I point out which workers are hired and what noncontractual privileges they have. I also discuss why some farmers avoid open, explicit, and informative negotiations and the apparent consequences of obscuring contractual terms. Since some technical requirements dictate the nature of specific contracts and management strategies, they are outlined when relevant. To appreciate the pressures felt by local laborers when they negotiate with farmers, readers should refer to appendix C, which gives information on family income and household budgets.

A full understanding of market dynamics would ideally require longitudinal information on wages and variations of contractual terms. Unhappily, in this study only data on the cash components of day wage and piece-rate contracts are available. No records are kept on the total cost of each type of contract, and the noncash elements of these contracts are not itemized. The only longitudinal information available is that of Errazuriz's (1989b) analysis of average day wages. I refer to her conclusion in the section on harvest contracts.

An institutional approach that takes into account the whole range of labor-management hiring strategies, the availability of legal protection, and the social conditions of the transacting parties is much more appropriate to this case study than are tighter and neater economic models. The institutional approach enables integration of customs and conceptualizations of fairness and consideration of how these elements affect supply response and contractual preferences. This approach does not negate economists' contention that in the long run wages and contracts reflect market conditions and the productivity of labor, but it questions the universal validity of their proposition. While farmers cannot avoid the realities of commodity prices and cost of production, they need not respond to them by altering wages. For example, farmers can reduce the cost of other inputs or gain greater productivity by reorganizing how they manage their farms. Some of the managerial strategies are only appropriate to farms of a certain size, while other strategies reward only farmers with considerable political power. All of these issues are discussed in this chapter with reference to types of contracts used in coffee agriculture in the local markets of this study.

7.1   Harvest Contracts

Farmers want laborers to work a full day, from early in the morning until sundown, when they must carry what they have harvested to the weighing stations and wait until a supervisor records the amount bagged. Farmers also want laborers to harvest the coffee before it falls to the ground but to do so without damaging trees. Growers are aware that custom dictates that meals and snacks must be made available for a fee to all laborers who want to eat and that free lodging must be offered to nonresident laborers. These rules and services as well as pay are clearly, though often summarily, spelled out when hiring workers. However, only experience will tell laborers about working conditions, quality of food and lodging, and earning possibilities at any particular farm. Thus, laborers may have to shift from farm to farm until they find one that matches their aspirations; if possible, workers will return to this farm year after year until they become once again dissatisfied with the condition of the coffee groves or the treatment and pay.

Farmers are concerned not only about quality of labor but also about supply. During the harvest they must attract a labor pool that is more than twice the size of the required maintenance labor pool (see section 6.2). They know that for the harvest they have to entice as many local residents as possible and attract laborers who reside elsewhere. To attract workers in the market, farmers must allow wages to float upward. At the same time, they have to control production costs, especially during periods of low coffee prices (see section 3.6). Since the harvest is a very tense and hurried period, managers of enterprise farms are more likely to use impersonal management strategies and wage enticements, while owners of smaller farms may have the time and inclination to be more involved with the laborers they hire.

Harvesters, conversely, want to earn what they consider to be an appealing income. An appealing harvest income must cover not only weekly food costs but also allow them to pay off debts, make necessary annual purchases, and cover future periods of unemployment. The wage component is thus a very important element of the harvest contract, albeit not the only one (see section 6.2).

During the harvest on most farms, wages are set according to how many kilos laborers harvest.[1] Once the piece rate is set to clear the basic nonharvest daily wage, it can be adjusted when demand conditions warrant. But what concerns trigger changes in wage rates? And to what extent do commodity prices affect payments to laborers?

When farmers and administrators of large enterprise coffee farms in Risaralda were asked whether they considered coffee prices or harvesting costs as criteria for setting the piece rate, all said no. They explained that they started at the same level as the previous year. One administrator told me that farmers checked what had been paid in a nearby municipality where the harvest had just finished. Those growers with trees that matured a bit later said that they paid the prevailing rate. On one big farm, I was told by the administrator that the owner, who lived far away, set pay rates.[2]

Some owners of medium-size farms also said that they asked around to see what was being paid. Others explained that they automatically started the season offering the same rate paid when harvesters were last hired. All farmers agreed that once the initial rate per kilo was set using whatever formula was favored, adjustments were made according to demand circumstances. As one farmer explained,

> Seeing that there were problems, that [laborers] were becoming obsti-
> nate about the price, and because the [maturation] of the coffee was
> pushing us, I rushed it to ten pesos a kilo, and there I left it. Never go
> back on a price. The rest of the year I will pay ten pesos.

On this farm they started the season paying eight pesos per kilo and then
raised the rate to 8.50 pesos, nine pesos, and finally ten pesos.

Owners of small coffee farms must rely on advances from traders to
pay wages at the beginning of the harvest and have to make piece-rate
decisions before becoming fully aware of what price their coffee will bring.
Thus, farmers in more precarious financial positions—and certainly
poorer farmers with less than five hectares of land—often start at a lower
piece rate than do larger farms and slowly allow the pay rate to float
upward. Many of these small farmers can hold on longer to the lower rates
since they harvest most of the coffee themselves or with the help of their
sons. Most of these smaller farmers did not pay more than eight pesos per
kilo in 1985.

Climatic conditions affect rates of maturation and the fall of ripened
berries. Competition for harvesters thus varies from year to year and from
one slope to another. During some years, some farms have to keep raising
the rate paid, but in other years the same farms may be able sustain the initial rate with only minimal adjustments. In 1985, while the farmer quoted
previously had to keep adjusting rates, another equally successful farmer
kept his rate between eight and nine pesos.

Farm conditions also affect rates.[3] Low-yielding coffee groves (those
not well kept or recently renovated) or those located on steeply sloped terrain may have to offer higher rates. But such is not always the case. Since
berries mature more slowly on the lower-yielding traditional coffee farms,
there is a more even demand for fewer workers. Low-yielding farms may
not get the best pickers or the migrants who are eager to earn as much as
possible, but these establishments attract older workers willing to trade
higher income for steadier employment. Farms close to town and those
surrounded by small farms or rural hamlets are privileged because they
can often count on a supply of laborers who prefer to sleep at home and
can save money by having food delivered from their own kitchens.

As a general rule, farmers assume that the piece rate paid at the end of
the last harvest season is the lowest rate that will be acceptable to laborers.
At the end and beginning of the season, harvesting conditions are similar.
There are few berries to pick and, unless the piece rate is high enough,

laborers would not clear what they earn as day workers. Although it is obvious that starting at the higher end of the previous season's rate pushes up the forthcoming season's average nominal earnings, farmers do so for two reasons. First, they are aware that offering less than what was previously earned is demeaning to laborers and not a good way to start a tense season. Second, because it is clear that persistent inflation has eroded the real value of the wage, the higher rate might push weekly income closer to laborers' reservation wages. Farmers aspire to retain this initial rate throughout the season. However, they are well aware that such is unlikely to be the case. They must decide at what point they will balk when laborers either implicitly or explicitly bargain for higher rates. This upper limit represents their reservation rate. The gap between the aspiration value and the reservation value is likely to be widest for wealthier farmers than for farmers with cash-flow problems or coffee grown under shade. The largest enterprise farm in one of the Risaralda municipalities had to pay eleven pesos for most of the coffee harvested, two pesos more than at the beginning of the harvest. The average paid on this farm per kilo harvested during the 1985–86 season was 10.81 pesos. On another smaller enterprise farm, the manager started paying only eight pesos per kilo and was able to keep the rate to an average of 9.12 pesos per kilo during the same season by delaying a final hike to ten pesos per kilo.

Harvesters, of course, want to attain a rate that they think will bring them a desired harvest income. This aspired-to rate is based on what they will need to meet their obligations, their appreciation of market conditions, and the quality of the coffee grove. Harvesters from elsewhere are likely to aspire to higher rates since they also have to cover transportation and food costs. Personal considerations and a realistic appreciation of abilities also determine what harvesters hope to earn. Laborers, even those on a single farm, thus have a range of aspiration rates.

During the survey, laborers were asked what they expected to earn during the height of the harvest. Since their responses did not reflect what they had earned in the past week, I assumed that their estimates reflected the income to which they realistically aspired. The two incomes most frequently mentioned by all male laborers were eight hundred pesos a day (by 17.7 percent) and one thousand pesos a day (15.9 percent): nearly 41 percent of all male laborers expected to earn between those two rates. About 16 percent expected to earn more, and almost twice as many expected to earn less. Some of those who expected a very low wage were supervisors who anticipated receiving a bonus. A significant proportion of harvesters who came from elsewhere (11 percent) mentioned that they expected to earn 1,500 pesos a day.

How close these workers come to meeting their desired wage depends not only on their ability and the condition of the farm but also on the piece rate that they are paid. By shifting the piece rate, a farmer can access a larger pool of harvesters and ease his own supply pressures. Figure 13 illustrates this point for one of the largest enterprise farms in Risaralda. This farm started paying nine pesos a kilo, moved the rate up to ten pesos a kilo when the ripening process accelerated and the supply pressure began to be felt, and one week later raised the rate to eleven pesos a kilo. In this way they were able to attract more demanding nonresident laborers.

Although laborers are in a position to bargain the income to which they aspire during the harvest, they often have to accept piece rates that will not net that amount. The workers are handicapped by the limited opportunities for collective bargaining and the unwillingness of farmers to pay differential rates. The most effective recourse available to laborers is to look for different jobs when it becomes clear that the coffee grove is not in good enough condition to net the desired income. Such action may not be as effective as a strike but may eventually move farmers to increase piece rates if faced with absenteeism and desertion. Laborers who protest by quitting may later reap the benefits of their action at different farms, since all farmers compete for the same pool of laborers. These essentially dyadic bargaining procedures are reinforced by the collective appreciation of the quality of the harvest, coffee prices, and the cost of living. The harvest is a busy season of intense human contact, and information about rates flows quickly. Laborers on occasion explicitly and collectively bargain for higher rates or better conditions. They approach the manager and threaten to stop midday if their requests are not met. However, it is less risky to act individually than collectively. It is also less costly to leave early one day and look for a job for the following day than to miss a day or two of work while waiting for a farmer to accede to a higher piece rate. Although farmers spoke of past walkouts, they would not discuss them, and laborers also failed to offer information on the subject.

Dyadic bargaining models suggest that the eventual settlement will fall between laborers' aspiration wages and farmers' upper-limit value (Nash 1950). Other behaviorally oriented research suggests that the reservation reference point might be a more important focus than the aspiration point in a bargaining situation (White et al. 1994). The prevailing daily wage at the beginning of the harvest was five hundred pesos a day,

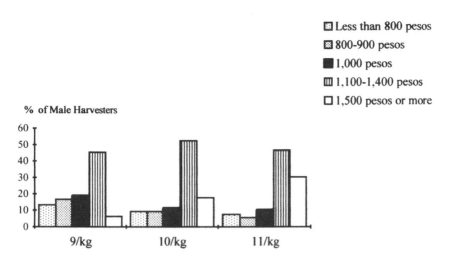

Fig. 13. Projected daily income of harvesters on a large enterprise farm in Belén, 1985. Based on the weekly amount harvested by each male laborer during the first week of December, according to account books. The daily incomes were estimated on the basis of a 5.5-day week at this farm's rates per kilo, listed along the horizontal axis.

and I assume that this figure represents the reservation daily income of laborers, although it does not fully cover the cost of living for a family (see section 7.6). As noted previously, the aspiration income in 1985 ranged from eight hundred to a thousand pesos a day for local harvesters and had an upper limit of 1,500 pesos a day for migrants. The aspiration labor cost for farmers was expressed by the piece rate at the beginning of the harvest, which in 1985 was eight pesos per kilo of berries harvested. It was not possible, however, to determine how farmers set their reservation rates. It is reasonable to expect that they might relate to prices, price trends, or cost of production. However, it is not clear that farmers have such figures in mind when bargaining with laborers, and Errazuriz's (1989b) correlations minimize the significance of prices in the short run.

While it is not possible to test the bargaining models described in the previous paragraph, the distribution of earnings and aspiration income of laborers in the same large enterprise farm shown in figure 14 is instructive. The farm in the graph has a good reputation in the area but is large enough to need to attract a fair number of nonresident harvesters as well as many locals. In the graph the distribution of day earnings for the male laborers

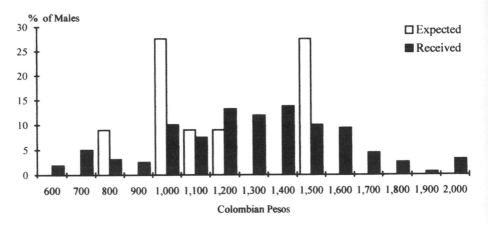

Fig. 14.   Range of expected and received daily wages of male harvesters on a large enterprise farm in Belén, 1985.   The expected percentages are based on laborers' answers to a survey question about what they expected to earn at the height of the harvest. The received daily wages are based on average earnings of laborers during a week at the height of the harvest. I have assumed that each man worked for 5.5 days. Some harvesters may not have worked a full week, which results in low daily earnings. It is also not clear why some laborers expected to earn four hundred pesos. The distribution of expected income is independent of the distribution of incomes received. For example, the column for one thousand pesos should not be interpreted to indicate that of the nearly 30 percent of those who aspired to receive that income, only 10 percent did so.

was based on the rate paid when the harvest was in full swing (eleven pesos a kilo). At that time the manager matched the aspiration income of non-resident harvesters. At the beginning of the harvest, when he was paying only nine pesos a kilo, he failed to satisfy the aspirations of a quarter of his labor force. Within a week he moved to eleven pesos a kilo, a decision that supports the bargaining model suggested by Nash.

Not all farmers are so obliging. On another equally well-run farm, less than half of the laborers who aspired to earn one thousand pesos a day managed to do so. All of them, however, did earn above their reservation wages (see fig. 15). This case illustrates the point made in literature on bargaining that the reservation price represents a more absolute limit to the negotiator while an aspiration may be violated if there is an opportunity for a quick settlement (White et al. 1994: 438) or for satisfying other aspirations (Devine and Kiefer 1991: 299). After observing how their subjects solved bargaining problems, White and Neal (1994: 307) concluded,

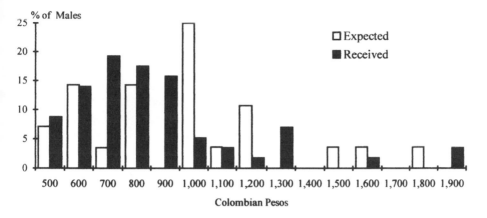

Fig. 15. Range of expected and received daily wages of male harvesters on an enterprise farm in Marsella, 1985. The percentages for expected earnings are based on answers to a question about what laborers expected to earn. The received daily wages are based on the weekly earnings of each laborer and the number of days worked during that week. For the estimates, I selected a week at the height of the harvest when sixty men were hired. The distribution of expected income is independent of the distribution of income received, as noted in figure 14.

While a negotiator may be capable of calculating his/her reservation price objectively, it is our argument that the same negotiator can fall victim to social cognitive biases that pervade the negotiator interaction. In this sense, the relationship changes from one of maximizing expected value to one that is influenced by the social interchange within the bargaining situation.

Although wage adjustments on two farms do not offer enough robust data to test any hypothesis, the evidence supports the suggestion that nonmarket factors must be considered to understand striking variations in the match between aspired and received daily wage. On the farm in figure 15 a desire for rapid settlement may have contributed to the acceptance of a lower rate. More relevant was the reasonable treatment of laborers on this farm and the security of employment it offered. The coffee grove was located at medium altitude, which allowed the farmer to spread the harvesting period over a longer period. He consciously tried not to rush the harvesting process and to keep a steady regular crew of workers most of the year. Most of the harvesters were local residents, and a high proportion of them were retained for a period of seven months. In chapter 5, I note other less pressing considerations that may influence the acceptance of incomes below those desired.

The contrast between these two farms illustrates that farmers respond differently to market pressures. The first farm required a large crew of laborers and could not hope to rely on local harvesters. The second farm was located in an ecological niche that permitted the farmer to hire smaller crews for a longer period of time. Both of these owners were well-off and had good access to credit. It is reasonable to expect that other farmers who have cash-flow constraints will try to attract and retain good laborers through a variety of noncash incentives. Thus, some dispersion of daily incomes during the harvest can be expected despite the intense competition for laborers.

Although managers and farmers were adamant in saying that they did not take coffee prices into account, it is reasonable to expect that prices played a role in determining the highest piece rate that growers would be willing to pay, since about one-third of production costs are harvest costs. Yet there seems to be no close connection between coffee prices and wages. Errazuriz (1989b) came to a similar conclusion after an analysis of national and regional wage trends in coffee agriculture between 1977 and 1987. She observed that real day wages (deflated by the cost of food in each municipality) remained high even after farmers' real coffee prices (deflated by the cost of living index) began to drop in 1977. Furthermore, the moderate increase in prices during the 1986–87 season had no effect on wages (Errazuriz 1989b, graph 20). Wages in Marsella and Belén followed a similar path (see fig. 16). It is also relevant that coffee wages were higher than wages for other crops and for construction work.

Errazuriz's analysis in part supports farmers' insistence that demand pressures and cost-of-living hikes force the raising of piece rates when the laborers demand it. She noticed that wages varied a great deal from municipality to municipality and that in 1985 the municipalities with greater production and higher rural food costs had higher wages.[4] However, a similar comparison for 1977 gave different results. Although during that year the municipalities in the vanguard of modernizing coffee groves had to offer higher wages, wage differences among coffee municipalities did not correlate with differences in cost of living twelve years later. Wage differences did correlate with variations in the population of the municipality.[5] Errazuriz explained the insignificance of difference in cost of living by pointing out that in 1977 the real value of the wage was

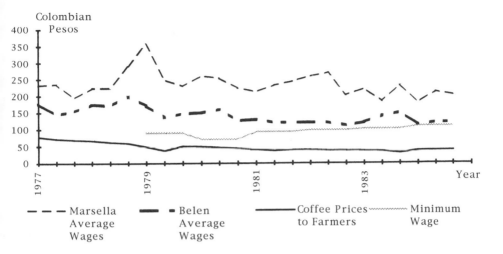

Fig. 16. Real wages paid to laborers in Marsella and Belén, minimum wage, and FNCC coffee prices to farmers, 1977–84. Wages were deflated by the rural cost of food derived from the difference between wages with and without food and indexed to the third trimester of 1978. This wage series is used to calculate the national average. The price of coffee is based on the series used by Errazuriz except that it is averaged by trimester and estimated by kilo. The minimum wage and price were deflated by the cost-of-living index for December 1978.

much higher than in 1985. By 1985 laborers were not approximating what they needed to cover basic food needs and were much more adamant in their demands. Errazuriz's findings are corroborated by the correlations carried out by Montenegro (1993: 390) and Corchuelo (quoted in Junguito and Pizano 1991: 174–76). All authors conclude that fluctuations in the prices paid to the farmers have only a delayed impact on wages. Montenegro and Corchuelo believe that FNCC policies that stimulate or discourage expansions and renovations directly influence wage rates by affecting demand for labor.

There is also a weak correlation between productivity and wages. Montenegro points out that between 1970 and 1975 the productivity of labor increased at a higher rate than did wages. However, as wages skyrocketed during the late 1970s, farmers faced costlier harvests and became less competitive in the international market. Only during the brief period from 1985 to 1987 did farmers enjoy a more fortunate ratio of wages to productivity. Otherwise, the drop in prices and production between 1988 and 1990 without a concomitant drop in wages accounted for the farmers' plight (Errazuriz 1993).

Corchuelo's disregard of the significant role of cost of living (see Junguito and Pizano 1991) leaves out laborers' role in wage settlement. Harvesters are not pawns of disembodied economic factors. They are individuals with aspirations and obligations, as anthropologists and job-search theorists are apt to point out. When in a position to assert themselves, workers will seek to attain their hopes and meet their needs. The obligation to feed a family is a keenly felt consideration. While farmers are interested in reducing costs to attain higher incomes, they know the harvest is not the best time to attempt to do so. They are well aware that they have other management options during the maintenance season that will allow recovery (see section 7.3).

I believe that coffee farmers are reluctant piece-rate setters who respond to demands of laborers only when the pressures of the harvest are great and workers have some bargaining power. Growers do not acknowledge a response to coffee prices or the efficiency of labor. However, eventually they may have to attend to price changes. The impact of prices for the period under consideration has been two pronged. First, higher prices have stimulated the conversion of land from food crops to coffee and thus have had an inflationary effect on the rural cost of living. Second, higher prices encouraged conversion of land to coffee production and the renovation of groves, which eventually led to higher productivity and greater demand for harvesters (see fig. 2). The higher efficiency of labor in modernized coffee groves assured high profits to the owners of enterprise farms (see section 3.6), allowing them to raise the harvest piece rate. Even when prices fell during the 1970s, returns to investment remained respectable according to Arango's conservative estimates (see table 9). It is important to remember that enterprise farms set the rates with which other farms compete. The more drastic recent drop in prices, however, must have affected the harvest piece rate (see section 2.4). Thus, prices and the productivity of labor impact on harvest wage levels but do so only indirectly and when they are smoothed over the long run.

Market conditions, laborers' preferences, and their ability to bargain during the harvest thus have a clear but complex impact on the rate paid per kilo of coffee harvested. But if these factors are to be a central facet of the argument, they should explain not only the swing in wages but also the contract format. In other words, why are harvesters paid by kilo of beans brought to the weighing station rather than by the day, as occurs during the rest of the year? What advantages does this form of payment offer farmers and/or laborers? Do these advantages warrant a seasonal change in contractual arrangements?

Researchers have viewed the prevalence of harvest piece-rate payment as the most efficient type of contract for farmers. The most common suggestion is that this type of contract stimulates laborers' productivity, inducing them to work faster and thus avoid possible losses when beans fall to the ground. At the turn of the century, when laborers received part of their payment in food, productivity was also stimulated by requiring a minimum number of cans of beans to receive meals (Palacios 1983: 213). This strategy solved the problem of monitoring work intensity. As the owner of one of the largest farms said, "If he works, he earns; if he does not [work], he does not earn." Another advantage for farmers is that the piece rate allows them to avoid paying for the time laborers spend transporting beans to the weighing station and the time lost while workers await their turns. However, piece rates complicate administrative tasks. Supervisors must be hired to ensure that no green berries are plucked and that speed and greed do not encourage harvesters to be careless with trees.

Alternative explanations revolve around the pressure to mobilize a large supply of laborers without incurring extra costs (Brown and Phillips 1986). To diminish the pressure of attracting harvesters from elsewhere, it is important to first tap all sectors of the local population. To entice a wide range of local laborers, daily rates not only have to be high enough to attract men otherwise employed but also must be low enough to make it possible to hire those with little experience or ability. Schoolchildren may skip classes, but more can come if they can work after school. Married women and even young girls may join crews if they can do so after they complete their household tasks. Older people, who are not certain of how many days or hours they can tolerate under hot sun or pouring rain, may ask for employment if no fixed time commitments are required. Some of these fringe harvesters are not very efficient and would probably be excluded if they were paid by the day. Paying them by weight harvested assures that they are paid according to their efficiency.

The piece rate also makes it possible to include those who are willing to come only as helpers. Men who are not adept at plucking berries are likely to entice their wives and daughters to help them. That extra effort will be acknowledged, though the helper does not receive direct remuneration. Wives and daughters were willing to help considerate heads of households and to accompany them whenever possible; mothers bring children old enough to help. In the two municipalities studied, 20 percent of all harvesters had at least one family helper on the day they were interviewed. Men and women were more comfortable encouraging dependents to help if the farm was small or the personnel familiar. From the account books of the one medium enterprise farm that used families from the neighboring hamlet, I estimated that 32.5 percent of male harvesters brought helpers. Wives constituted 20 percent of the helpers, sons or daughters 41 percent, siblings 31 percent, and other family members the rest. Harvesters' followers are a common institution in Europe (Morgan 1982) and are known in other Colombian coffee regions.

If the piece rate efficiently mobilizes all local labor pools, it also serves to stimulate the supply of able pickers who live elsewhere. These men would come only if they could earn more than they would at their regular jobs. During the harvest of 1985 construction workers or persons employed in the service sector or commerce could profit from working on a coffee farm away from home since they could earn two thousand pesos a day doing so. This sum certainly compares favorably with the seven hundred pesos a day maximum agricultural wage. Not all who came would earn that much. The less able harvesters were often unemployed agricultural laborers from areas where the harvest had not yet started or had just finished and were usually earning very low incomes (see section 6.2c). They represented about 28 percent of the migrant population. This group includes not only the unemployed but also some young men who were anxious to travel to other areas, explore other options, or even to visit friends and kin.

Another reason for favoring a piece-rate contract is that it allows for an automatic reduction of daily earnings as the harvest slows down. If workers were paid by the day, farmers would face resistance when they wanted to lower wages at the end of the harvest. However, when laborers are paid by amount harvested, their day earnings automatically decrease toward the end of the harvest because it becomes harder and takes longer to bag a kilo of berries. When earnings fall below the preharvest wage, this form of contract is terminated, and laborers receive daily wages. Although this transition did not seem problematic in Colombia, such is not always the case, judging from Wells's (1996: 192) depiction of the strawberry industry in California.

It would appear that piece rate contracts allow for small adjustments, help to mask wage differentials, and ease the transition to a market with an oversupply of laborers. Flexibility in its adjustment to supply and demand conditions and its ability to stimulate at a minimum cost a number of supply sectors are probably central to its continued use. Just as important is the laborers' preference for this form of contract. Except for the most inefficient harvesters, laborers prefer the piece-rate system because they feel in control of what they earn and the hours they work. They can come and go according to the state of the harvest, perhaps working only a half day. They can search for better jobs without losing an entire day of work. Women find it easier to attend to their domestic duties when their pay is not linked to entry and departure times.

As Marx has noted (1977: 697), the piece-rate system gives laborers a sense of liberty and individuality. When they rule, laborers do not mind the competitive market. The impersonality of market relations during the harvest is very much forged by this type of contract. However, laborers have not always preferred piece rates, and their prevalence was one of the issues raised by laborers during the confrontations of the 1930s. At the time, powerful landlords used piece rates to exploit vulnerable laborers. Once demand conditions changed and power in the market became more balanced, the piece-rate contracts offered laborers a greater sense of control.

The piece rate also leads to some unpleasant consequences, such as differential incomes, pushing some workers below the minimum nonharvest wage. Piece rates also increase the competition and tensions among coworkers. The theft of bagged berries is frequent enough for large farms to police the areas where laborers store harvested berries. It is not a climate that encourages collaboration or the coordination of strikes.

Another serious consequence is that the piece-rate system may lead to lower earnings among powerless constituents. Farmers will raise rates as the harvest dwindles, when most of their laborers are men, eventually switching to a day rate. No farmer would keep male workers while paying them below subsistence level. But not all workers have their needs recognized. Female harvesters, who work in all-women crews throughout the year, are always paid by the kilo. During many months they earn a miserable wage. They are willing to continue to work only because they have few other opportunities and are not considered their families' wage earners, even when they provide the household's main support.

7.2 Day-Wage Contracts

After the harvest, most pruning, fertilizing, weeding, and even picking whatever berries ripen is done by workers who are paid a day wage, even when the laborers reside on the coffee farm. The two exceptions to this rule are job contracts (discussed in section 7.4) and payment to those women who continue to harvest (see section 7.2).

The nonharvest period is relatively bleak (see section 6.2). Laborers must struggle to find work in a market limited by a progressively shrinking demand. The estimated unemployment rate for men over the age of fourteen reached 31.4 percent during the nonharvest period of 1985–86. This estimate is in line with those given by the FNCC, which calculated the average annual unemployment rate for 1984 at around 15.6 percent, with a range from zero to 32 percent. Only during years when farmers decide to renovate their coffee groves are laborers likely to be employed most of the time. The bleakness of the market often forces laborers to accept contracts that are totally out of step with what is offered at other farms, a fact that serves as a reminder that noncompetitive markets with high rates of unemployment can tolerate a wide range of modes of remunerating laborers and a considerable dispersion of wages (see appendix B). Wages also fluctuate by 3 to 6 percent from month to month during the maintenance season. Given these realities, laborers search to find jobs and security rather than to find jobs that meet their aspiration or even reservation wages. In fact, very few of the day wages are above a subsistence-based reservation wage. A young husband who had not yet become a father needed about 550 pesos a day to fulfill his obligation in 1985 (see appendix C). This amount was a hundred pesos more than the legal minimum wage and fifty pesos more than the average wage for July 1985, according to the census figures (Departamento Nacional 1985c).

Whereas harvest contracts are always clearly spelled out, day-wage contracts are not necessarily itemized. Many laborers were not sure how much they would be paid when they first started working on a farm; they were often surprised at the low amounts received. How laborers are approached, what information is exchanged, and what questions laborers themselves raise depend on relations between buyers and sellers, market conditions, and farmers' management styles.

Large, more bureaucratized farms with resident managers prefer to standardize wage payments throughout the maintenance season and to maintain a crew of nonresident laborers at or above the legal minimum wage. Most work is performed by this crew, and tasks are scheduled in such a way that all of these laborers can be maintained most of the year. These farmers pay higher wages than other farmers, contrary to the findings from India (Pal 1996). The wage payment is reviewed only once a year, usually right after the harvest. It is not clear how the wage is set or how increases are estimated. My impression is that these wages are not negotiated openly with laborers but are set unilaterally. These are prized jobs, available only on the enterprise farms (see section 3.5a). In many instances these laborers are offered not only clearly itemized contracts but also some of the fringe benefits to which they are entitled by law. When the cost of these benefits is added to the daily payment, the total wage earned is at the top of the range of offers. Altogether, these workers probably represent about 16 percent of the total unskilled maintenance-labor force (see appendix A).

On these farms, the laborers are told the hours they are expected to work and whether food is available and at what price. The tasks to be performed are not always spelled out and vary considerably throughout the season. Laborers must renegotiate their contracts if they believe that the assigned tasks deserve higher remuneration. For example, many laborers will not fumigate unless they receive a premium, and some of them will not fumigate under any conditions. Such issues are sometimes resolved by enticing willing laborers to perform the task for higher pay and retaining reluctant laborers for other tasks. On the two large enterprise farms in the sample, managers accommodated reliable workers' requests as long as they did not interfere with the organization of maintenance work. Managers also tolerated some absenteeism and offered help in cases of illness in the family. All of these exchanges are not considered part of the work contract but are rather managers' benevolent acts in response to requests.

These managers gave a number of different reasons for paying the legal wage rather than the equilibrium or prevailing lower wage. Their explanations shared the language used, couched in legal and moral terms: "It is the law"; "We want to treat them right." Legal propriety was a dubious explanation, since these farms do not necessarily abide by all labor laws. These managers may have feared the attention of labor organizers, having experienced labor conflicts and remaining aware that these farms' prominence made them vulnerable to further disruptions. The managers probably also wanted to convey an image of benevolence and security to exact a greater commitment on the part of laborers (see section 8.2c for a discussion of this point).

Medium and small farms, in contrast, let market conditions set the stage for how individual laborers are hired. When faced by financial difficulties, these farmers are tempted to salvage their farms by paying less than the minimum wage and what other farmers pay. Instead of openly challenging the ongoing wage, these growers manipulate the hiring process to avoid stating a rate of pay. Instead of searching for laborers, these farmers wait until they are approached and treat a job query as a request for help. They respond by granting permission to work. When I was present at such encounters, I was told that these applicants were hired to help them out. These exchanges can at best be described as undisclosed contracts that share some of the characteristics of a gift exchange (Akerloff 1982).

Laborers have grown accustomed to this practice. One man explained that this is how things work; if laborers ask too many questions, farmers complain that there are too many conditions and will offer the job to someone else. Undoubtedly, custom and market conditions do limit laborers' ability to bargain. However, custom does not fully explain nonnegotiable contracts. The same man who submissively approaches a farmer during the maintenance season also asks the farmer how much he pays per kilo of berries harvested. The scarcity of jobs gives farmers the power to manipulate job solicitation to their advantage. Focusing the analysis on how that power is gained and how it enhances customary behavior may provide a better understanding of why certain contracts prevail than narrowly focusing on the rigidity of customary institutions. The idea in the economic literature that institutions are rigid and impede the effective role of the market hinders an intelligent consideration of all variables affecting wages and contracts (Binswanger and Rosenzweig 1984: 30–31).

Not all farmers placed laborers in such demeaning positions. The farmers with very small coffee groves were particularly mindful of not abusing their advantage. Many of them had been laborers and were aware of how difficult it is to feed a family on a day wage. They avoided paying the lowest wages (offering six hundred pesos instead of five hundred pesos) and provided better-quality food. They also expressed a concern for the families of workers hired.

Other farmers avoided low-wage undisclosed contracts because they encourage low effort. When laborers accept jobs they expect to receive wages or wages plus fringe benefits that come close to their reservation wages. If they receive payment below that figure and are not enticed with other benefits, they will perform at standards below farmers' expectations. Mutual disappointment leads to tensions and laborers' shirking work. While they can be replaced with other workers, there is no guarantee that the replacement will be any better. Disappointed laborers are also less likely to respond quickly when called to work during the harvest. A nonnegotiable undisclosed contract allows farmers to pay lower wages but also lowers productivity and responsibility.

Despite these disadvantages, some cash-starved farmers use these nonnegotiable undisclosed low wage contracts when hiring laborers. If productivity and responsibility are important issues, these farmers try to control shirking in other ways. They personalize their relations with the laborers and offer noncash benefits: free plantains and small services.[6] These efforts are likely to be effective only if laborers live nearby, if they have few other employment options, and if laborers and farmers have frequent contact with each other. Older heads of households are more likely to profit from multistranded undisclosed exchanges and respond to them in appropriate ways. Young men are more interested in cash wages and can afford to be unemployed. Farmers who use these contracts consider young men to be irresponsible, to be hard to manage, and to need costly supervision. Thus, day wages will depend on the representation of this cohort among the available workers.

It may be argued that laborers learn what the farmers in their neighborhoods pay and from the beginning adjust their performance accordingly. It is of course true that some farmers have a bad reputation and that laborers either avoid working for them or shirk on the job. But few laborers who work for these farmers all the time are likely to be fully aware of the range of rates they pay, since wages fluctuate from month to month on all of the medium farms. Furthermore, as the maintenance season progresses, laborers must search beyond the area with which they are most familiar and are likely to face some surprises.

Farmers concerned by the quality and efficiency of their laborers have three choices: they can meet laborers' reservation wages, engage in multistranded transactions, or hire supervisors to monitor performance. The second choice recalls Bardhan's argument about the rationality of interlinked contracts and the attachment of laborers to the farm (see section 1.1). His argument, however, disregards the tensions inherent in these contracts and laborers' inability to negotiate a contract of their preference. Thus, day wages during maintenance season depends on demand, which in turn depends on stimulus to renovate coffee groves, the financial ability of farmers, the demographic structure of the population, and the representativeness of enterprise farms in the local market.

7.3 Job Contracts

Instead of paying day wages during the nonharvest season, some farmers and laborers prefer to contract by the job. Doing so simplifies the management of labor for farmers but brings the risk of having to pay for a poorly performed job. Farmers who do not reside on their property or who have several small lots find the risk worth taking. It is a more common arrangement on small and medium-size farms than on large ones, and it is more often used for weeding than for spraying or fertilizing.

Some laborers who prefer contract work explain that they can incorporate their sons and thereby realize a higher collective income. It is a useful mode once a familial working group has an established reputation. Other laborers prefer contract work to avoid rude supervisors or time-keeping bosses. Many workers are fast and able and can move rapidly from job to job during the active part of the postharvest season and realize enough money to sustain days of rest or unemployment. But for others, the acceptance of contracts is disastrous. Unable to correctly estimate work requirements, they accept payments that are exploitative. Even the most experienced and shrewd individuals err on occasion. Inexperienced laborers are taken for a ride and may give up accepting contracts after a few failures. Once jobs are completed, farmers do not allow laborers to renegotiate pay.

Laborers generally believe that the job-contracting system prevails among farmers who want to take advantage of workers. This belief is substantiated by the prevalence of job contracts for a large number of maintenance season tasks in 1992, when farmers were desperate to reduce costs (Arango 1993: 206–8). Only those laborers who are sharp, experienced, and aggressive can counterbalance the demands of farmers and bargain a contract that is either to their advantage or to the satisfaction of both parties. When less confident and less experienced laborers fail to estimate correctly or to bargain effectively, they reduce their efforts to attain their daily reservation wage. Cheap contracts lead to shoddy work. Farmers who want to save money are willing to take the risk. It would have been interesting to record negotiations and quality of performance, but this task proved impossible.

Other more specific and routinized tasks are sometimes contracted out, for example, the preparation of bags for the germinating of seedlings, the planting of coffee trees, and the renovation of coffee groves by cutting back the bushes to one-foot stumps. If farmers decide to raise their own seedlings, they will contract unskilled laborers to fill small plastic bags with dirt, with payment based on the number of bags to be filled. A fast worker can earn above the prevailing wage rate for a long day of work. On some enterprise and medium farms, contractors who bring and supervise their own crews are hired to renovate established coffee groves. Contractors are told what to do and, after examining the area to be renovated, a price agreement is reached based on the number of trees to be cut down. These contracts as well as those described in the following section, are carefully and explicitly outlined at the onset and typically are less likely to cause ill feelings.

On some local enterprise farms, the sensitive task of replanting and planting new trees is contracted out. These contractors are willing to assume the managerial responsibility of bringing together a crew of perhaps fifteen men who work well together. Their most important assets are the ability to judge how best to trace lines in a field, to measure accurately, and to direct the crews to coordinate the work of marking, digging, and setting of seedlings so that there are no slack periods and no seedlings left unattended lest roots dry out. Contractors work along with the crew and supervise the work. They charge by the tree planted and demand an advance to pay their crews' wages. These contractors usually clear above the daily wage by driving their crew members—who for the most part receive piece-rate wages—to work very quickly.

To my surprise, these contractors in the municipalities of Risaralda were not always highly trained individuals, though the ones in Belén had attended extension courses. Many contractors in Risaralda started as day laborers and learned their trade either from observing how it was done on well-kept farms or from their fathers. On occasion, minor contractors return to work as laborers or offer themselves as crew members to other contractors. These workers complain that they are not paid enough because of collusive agreements among farmers and that earnings are not much above those of a day laborer. Yet from information obtained from several of these contractors, it appears that they must earn at least one thousand to three thousand pesos a day, which is far above the general postharvest wage and more in line with daily harvest earnings. However, contractors' income is limited by their ability to search for and attract contracts as well as the readiness of farmers to renovate or expand areas planted with coffee. Very few men specialize in this kind of work, so the competition is not very keen. It was not possible to determine how many individuals had attempted to enter this market and had failed.

In some municipalities, contractors attend workshops organized by the FNCC. Once trained, these laborers assume a more professional status, taking on more responsibilities and expanding the scope of their enterprises. Such was the case with one of the major contractors in Belén, who provided seedlings, planted them, and watered and fertilized the growing trees until they were well established. He was rewarded with higher pay per tree planted. He was responsible for about 30 percent of the new variety of *colombian* seedlings planted in Belén and had raised about 60 percent of all of the seedlings that were in production in that municipality. He worked for eighteen farmers who owned medium or large farms, among them the proprietor of one of the largest and most productive farms in the area. The entrepreneurial success of these individuals depends on the number of area farms interested in such services. More to the point, local FNCC agronomists can help these contractors build clientele by recommending their services. The municipalities where the FNCC develops training centers or workshops are more likely to have contractors than municipalities with more lethargic municipal FNCC committees.

The time required for all maintenance tasks could be estimated if farmers and laborers jointly reviewed the field conditions, but only if they shared an appreciation of appropriate work effort. This collaboration is unlikely to occur when class differences shape perceptions of trust. Furthermore, while laborers are more concerned with fairness and their reputations, farmers are often more concerned about costs. Thus, job contracts are satisfactory to both parties only when they share the same goals, trust each other, collaborate, and when renegotiations are allowed. When there are strong imbalances in negotiating power, these contracts are likely to be exploitative tools for farmers. Contractors in turn pass the burden of the exploitation onto their hired day laborers.

7.4   Resident-Laborer Contracts

Contracts between farmers and resident laborers have been profoundly transformed since they were first adopted at the turn of the century, when they were used to open up and maintain large coffee farms. The most significant changes have occurred in response to political events and government regulatory practices rather than to market conditions (see section 2.1). *Agregados* were assigned a house and an allotment where they could grow crops for their own subsistence and for sale to the landlord or in the local market. In exchange, they had to work two to three days a week and be available to work at a day rate during the harvest (Arango 1981: 134; Palacios 1983: 193). While working to repay their land rent, the *agregados* received half the ongoing wage (Palacios 1983: 215). In Cundinamarca, the *arrendatarios*—the name given to resident farm laborers in this region— often lived on the allotment, whereas in the central coffee region their houses were far from their fields. If they failed to come to work, they could be evicted by the local authorities or by the powerful landlords. It is not clear from the historical record how much land resident laborers received for the assigned number of days of work, and there is a lack of information about how the terms of these contracts varied with other factors. It is clear, nevertheless, that these arrangements were one of the major modes of attracting and contracting labor. This system is still in use on one of the Risaralda farms and on some farms in Cundinamarca. On the Risaralda farm, the attached families live away from the allotment and are obliged to work for wages for the landlord when needed. These *agregados* receive a wage rate comparable to those paid at other neighboring farms. One of these *agregados* claimed that it was no longer profitable to work on the allotment except to grow a few crops for home use. On the Cundinamarca farms, the families were once assigned one hectare of land to use as they wanted as long as they either paid a rent of two hundred pesos or weeded a specific acreage of the owner's land (twenty-six *cuadras*). Now these *arrendatarios* receive a house and enough land only to plant food for home consumption. They are expected to be available to work for a wage when called.

On most other farms in Risaralda, *agregados* no longer have the right to plant crops or even to have a small vegetable garden. They are also not allowed to keep animals except dogs, cats, and a few chickens. Furthermore, the number of laborers hired as *agregados* has decreased considerably in recent years, but it is not possible to determine when the reduction happened or when the format of the contract changed.

Although the term *agregado* is still used locally, the term *attached laborer,* which is used in the literature on Asia, might be more appropriate. The attachment is contractual and can be broken by laborers quitting or being fired. While laborers are attached, they are morally obliged to work for farmers at a daily wage that is similar to the one paid to occasional workers. When not needed, attached laborers are free to work elsewhere. Although the contracts can be broken, there is an expectation of indefinite continuity and of nearly full yearly employment. Most attached laborers receive a house and a wage, but not all families who are allowed to stay in empty houses are necessarily attached to the farm. Farmers who have dismissed a large number of *agregados* may have empty buildings and be willing to lend them to families in need. Unless there is a verbal contract, these laborers cannot count on assured employment on the farm. Attached laborers are now used as supervisors, drivers, and food providers for other laborers. Rarely do they constitute the bulk of the labor force, even on farms that have trouble attracting piece-rate harvesters. The Risaralda farms of greater than sixty hectares had between ten and twenty attached laborers. The medium enterprise farms had two to three attached laborers. Smaller farms have attached laborers only if the owners reside elsewhere.

The government regards attached laborers as permanent workers, and landlords are expected to abide by the relevant labor legislation. They are obliged to cover the cost of the education of laborers' children younger than age fourteen through a monthly family subsidy. Since these laborers are also entitled to social security benefits, landlords must register all permanent laborers at the Instituto de Seguridad Social (Social Security Institute) and add a contribution to what is deducted from their laborers' weekly pay. Social security benefits insure some coverage of medical costs and disability compensation. The enterprise farms are large enough to also be required to assume financial responsibility for other medical costs: full coverage of drugs and medical treatment for two years following a work-related accident. In the case of non-work-related illness, medical costs are covered for only six months: growers must indemnify laborers with two-thirds of their salary for ninety days and half of their salary for the subsequent ninety days. Permanent laborers on all farms must receive a compensation commensurate with their years of service if fired without due cause—one month for each year employed. This payment is very important since there are no unemployment benefits available to dismissed workers to cover subsistence needs while searching for another job. The laborers' rights to these benefits apply regardless of whether they reside on the farm; in other words, such benefits also apply to other permanent workers (see section 2.6). Smaller enterprises are not expected to assume all these benefits. The list varies according to farms' capital assets. Hence, the actual value of these benefits ranges from 15 to 30 percent of what the landlord pays in wages (Gomez 1976: 99–108; Ortega Torres 1980: 330–31). Most if not all farms that have attached laborers or permanent nonresident workers are large enough to be compelled legally to contribute at least a share of their medical costs, free lodging, and severance pay.

Thus, the state has officially transformed contracts between landlords and attached laborers from a predominantly land-labor contract with a minor wage component to a predominantly wage contract with a housing and welfare component. Landlords are no longer the sole arbiters of contractual terms. The freedom to negotiate is now circumscribed by law, and, at least in theory, laborers' rights are backed by governmental institutions. One would now expect the wage to reflect more clearly the market conditions, responsibilities assigned, human capital endowment of laborers, cost of housing, and fringe benefits. Legal sanction should also help balance the power of negotiating parties and assure that laborers are able to exact benefits pertinent to their condition. However, the realities are quite different.

The weekly wages of the attached laborers seldom comply with minimum legal levels. The pay received ranged widely from farm to farm and from case to case. Attached laborers with no significant responsibilities earned from a low of 2,640 pesos to a high of 3,800 pesos a week. Married laborers received an additional amount if their wives cooked food for other workers (see appendix B). Attached laborers with supervisory responsibilities were often paid higher weekly wages ranging from 3,300 to 4,200 pesos; they are the only ones likely to receive fringe benefits and to receive a bonus for the amount of coffee their crews harvest (see section 3.5a and appendix B). Workers in charge of processing harvested beans are often paid a higher wage to discourage them from stealing some of the harvest. Thus, one of them received four thousand pesos a week during the harvest as well as a bonus; however, others received wages similar to those of unskilled attached laborers. The variation is so great that the most that can be said is that each of these rates can be understood only within the context of the situation: the size of the farm, the individuals involved, and the negotiation procedures used.

Social security benefits, which landlords consider an unfair burden, are infrequently extended to all attached or permanent nonresident laborers. This belief holds true not only for the coffee region but also throughout rural Colombia. In 1983 95 percent of Colombian rural laborers received no social security benefits. In the two Risaralda municipalities investigated, only a few attached laborers were registered at the Instituto de Seguridad Social. For November 1985, the official records listed only 616 registered laborers in 459 agricultural enterprises for all of Risaralda. In Belén and Marsella there must be about 1,118 laborers attached to farms plus others who have contracts as permanent day laborers. Landlords openly acknowledge not registering workers or not doing so for all of them. Growers calculated that avoiding fringe-benefits requirements saved from 300 to 575 pesos per worker per week. Some laborers did not mind not being covered by social security because they believed that they were unlikely to receive enough medical coverage and disability payments to warrant a pay deduction. The deduction for social security and other fringe benefits could amount to 106 pesos per week for an attached laborer earning a top weekly wage of four thousand pesos.

The fringe benefit highly valued by laborers and most feared by landlords is severance compensation. This severance pay pegged to years in service after a sixty-day trial period encourages farmers not to prolong contracts. Severance compensation must also cover any improvements that laborers make to the landlord's property. Liability for improvements is the reason given by farmers for not allowing laborers to plant crops. By taking advantage of legal loopholes, many landlords avoid paying severance benefits. Others openly flaunt regulation with little concern for laborers or for the possibility that complaints will be lodged with the labor affairs tribunal. Among the fifty-four laboring families interviewed in their homes in Risaralda, twenty-three had served as resident laborers at least once, but only ten had ever received severance pay or any welfare benefits. Laborers bitterly resent the loss of severance pay.

Although laborers can appeal for nonpayment of compensation or family subsidies, very few do so. Most laborers are unaware of all their legal entitlements. Those who are aware believe that it is a waste of time to lodge a complaint at the labor office in Pereira. According to the books of the regional labor office, attached laborers in Risaralda filed eleven complaints of unfair dismissal during 1985–86, but only one was favorably settled. The labor office also ruled against nine complaints for nonpayment of salaries or family subsidies. Only larger, more efficiently run farms are likely to provide some of the benefits accorded by the labor laws. The argument that labor legislation is counterproductive because it encourages a shift to occasional contracts (Schaffner 1993) has relevance only when the legislation cannot be ignored or when the cost of the fringe benefits does not result in an increase in the productivity of laborers.

The lack of compliance with labor laws attests to the unwillingness of government bodies to intervene and to the political power and personal links of many landlords. It also raises the question of why laborers agree to attach themselves to farms where they may receive day wages even during the harvest, may not receive social security, and may be dismissed without severance pay. Bardhan (1984: 73–85) has argued that a desire for security explains a preference for attachment even when the wage received is lower than that paid to occasional workers. Pal (1996) suggests that wage advancements may also be responsible for the attractiveness of farm attachment. While in Risaralda wages paid to attached laborers were about the same as those paid to occasional workers during the mainte-

nance season, attached laborers were unlikely to earn as much as harvesters during the peak weeks of that season. The main attractions of a
contract as an attached laborer were greater income security; increased
chance of employment for sons; opportunities for wives and daughters to
earn an income preparing food for laborers (see section 3.5); and availability of a rent-free residence. Not all of these benefits were equally
significant to all laborers. Furthermore, it was not possible to estimate
what income laborers had to forgo when they attached themselves to a
farm. It is thus impossible to evaluate the rationality of the laborers' preference, for example, whether laborers who sought attached contracts were
less adept at picking berries and hence less likely to profit from harvest
piece-rate payments. It is clear, however, that many of these contracts are
disappointing to the applicants.

Bardhan's (1984) argument about the rationality of attachment to a
farm also assumes that laborers are aware of the terms of these contracts.
However, initially what is known to each of the soliciting laborers is the
pay, the condition of the living quarters, and which farm resources (wood
and plantains) they are allowed to use. This last point is most clearly itemized as administrators and landlords try to avoid misunderstandings. Only
on larger, more bureaucratized farms is the policy regarding fringe benefits
clearly spelled out and consistent. On these farms, attached laborers
receive some help with medical costs, a family subsidy, and social security.
Length of contract and future severance pay benefits are two issues that
laborers never raise during negotiations and that managers, even on larger
farms, never spell out. Yet these two concerns are vital reasons for entering into such contracts. Laborers do not ask because they fear that they
will be regarded as troublemakers and will not be hired. Instead, workers
bide their time while keeping track of how long others have remained on
the farm and what payments they receive on departure. However, even this
information may not foretell laborers' fates since farmers may keep only a
few of workers for a long time and terminate others routinely after a few
years to avoid hefty severance payments. One attached laborer confessed
to me that he was not sure how much he would receive when he eventually
retired; he had been on the same farm for fourteen years. The administrator of one large farm admitted that after three to four years he asks his
most loyal resident laborer to leave for a while, promising to rehire him
after a few months.

Owners and managers prefer to express their relationship to their
attached laborers in personal terms rather than as a set of explicit mutual
contractual obligations. By so doing, landlords make it difficult for labor

ers to openly negotiate for fringe benefits not yet received or specified when hired. For example, according to the law, permanent laborers have a right to receive an extra monthly wage a year, to be paid in two installments. Rarely is that benefit formally accorded. Instead, landlords transform these payments into gifts to celebrate the birth of Christ. Landlords exaggerate the value of the gifts, and attached laborers often dismiss their financial significance. Landlords claim turkeys, clothing, furniture, and even sewing machines as contributions to attached families' seasonal merriment. The landlords want these gifts to convey attention to laborers' needs. Likewise, when laborers become ill, they request help from landowners rather than demanding a legal right. These requests are often but not always attended to. "We like to collaborate with them," a farmer told me proudly. Yet, one attached laborer discovered to his chagrin that his landlord refused to help when the worker's son got sick and had to be hospitalized.

Through these patronizing responses, landlords hope to buy the loyalty and submission of the permanent laborers who make up the core of the labor force. Growers complain bitterly when they feel rebuffed. Compliance, however, is not the only intended goal. Landlords also mean to convey another significant element of a paternalistic relation: control. In a region where control over others has been associated with abusive power, dependency heightens uncertainty and fosters tensions between farmers and laborers. Paternalistic, undefined attached contracts satisfy both parties only in cultures that value or at least tolerate subordination. (See Hart 1986; Hefner 1990; Wells 1996 for contrasting examples in Java and California.) Of course, some coffee landlords in Risaralda are sincerely concerned at least about those laborers with whom friendly and collaborative relations have been forged. But these owners are not in the majority. Thus, for every loyal resident worker, there are many who leave in resentment.

Bardhan's (1984) argument about the rationality of attaching laborers to a farm spells out not only the preferences of laborers but also those of farmers. As chapter 1 discusses, he argues that landlords attach workers either to insure their availability when needed or to insure their loyalty as supervisors. Why then do the landlords of Risaralda mar their paternalistic relation by behaving inconsistently? I do not think that the answer lies in a model of rational market behavior. Social perception, political animosities, and past experiences are more central to the definition of the landlord-laborer relation, as reflected in the quotations in chapter 3. In other words, the market does not explain the totality of the labor process.

Chapter 8

Conclusion

Many policymakers and economists regard the modernization and intensification of agricultural exports as a necessary step for rural welfare. They predict that the growth of exports will bring fuller employment and higher wages. However, many social scientists have criticized agricultural modernization policies for disregarding other negative impacts: the marginalization of peasants and small farmers, the seasonality of most labor contracts, the instability of rural populations and the weakening of the social fabric, and the impersonality of labor relations. Most of these criticisms are based on case studies where the modernization agriculture has been accompanied by free market neoliberal policies. This was the case for Chile's fruit industry but not for coffee in Colombia. The international and national market for coffee was highly regulated and the modernization of coffee groves was subsidized. Thus, Colombia offers a valuable contrasting study that should address the points raised by supporters and detractors of modernization and free-market policies. In the first part of this chapter, I examine some apparent consequences of the intensification of coffee production and highlight those that have been central to the controversies on modernization and deregulation.

According to the classical definition, the labor market is the place where the labor demand and supply interact and where wages are determined by competitive bidding. This definition disregards one of this study's central findings: the market interaction is not between demand and supply but between socialized and politicized individuals who only sometimes openly negotiate their interaction. What emerges is a partial agreement with incomplete information rather than a bargained optimal exchange. This agreement is likely to best suit the interests of the party that has greater power at the time of the negotiations: perhaps the laborer during the height of the harvest, the farmer during the rest of the year. If the market is to be an effective and fair instrument to mediate transactions between producers and laborers, then formal and informal mechanisms must be in place to insure that bargaining does take place and that it is not affected by inordinate power imbalances.

But that is only half of the story. Laborers must monitor that farmers keep their promises. Workers will either behave in ways that will anticipate farmers' compliance or use sanctions to force them to comply. Farmers have to create conditions that will realize the labor power they have contracted and must do so on farms rather than in the market. Farmers have several options for attaining the efficient deliverance of quality labor at the appointed time: they can ruthlessly coerce laborers, they can engage laborers in social relations that may enhance loyalty and responsibility (that is, patron-client relations) or offer sufficiently attractive contracts that workers will fear losing their jobs. Alternatively, farmers can avoid the personalization of working relations and realize the contracted labor power by organizing work activities in ways that can be effectively controlled and supervised without undue coercion, for example, the giant lettuce-wrapping machines in the United States that follow and set the pace for laborers who cut lettuce (R. J. Thomas 1985). Farmers and laborers keep these considerations in mind when encountering each other in the local market or at the farm gate. Considerations about conformity and compliance will determine how laborers are hired, perform, and survive. A clear picture of what transpires at the local market and on the farm will help determine the competitiveness of the agricultural labor market in question and the appropriateness of those regulatory systems that are intended to enhance farm profitability and laborers' welfare.

In the second section of this chapter I address the above issues and how seasonal fluctuations in the farmers' and laborers' market power have impinged on contract terms. I also illustrate how each type of contract is linked to certain managerial practices and their related costs and benefits. The discussion of these and other points revolves around problematic stages in the labor process that require a decision. Each stage is discussed in a separate subsection that includes comparative examples from commercial agricultural activities in other regions of the Americas. In considering choices, I have assumed that farmers are guided by a desire to satisfactorily resolve their investment-managerial problem. This assumption does not imply that farmers' decisions are rational in the narrow sense of the term used by economists but that growers reason their decisions to attain their goals (Ortiz 1983). Although the summary section takes the farmers' perspective, this discussion incorporates laborers' reactions, their occasional power to narrow the options open to farmers, and the contractual terms that farmers must offer to attract laborers.

8.1 Global Markets and the National Nexus:
The Impact of Agricultural Expansion and Intensification
on Laboring Families

With the negotiation of the International Coffee Agreement, the FNCC gained extraordinary economic and political power, which it used to launch a campaign that has transformed Colombia's countryside. While the majestic shade trees have disappeared from the coffee groves, rural neighborhoods and towns have been revived. This expansion was engineered and sustained by a national agency with national capital and the capacity to store coffee and organize its commercialization in the international market. Only for a short time, between 1973 and 1979, was the boom fueled by rising international prices. After 1987, when coffee prices in New York dropped to a new low, the expansion could only be sustained with the FNCC's support prices and subsidies. For a few years after that event, in the then unregulated market, this organization decided to continue to protect producers.

To what extent can the fate of Colombian coffee farmers and laborers be compared to that of producers who are not protected by similar trade organizations? What lessons can be learned from this case study about the impact of dramatic commodity price swings on labor markets? How has this modernization affected the earnings and welfare of coffee laborers? Answers to these broad questions are beyond the scope of this book, but some suggestive comparisons may place this case study in the midst of ongoing controversies about globalization and technologically induced intensification of production.

Although in each of the Latin American coffee-producing countries, growers have associations to represent them, none of these groups is as powerful and financially well endowed as the FNCC. In El Salvador, in 1979, coffee growers were not able to block government policies that they considered detrimental to their interests (Paige 1997: 187–218). In Costa Rica, producers and processors are two separate groups of entrepreneurs with conflicting interests that were not resolved until 1961 (Paige 1997: 232–37). Perhaps only in Brazil is there an organization with functions similar to those of the FNCC (Bates 1997: 44–45).

In Colombia, the price that farmers received for their coffee until 1988 was lower but less erratic than the international price. More benign price swings, subsidies, the adoption of a new agrotechnology, and the stringent supervision of work performance increased the productivity of labor and allowed farmers to maintain high wages during the harvest season. During the maintenance season, however, some farmers responded to decreasing revenue by adopting contractual modes or hiring procedures that lowered the cost of labor per hectare. Changes in the international market did not seriously affect laborers in those enterprise farms that were expanding or renovating their coffee groves.

The introduction of new technologies has altered agricultural practices and the organization of work in the Americas. The success of many of these technologies depends on how carefully laborers follow the prescribed modes of tending trees or crops. To insure that these policies are followed, farmers must carefully supervise task performance. They also have to train at least some workers. The demand for hired hands often increases with the introduction of new agrotechnology unless some tasks can be mechanized. Another important consequence of agricultural intensification is farmers' increased reliance on credit institutions. In some cases, new agencies and actors enter the scene to provide the inputs directly or the capital to cover operating expenses. Increased production implies the growth of a more sophisticated commercial network capable of both moving larger volumes and finding new outlets. Growth in production also implies increased competitive pressures among growers to maintain their niche in national or international markets and often has been accompanied by a growth in the size of the units of production.

Not all of these developments apply to coffee production in Colombia. The FNCC assumed the commercial and financial burden of the technological revolution. This institution has been a main provider of credit and commercial services. It has assured farmers a buyer for all that is harvested. The characteristics of the crop have also allowed farmers and merchants to avoid certain costs, such as annual soil preparation and planting costs or careful packaging and refrigeration costs. Once the initial cost of tree planting is covered—31 to 37 percent of total costs for a six-year production cycle—farmers can protect themselves from low revenues by reducing some chemical inputs. The only expenses that they cannot forgo are the laborers' wages to maintain the health of the trees and harvest beans. Growers are also not in a position to mechanize tasks except for the washing and hulling of berries and the drying of beans. Although it is possible that some very small coffee farms have been consolidated, there has been no dramatic change in the average size of coffee farms or higher incidence of very large farms.

Coffee farmers in Colombia have avoided two other problems related to intensification that have been very instrumental in shaping the labor process in other crops and in other regions of the Americas. Colombia's coffee growers did not have to contend with labor unions and have avoided complying with onerous labor legislation.

Despite these characteristics, coffee agriculture in Colombia replicates some of the consequences of agricultural intensification in the rest of the Americas. There has been a significant sedentarization of migrants with the concomitant consolidation of localized labor markets. Towns and urban centers have grown in importance as labor pool centers for men who are seasonally available to work in the harvest. Job security has become more precarious, but the labor process has not necessarily become more impersonal, as is the case in industrial agriculture in the United States, Chile, or Argentina. One significant difference between Colombian coffee farmers and some other American producers is that Colombians have not searched for new, more vulnerable labor pools to lower the cost of this input (see section 8.2). Sections 8.1a to 8.1d examine these events comparatively.

8.1a *The Urbanization of the Labor Market*

During the coffee bonanza of the 1970s local rural residents could not harvest the crop on their own. Farmers had to draw from other constituencies. Among the first to be tapped were local town and city dwellers who were either unemployed or were engaged in lower-paying occupations (see section 5.7). As harvest demand increased, so did the participation of town and city dwellers. In some cities within the coffee region, new city neighborhoods emerged as pockets of labor supply (Errazuriz 1993: 171). In Líbano (Tolima), neighborhoods of laborers sprung up along entry routes (Errazuriz 1986: 272). In Caldas laborers live scattered throughout the urban clusters (Hataya 1992). Within the coffee-producing region, only the large cities with more than half a million inhabitants fail to send harvesters to the surrounding farms (Urrea 1976: 161).

Knight's cautionary remark is important: "it may be equally important not to distinguish some 'rural' proletariats from urban workers" (Knight 1972: 167). Knight studied the sugar industry in Colombia and noted that growers used trucks to bring field laborers to the field from the local towns and cities. By 1980 a similar pattern emerged in cotton agriculture (Deygout 1980: 111; Helmsing 1986: 231). A household survey corroborates this finding and generalizes it for Colombia as a whole: 23 percent of the active rural labor force reside in towns and cities (CIDSE 1989: 92–93).

A socially meaningful spatial framework enables avoidance of the easy generalization that rural work is performed by rural dwellers. It also enables understanding of the significance of agricultural job opportunities for industrial growth, and vice versa. Hataya has dramatically captured the role of coffee agriculture for the urban poor in her 1988–89 survey of some working-class neighborhoods in Manizales (the capital of the department of Caldas) and Chinchiná (a nearby urban cluster). Some of these neighborhoods were located on the periphery, others in the midst of each urban center. In both cases, 23.9 percent of the employed population of these areas worked in the coffee harvest and 15.63 percent worked in coffee agriculture all year round (Hataya 1992).[1] Those who worked only in the harvest combined agricultural work with jobs in construction, street vending, and commerce, a pattern that also reappeared in our survey. Some of these workers lived close enough to the farms to walk there every day. Others, who worked on more distant farms stayed there during the week and returned home on weekends.

Hataya also recognized that jobs on coffee farms allow recent arrivals time to search for permanent jobs in the city. A father's income as a farm laborer allows his sons and daughters to explore other possibilities. Households show a mix of employment strategies that Hataya explains in terms of length of residence in the city and dependency ratio of young household members to those old enough to participate in the labor market. In 12 percent of the 302 households that she surveyed, all members worked in agriculture; in 18 percent some worked in agriculture; the rest had urban jobs. Most other families had become completely dependent on urban markets (Hataya 1992).

This phenomenon is not unique to Colombia. Whiteford (1981) paints a similar picture for the recent migrants to northern Argentine cities, many of whom are Bolivians. Unable to find year round employment in agriculture, they move between cities and farms until they can permanently settle in cities like Salta and Jujuy. Urban residence may not, however, mean urban employment for all family members. They survive by adopting diversified occupational family strategies, as did the laborers interviewed by Hataya (Whiteford 1981). After coffee planters of São Paulo rescinded the system of tenancy and labor attachment, they had to bring roughly a quarter of the required labor force from regional cities (Stolcke 1988: 67, 126). The laborers in the commercial tomato farms of Autlan (a municipality in the department of Jalisco, Mexico) are mostly local town dwellers (Torres 1997). Peter Gregory even argues that many workers in Mexico have been engaged in both rural and urban occupations in the past forty years (1986: 109). Chile's fruit industry is in the hands of town dwellers who return to urban employment after the harvest ends (Venegas 1987; Gomez and Echenique 1988).

There are numerous other examples from commercial large-scale agriculture in other parts of the world. One of them is Grieco's historical study of the seasonal hop trains that carried Londoners to Kent until the harvest was mechanized between 1950 and 1960. The earnings of the wives and children in the hop fields supplemented the uncertain earnings of dockworker husbands and gave women greater financial independence (Grieco 1996). Sugar beet producers in Michigan during the 1920s used private agencies in Chicago, Detroit, Toledo, and Saginaw to advertise wages, contact workers, and announce when they were likely to be needed (Valdés 1991). The asparagus growers of Michigan, who cannot presently mobilize enough workers through their established networks, use the services of city employment agencies (Griffith and Kissam 1995: 129). Whitener (1985: 167) points out that about one-third of the migrant labor force in U.S. agriculture works in industry or the service sector for some part of the year, and another third goes to school at the end of the harvest season. Barnett (1978: 22) cites a similar proportion of nonagricultural job holders among harvesters in California. In each of these cases the interlinkage of urban and rural markets serves different purposes and has different origins. All writers point out that to understand recruitment strategies and job-search strategies, it is important to introduce the faces of laborers and their families as well as the conditions within the region where workers and farms are located.

When farmers limit the search to nearby locations and have done so for long enough to consolidate the localization of labor markets, it is possible to examine how the social world of the regional cities might affect relations within the farm. In Latin America, city and town workers are more likely to be literate and savvy about labor regulations and union activities. The towns in the local markets of these municipalities were not large enough for difference in education and information to be significant, but it is a point that should be examined in future comparative, localized labor-market studies. Are the laborers in Hataya's case study, who work and live all year round in cities, less likely to accept nonnegotiable job offers during the maintenance season? If farmers in the United States try to recruit vulnerable workers to avoid discipline problems, do they extend the search only to women and minorities in urban areas?

De Janvry and some of his colleagues have assumed that the inter-linkage of rural and urban markets in Latin America intensified with the expansion of commercial agriculture and the eviction of peasants and tenants (de Janvry, Sadoulet, and Young 1989: 416). While such has been the case in many Latin American regions and countries, it is too simple an explanation to be of general validity even for the region. The exodus of rural dwellers in the coffee region was probably related to the insecurity that many families experienced during the *violencia* (Schultz 1971:160) coupled with a contraction of labor demand. In more recent years, a preference for the amenities of towns and cities and the availability of housing have played significant roles in the urbanization of the labor force in Colombia (see section 4.1) as well as in the United States (Griffith and Kissam 1995; Nelson 1986). Whatever the reasons for the urbanization of agricultural workers and the participation of urban workers in agriculture, it has been a reality in the coffee region for quite some time. Results from our survey indicate that 77 percent of local, town-resident harvesters and 82 percent of migrant, town-dwelling harvesters had lived in cities and towns all their lives.

8.1b   The Sedentarization of the Laborers

Urrea (1976: 219–20) argued that the newly adopted technology allowed laborers to settle down because they could find year-round employment in coffee agriculture. He predicted that fewer migrants would be needed in the future. Ten years after his survey, the percentage of migrant harvesters had increased but had done so at a slower rate than the harvest.[2] In the municipalities surveyed, farmers had to attract only 10 percent more laborers than what Urrea indicated for the earlier period, yet coffee production had increased by about 30 percent. In 1973 Risaralda's rural population had begun to grow for the first time since the 1960s. With more work available throughout the year, fewer families left the area, and more seasonal migrants settled locally.[3] Another reflection of the sedentarization process is the disappearance of ambulant harvesters (see section 5.7).

The present balance between migrant and local harvesters is precarious, however. It rests on farmers' ability and willingness to continue renovations and labor-intensive upkeep modes. Judging from demand estimates, there seems to have been enough work available to retain the existing population. Between 1988 and 1992 the demand for labor for renovations grew by 4.3 percent, and the demand for maintenance work grew by 5.9 percent. The demand for harvest labor during the same period grew by 14 percent (Errazuriz 1993). But the future, after the crisis of 1992, might bring very different circumstances. The FNCC has become aware of the implications of employment opportunities for the retention of the labor force and has for some time financed projects that offer employment opportunities for the women of coffee-laboring families. The federation has also revived a policy of diversification that had previously been implemented only halfheartedly (see section 2.2).

The overall picture in U.S. agriculture is similar. The migrant stream is not as important now as it was in the 1950s, though there is no agreement about the actual numbers of past or present migrant farm workers (Martin 1988). The apparent decrease results in part from the ending of labor importation programs, the settlement of some families in urban and rural areas, and the mechanization of tasks that were previously performed by migrants. The decline has not implied a decrease in the demand for agricultural workers, which has either remained stable or has increased, depending on how it is calculated (Buttel, Larson, and Gillespie 1990).

Estimates for Argentina, another country that depends heavily on migrant streams from other regions within the country and from Bolivia, Chile, and Paraguay, paint a slightly different picture. Argentina's recent agricultural renaissance has also implied mechanization of numerous tasks, a process that had a dual effect on the market: it disrupted migratory streams and offered more permanent employment to a smaller number of workers (Ekboir, Fiorentino, and Lunardelli 1990). The mechanization of cereals, sugarcane, and some activities in the fruit industry has reduced the demand for these laborers. The cereal industry's labor force now consists of machine operators who reside locally and earn higher wages. The cane cutters of Tucumán who lost their jobs were rehired in the fast-growing regional fruit industry (Aguilera 1997; Aparicio and Benencia 1997). The women who used to wrap and box fruit before machines were introduced to perform these tasks are now unemployed (Bendini 1997). But not all agricultural activities have or could be mechanized. The horticultural region of the province of Buenos Aires still uses labor-intensive techniques that require an almost permanent labor force (Benencia 1997). To avoid responding to what remains of the Peronist labor legislation, many of these vegetable growers have engaged married sharecroppers who reside permanently on farms.

Thus, intensification of production can contribute to the sedentarization of the labor force and the consolidation of localized labor markets. But such intensification will not contribute to the formation of robust and large local labor markets if accompanied by considerable mechanization or by management strategies that exacerbate cyclical demand shifts, as has been the case for Californian agriculture (see section 8.3b). It is also important to remember that in many of these cases other policies have also contributed to the sedentarization of the labor force. In chapter 3 I describe some efforts to help potential laborers find local housing. A similar effort was made on behalf of laborers in tobacco agriculture in northern Argentina (Aparicio and Gras 1997). Former migrants were given title to small plots of land in periurban areas. From these new locations laborers could return to seasonal work in agriculture, combining it with temporary urban jobs. These and many other examples point to the importance of including sociopolitical scenarios within arguments on labor-market developments.

8.1c   Increased Reliance on Occasional Laborers

Many scholars have linked capitalist agricultural development with the withering away of permanent labor and land-tying arrangements like tenancy and sharecropping. Farmers who adopt the maximizing strategies that characterize capitalist entrepreneurs are expected to prefer more flexible and low-cost short-term wage contracts. These farmers are also expected to adopt new technology and strive to increase the productivity of labor through appropriate management strategies. When the productivity of labor increases, farmers will be in a position to allow wages to rise and reflect these increases. Thus, social scientists prognosticate that a capitalist transformation and modernization of agriculture will at first lead to unemployment and lower annual incomes in rural areas, followed by higher wages and fuller employment as more land is converted to intensive agricultural production. The story, however, is not so simple, even from the perspective of neoclassical models, as already mentioned in chapter 1.

One important consideration is whether the new technology adopted to intensify production is accompanied by greater variation in the seasonal demand for labor. The modernized, high yielding fruit industry in Chile, for example, has sharp demand swings despite fruit crop diversification and considerable expansion of production. Fruit growers have responded to labor requirement cycles by reducing the number of permanent laborers and hiring men and women who are engaged in other occupations for the harvest (Venegas 1995; Gomez and Echenique 1988).

In coffee agriculture in Colombia, new agrotechnology increased demand swings, particularly during the periods when coffee groves were neither expanded nor renovated. Farmers then had to devise means of attracting laborers for the harvest even though they could not employ most of them during the rest of the year. This task was made easier by the considerable increase in the productivity of labor on *caturra* plantations. Farmers could afford higher harvest wages than when coffee was grown under shade. Given all of these developments and the considerable increase in the price of land, one would expect that farmers would rationalize their use of labor and shift to occasional contracts.

Share contracts did indeed dwindle dramatically at the beginning of the *bonanza,* apparently confirming these predictions. The culturally established format of half shares, with tenants contributing only labor, became too expensive and was no longer commensurate with the cost of labor. Since productivity had greatly increased, a half share of the proceeds would have been much higher than the cost of laborers at prevailing wages. The new technology questioned the fundamental principle around which farmers and tenants bargained their shares. Strangely enough, it has never occurred to farmers that shares could be renegotiated and altered. Only in Antioquia were share contracts retained (Arango, Aubad, and Piedrahita 1983: 29–36); they are still in use, particularly since the crisis of 1992 (Arango 1993).[4]

I was also told that there had been a reduction in the number of permanent resident and nonresident laborers hired by farmers; however, I was not able to corroborate the decline with figures. I was only able to confirm that on only one farm were resident laborers still allowed to grow crops in 1985 and that there were many empty houses on large farms. Coffee growers explained to me that they reduced the number of resident laborers only out of fear of recent legislation that pegged compensation to improvements and length of residence; they gave the same reason for discontinuing permission to plant crops. Researchers and agronomists have added that land had become too valuable to allow laborers to use it. The decline in the number of permanent laborers certainly gave farmers greater flexibility in how they could use workers.

Although there is evidence that the number of permanent laborers has decreased, it is also clear that some were retained. In section 3.5, I describe *agregados* or attached laborers as supportive personnel for managers and absentee owners. But I do not tackle the thornier issue of why there is considerable farm-to-farm variation in the number of attached laborers, except to relate the number of *agregados* to the size of the farm and the absence of its owner. Optimal-contract theorists offer a helpful hypothesis. Bardhan (1984) pointed out that since resident laborers are often paid less than occasional laborers (which is not necessarily the case in coffee agriculture), farmers gain efficiency and quality labor at a small cost. More pertinent to the coffee region of Colombia, Eswaran and Kotwal (1985) suggest that farmers use long-term contracts, with or without residential requirements, when monitoring of work is either progressively more difficult or more costly (see also Chomitz 1990). Bardhan (1984) had already suggested that landlords are more likely to attach laborers during periods of development, when yield-increasing improvements are implemented. Optimal-contract theorists also add that risk-averse laborers prize these contracts and are willing to invest energy and loyalty to avoid losing them (Bardhan and Rudra 1979). These two related arguments might explain why some farmers retained most permanent workers at the beginning of the coffee expansion, when the market was tight and careful performance was important. It also explains why by 1985, when the local pool of laborers increased and the rate of renovations decreased, farms had fewer attached resident laborers. However, as Rosenzweig (1988) has pointed out, permanent labor contracts are not always present where expected. He suggests that there may also be other, better contracts that will attain the same goals. I suggest instead that these various permanent contracts be examined within the context of the labor process to determine when they bring compliance and the availability of laborers and when they fail to do so. The managerial problems associated with each type of contract should also be examined.

Permanent workers are not only those who are offered a residences on farms. Some managers of large farms also offer year-round employment to laborers, paying them the ongoing rate and perhaps even some fringe benefits. These coffee growers are probably willing to incur this extra cost to gain greater loyalty and commitment. They did not, however, expect the employees to work well and hard on their own. All of these workers were supervised. One manager gave two other related explanations: he wanted to be known as a man who took care of his laborers; and he wanted to work with a group of men whom he knew to be good and reliable.

Whereas this manager talked about the advantages of working with a stable group of workers, tomato growers in Mexico spoke of tense relations with trusted employees over how much authority the central administration has and who is in a better position to pass judgment on technical matters (Torres 1997). Many Colombian coffee farmers favor an active managerial style and like to control the productivity of their investments. However, none of them alluded to the points mentioned by Torres. They also do not have to contend with the danger that their permanent personnel may join a union, since none were then present in the region. Conversely, sugar producers in the neighboring department of Valle had good reason to fear unions and, according to Knight (1972), switched from a large labor force of permanent workers to one where occasional workers predominated. By 1986, when wage increases outstripped productivity increases, the manager mentioned previously who maintained his coffee grove with a crew of permanent workers was rumored to be considering terminating the yearlong contracts, according to his laborers. (The manager avoided our questions.) According to Arango (1993), in 1992, when commodity prices dropped, coffee farmers in Antioquia reduced the number of permanent nonresident laborers hired. Retrenchment of the permanent labor forces was the result of falling incomes rather than of a drive to reduce labor costs or enhance managerial control.

The prominence of permanent contracts depends also on their attractiveness to laborers. In Risaralda, nonresident permanent laborers who worked on the few large farms that offered permanent jobs gained not only security but also higher earnings. Attached laborers (*agregados*) at best gained only security. In chapter 7, I explained why some laborers accepted a position as *agregado* despite the uncertainties of this contractual arrangement. I also discussed how the farmers' demand was met by the needs of a particular subgroup of laborers in the supply sector: recently arrived homeless men with large families.

What is the likelihood that farmers, as they modernize their production, will continue to shed permanent workers and hire them only when needed? If the explanation given by one manager of a large farm is a guide, crews of permanent laborers are likely to be retained as long as highly productive coffee groves remain rewarding investments and the demand for laborers during the maintenance season is high. Better monitoring of fringe benefits or the appearance of unions, both rather unlikely in this area, would encourage coffee farmers to shorten the time for which they hire laborers. There are, of course, other ways of bypassing regulations and union activities. Landowners can delegate the task of hiring to contractors, as mentioned earlier. A more creative strategy is the one used in Argentina, where contracting companies use the subterfuge of cooperativization. In northern Argentina harvesting cooperatives often have assumed responsibility for bringing laborers and the necessary equipment to harvest fruit. To get a job, laborers must join the cooperatives and pay regular dues and social security premiums (Aguilera 1997). Whether this pattern will be replicated in other industries will depend on technical, legal, and managerial issues. Any monolithic prediction is unwarranted.

8.1d When Women Harvest

Letters from landlords and administrators written over the past century often mention female harvesters. Their names crowd the account books collected by historians. Most of these women were wives and daughters of tenants and *agregados.* Some came with their husbands from afar for the harvesting season. However, few historians with access to old records have bothered to tabulate the gender of the laborers, so there is a general impression about women's presence but no precise account of where they prevailed and how significant was their contribution.

As time went by, women began to avoid the damp and shaded coffee groves. Most local people today seem ignorant of the history and describe the harvest as a man's world. It is difficult to pinpoint the moment when women became more housebound and less willing to work for wages on someone else's farm. My guess is that in the central coffee region the eviction of tenants and *agregados* discouraged women from participating in the harvest. It was easier for women to flaunt the strong cultural sanctions when their houses were located on coffee farms. But once women had to walk down public roads to harvest someone else's trees, fear of condemnation discouraged many from seeking jobs (see section 4.3). Medrano (1980: 86) suggests that in southern Antioquia all-female harvesting gangs probably disappeared about 1965, a period when labor demand may have been lower because coffee trees were older and less productive. Women were likely to be the last ones to be tapped and the first to be dismissed, given cultural ideas about gender propriety. In the regions that were heavily affected by the *violencia,* women were probably too afraid to venture out of their homes and stopped working in the fields even before the 1960s. Later, the high wages of the bonanza allowed husbands to insist that "their women" stay at home, which may explain why Arango noted a sharp reduction in the participation of Antioqueño women on family farms between the boom years of 1975 and 1977 (Arango, Aubad, and Piedrahita 1983:153–55). Urrea (1976: 146) also reported low (6.9 percent) participation of women in the central coffee region during the 1975 harvest. By the 1980s, it was possible to travel throughout the coffee region and see hardly any women harvesting.

Yet, women are once again harvesting coffee as wage laborers in some local labor markets (see section 5.7b). Are owners or managers using women to lower the cost of labor, as has been argued in the literature on gender and the labor process? Is this strategy related to the expansion and intensification of a crop that has always required considerable amount of experienced labor? Why, then, is this the case in only some of the local markets within the same cultural region? Although this case study cannot offer definitive answers to these questions since even at present very few women participate in the harvest, I can offer some suggestions.

Many researchers who have studied fruit and vegetable production in the Americas have pointed out that women are often targeted for specific tasks and often receive lower wages. Because export fruit and vegetable industries have high labor costs and face strong competitive pressures, scholars have been tempted to explain the frequent use of women workers as a strategy to cheapen labor or to insure its docility. While such is often the case, not all women harvesters earn less than men, and women are not necessarily less likely to protest. Collins (1995) also points out that there is a great variation in the use of women from industry to industry and from region to region. She adds that to understand why women are sometimes selected but at other times are barred from certain jobs, it is necessary to examine local conditions and farmers' need for a particular kind of labor at a particular price. It is also important to consider whether other strategies available to farmers are not just as effective and easier to adopt, a point I discuss in other sections of this chapter.

It is not always simple or easy to negotiate shifts in hiring practices or populations to be tapped as sources of labor supply (Downs 1995). Both women and employers often have to surmount cultural ideas about family relations, family responsibilities, and the characterization of jobs. As long as the coffee farms carry the image of disease and the harvest continues to be depicted as a time of tension and danger, it is unlikely that the presence of women in harvesting crews will become significant. Farms will have to be linked more closely to the world of the household than is presently the case. Farmers will have to make the management adjustments necessary to attract women, following the guidelines of the manager in Belén (see section 5.7b).

At the moment the women who harvest or are willing to harvest are not numerous enough to significantly lower the labor cost of coffee production. Other reasons would have to tempt farmers and managers to make the necessary changes to attract female workers. The manager of the farm in Belén might have been prompted by a desire to thwart labor unrest. Demographic constraints probably also contributed to the greater presence of women in Belén. Marsella was closer to the departmental capital, where women who wanted to work had many more appropriate employment opportunities. Farmers in Belén also had a smaller pool of local male laborers proportionate to their demand needs than did their counterparts in Marsella. Two other recent developments may encourage farmers to reconsider and reorganize the harvest labor process. Harvest costs are increasing faster than the productivity of labor. Women are also marrying later, value their independence, and want to have an income they control (see section 4.3). If enough women show interest in the harvest, farmers may be able to lessen reliance on migrant laborers, who are considered problematic and who are more expensive (see section 7.2). Whether women show an interest in the harvest will depend on the availability of other, more prestigious occupations.

8.3   Farmers and Laborers at the Local Markets (1985–1986)

An unskilled labor market, like the one discussed here, is often represented as a depersonalized interchangeable set of units of labor. Nothing can be farther from reality, as must now be apparent. Farmers have to realize the labor power by tailoring their management strategies to satisfy the requirements or expectations of their supply sectors. Young men have different needs than do older married men, and both of those groups' requirements differ from those of the women in their families. Likewise, workers known and valued by farmers cannot be equated with unknown migrants. I would not have been able to explain farmers' strategies and the emerging market structure had I not allowed their faces and voices to enter my analysis.

At the time of the survey and interviews, the economic situation was difficult for laborers and uncertain for farmers. The brunt of the recession was suffered by laborers, who were facing a sequence of years with distinct "hunger months." By 1986 some coffee groves had to be renovated if they were to continue to be as productive as they had been previously. At the same time, farmers were beginning to feel the pinch of lower prices. The management strategies observed and discussed in this study reflected the farmers' quandary.

The impact of economic pressures can be seen most clearly during the harvest, when laborers have considerable market power and farmers must compete with each other for the same pool of men. Although farmers were forced to allow wages to respond to tight supply conditions, they could control harvest costs by assuring quality performance and by accurately estimating the appropriate crew size. In section 8.3b I describe the parameters of crew size and the headaches it causes. Quality can be insured through supervision and sanctions rather than through screening at hiring time, as I discuss in section 8.3d. This process entailed building a hierarchical management system and ensuring the loyalty of supervisors. Farmers offered long-term contracts and perks to supervisors to achieve that end (see section 8.3e).

The high cost of the harvest season can also be balanced by conservative investments (see section 8.3c) and frugal wages during the maintenance season, when laborers have very limited market power and few alternative options. Farmers space tasks carefully to avoid competition for laborers. They also reduce the application of chemicals. Some farmers enhance their power by further diluting the bargaining position of occasional laborers. The owners of medium-size farms who are most concerned about costs are most likely to use exploitative undisclosed contracts. These growers present themselves as saving laborers from hunger and recast the relationship as a helpful social exchange. Alternatively, these owners offer task contracts to a small group of workers with the awareness that exact labor time estimates are easier for farmers than for laborers to calculate. Unless backed by long-standing and rewarding social relations, the last two strategies are likely to result in quality losses for farmers and hence are not favored by coffee growers in better financial situations or particularly concerned about productivity. In sections 8.3d and 8.3e I discuss in more detail the implications of these strategies (see also section 8.2c).

The impact of culture and social relations was also evident in the design and prominence of strategies. The differential participation of women in Cundinamarca and Risaralda (see section 8.2a) illustrates this point. In other, more marginal Colombian coffee municipalities, it was possible to bring in Indians from nearby settlements; farmers thus used ethnicity to break the bargaining power of laborers, very much in the manner depicted by Bossen (1982) and by Bourgois (1989) for Central America. Another more dramatic example of how culture shapes management styles is seen in Wells's account of strawberry producers in California. Japanese growers practice micromanagement, Anglos try to build businesses, and Mexicans manage farms to maintain them (Wells 1996: 131–38). However, privileging culture can obfuscate other important variables. As Wells points out, Mexican growers may have a different cultural perception of the world around them, but they are also less endowed with financial and human capital. Unlike Anglos and Japanese growers, their connections to sources of power and information are asymmetrical. Similarly, owners of the large coffee enterprises, while culturally and ideologically more removed from the laboring class than the owners of smaller farms, were also better endowed financially. Nevertheless, class differences cannot be neglected since they interfered with farmers' attempts to personalize labor relations. The efforts of the better-off coffee farmers were shrouded by shared mistrust and disappointing experiences. Poor small farmers, conversely, could call on trusted kin to work unsupervised in the coffee groves. The choice of contracts and management styles is clearly affected by culture, class, political power, and local social networks.

Some of the farmers' cost-saving strategies resulted in lower annual incomes and longer periods of unemployment for laborers. I did not detect any dramatic changes in job-search patterns or rates of mobility during either the harvest or the low season. It is quite possible that laborers in 1986 had become less aggressive than formerly in approaching farmers and in requesting to negotiate contracts. Workers were certainly more assiduous in searching for jobs and more resentful of their condition. Eventually, this resentment will spill over to their performance, if it has not done so already. The usual statement was, "This is the way it has always been." Their poverty and dissatisfaction were expressed in more undercover ways that rendered some contracts expensive from the point of view of quality performance. I integrate the laborers' responses to their plight at appropriate points in my discussion of farmers' strategies.

8.3a   Mobilizing a Supply of Laborers

The population of the Risaralda municipalities studied has waxed and waned with the birth of new generations, cycles of political unrest, and economic distress. However, since 1960 population has grown slowly but consistently (see appendix A and table 19).

Labor-supply problems emerge only during the harvest, when demand more than doubles (see figures 11 and 12). The local population no longer suffices (see appendix A). Farmers must then tap all possible local sectors and attract laborers from elsewhere. When demand oscillates greatly and the harvest requires large numbers of workers, commercial farmers often rely on contractors to make up for a shortage of local workers and to avoid having to retain permanent workers as supervisors (Griffith and Kissam 1995). Martin (1988: 130) stresses this point and adds that except for some large companies, fruit and vegetable producers in the United States "have turned over the labor market to such intermediaries." However, instead of using labor contractors, as is the case in the sugar industry in a neighboring department (Knight 1972), Colombian coffee growers prefer to attract laborers with appropriate wages.

One possible objection is that the use of contractors ties the farmers to specific crews and to contractors' supervisory styles. Farmers then lose control over the labor process and cannot easily protect themselves from careless and destructive harvesters. In a comparative study of U.S. agricultural industries, Griffith and Kissam (1995) confirm that contractors are often known to be careless supervisors. The Risaralda farmers are concerned about damage to trees and have access to cheaper overseers, their attached laborers. Unlike Argentine farmers, Colombian growers can disregard many fringe benefits required by law. Each of these arguments, however, can be countered with examples from either Colombia or elsewhere, as Wells (1996) discovered when she tried to explain why some strawberry farmers used contractors while others did not.

According to the farmers, contractors are expensive and unnecessary because harvesters will come on their own. It is a curious position given that it has often been argued that contractors bring cheaper workers: cheap cane cutters from southern Colombia, vulnerable Indians in Guatemala or Peru, and immigrants in U.S. agriculture. Furthermore, Colombian farmers attract enough harvesters but do so by paying wages that are higher than those for other crops.

The contrast between this matter-of-fact explanation and the well-reasoned list of speculations illustrates the limited number of issues that managers consider and the saliency of some of them. Basically, farmers did not think supply to be a problem that required a solution. They mobilized laborers through their social networks and waited for others to come. For these growers, the failure of laborers to show up on an appointed day resulted from irresponsibility rather than availability, and contractors would not solve this problem. The harvest was complicated enough as it was. The farmers' response highlights another point that I have made throughout the book: farmers do not choose "optimal" solutions even when such options exist. Growers scan possible satisfactory solutions and use the one that fits their managerial style and economic conditions.

It is also interesting to note that farmers avoid tying down prospective harvesters through debt, despite their complaints that laborers often violate an agreed-upon date of hire and may not even show up on subsequent days. When I asked why growers did not offer wage advances or loans during the maintenance season as way of coercing local laborers to show up when promised, the farmers responded that the strategy might not work and would make the organization of the harvest even more problematic than it was (see section 5.5). This position contrasts sharply with the argument, based on Indian case studies, that loans are extended to potential harvesters when supply is problematic and credit markets are tight (Bardhan and Rudra 1981; Bardhan 1980; Eswaran and Kotwal 1985).

To simplify the management of the harvest as much as possible, farmers first try to mobilize laborers through the networks of permanent workers and then hire whoever approaches. Farmers also avoid screening applicants who come to farm gates or who are hired on the town square. As a result, growers must rely heavily on supervision to insure quality work. The dual strategy of letting regular workers know that they will be needed and of hiring whoever approaches provides farmers with a core of fairly reliable workers and the flexibility needed to assemble the right size crew. It is not an easy job, and farmers complain loudly about it. Farmers with extensive social networks are thus in a better position to find satisfactory workers while laborers with such networks also profit from greater job possibilities.

8.3b The Size of the Harvesting Crew

Farmers must not only attract laborers at the appropriate moment but also estimate how many will be needed at any one time. Growers must keep several issues in mind. They must coordinate crew size with the capacity of the processing equipment. Weather conditions must also be considered; if there is a threat of rain, the harvest must be completed in a timely fashion using larger crews for a short period of time. Large crews are likely to include many migrants who have to be lodged. Crews with too many strangers also require different management skills from supervisors.

Fisher (1953) focused attention on the problems caused by overhiring in California. He noted that demand-supply pressures and low hiring costs led farmers to hire more laborers than crop and climate required. Instead of taking time to complete the harvest, growers used more workers to finish it as soon as possible. This strategy accounted for the constant complaint of labor shortages, which was used to manipulate political support for the importation of laborers. Fisher's measure of overhiring was the disparity between the farmers' estimates of the average number of laborers needed and the number of laborers actually hired. Using Fisher's mode of estimating—cross-checked with local agronomists' estimates—I identified only two farmers in our sample who overhired laborers on the day of our survey. Technical and capital cost constraints—the cost of upgrading processing equipment and its capacity—set clear limits on crew size and spared farmers from the temptation to overhire. Only students, construction workers, and self-employed persons generally profit from shorter and more accelerated harvest seasons (Sosnick 1978: 209–10). Farmers' avoidance of overhiring is consonant with their wish to retain a local labor pool of landless agricultural workers who need a long harvest season to balance the low earnings during the rest of the year.

Smaller crews also help to minimize tensions in the workplace and enhance performance, as Wells (1996: 162–66) noticed in strawberry farming and Torres (1997) determined for tomatoes. Members of smaller crews also realize that careful handling of trees is likely to be noticed and that they have a greater chance of being hired when few jobs are available. Nevertheless, these crews are supervised unless farmers work alongside their laborers or hire close kin.

Crew size is also relevant during the maintenance season. Larger crews can complete weeding and fertilizing tasks more quickly, thereby allowing farmers to rely on cheaper occasional workers. Yet large enterprise farms did not favor such a strategy. These farmers preferred and could afford to keep a core of working men employed throughout the year. Even medium farmers space jobs to help laborers, to avoid competition for workers, and to ease cash outflows.

Farmers thus tend to spread the demand for labor both during the harvest and, to a lesser extent, during the maintenance season. These managerial strategies assured 16 percent of local laborers almost full yearly employment in the large enterprises. Another 19 percent of workers gained a regular income as resident laborers. The rest served as occasional workers on medium farms and medium enterprises and faced periodic weeks of unemployment. The frequency of these periods depended not only on farmers' spacing tactics but also on their investment decisions, which I discuss in the next section.

8.4c   Investment Decisions

The central managerial decisions faced by farmers during the maintenance season are how much fertilizer to apply, how often to weed, how much chemical disease control to spray, and what proportion of the standing coffee grove to renovate. Farmers must also consider what labor contracts they can afford (see section 8.3a). For technical reasons, mechanization is not a viable labor-saving option.

The application of fertilizers is not a simple labor input decision but also requires capital to buy the chemicals and to pay laborers. Managers of large enterprises, who keep careful logs of inputs and yields per parcel, do carefully and rationally evaluate how much fertilizer to use and how many times to weed to attain specific returns. Other growers develop more general rules of thumb that pivot on profits from the previous harvest, fiscal solvency, and price trends. According to a farm survey in Risaralda (Federación Nacional 1980), only 16 percent of the farmers applied the recommended amount of fertilizer, even when the FNCC subsidized this input. Only 12 percent weeded the coffee groves as frequently as advised. In other words, all farmers balance high harvest labor inputs with less than optimal maintenance labor use. Arango (1993: 202) noted that in Antioquia, when prices and coffee incomes fell, so did the amount of fertilizer applied. This finding matches what medium farmers explained to me. They did not use technical guidelines or seem to have much faith in them. Instead, these growers decided how much fertilizer to use and how often to spray in terms of their financial resources. They did not cut down on the number of weedings, though they used their own formula rather than the FNCC prescription. Instead, they cut labor time by using machetes. A few wealthy farmers used chemical weed killers on occasion.

Maintenance demand for labor depends also on farmers' renovation and expansion strategies. The central criteria guiding this decision concern projected prices and subsidized credit. Errazuriz noticed that the high prices of the 1970s encouraged the conversion and renovation of coffee groves. These renovations slowed when prices began to drop and flourished again between 1985 and 1987, when the future once again seemed promising (Errazuriz 1989b: 70–74). A more recent study (Echavarría, Gaviria, and Téllez 1993) confirms that higher prices served to stimulate expansion but argues that subsidized credit was more influential. This work also points out that these incentives are balanced against the productivity of farmers' coffee trees. In the municipalities we studied, renovations slowed down during 1985–86.

8.3e *Contractual Choices and Control of Performance*

In this book I have discussed labor exchanges not as sales of labor but as complex contractual agreements that include a number of aspects: a wage component, considerations about length of employment, work rules, and so forth. Some elements of the contract—hours to be worked, how berries are to be picked—are clearly spelled out. The particulars of other elements—for example, the number of meals and how to weed with a machete—are assumed to be understood and to conform to what is socially fair and technically appropriate. Contracts thus include both explicit statements and tacit understandings. The balance between the two defines the overall nature of the contract. Contracts are explicit when the itemized conditions predominate and the tacit elements are clearly shared. These contracts can be effectively sanctioned and are openly bargained. An example of such a contract is the harvest piece rate.

Piece-rate contracts are associated exclusively with the harvest and are used by nearly all farmers. Tasks, work rules, rate, and units of measurement are clearly spelled out. Farmers prefer these contracts because they avoid the costs of screening, stimulate productivity, and allow farmers to tap all supply sectors without added costs and to adjust the size of the crews to the intermittent rate of maturation of the coffee beans. Laborers value these contracts because they provide a sense of control of the labor process and permit workers to sell their ability to harvest rather than the hours spent working in the coffee grove. These contracts also give workers freedom to search, move, and be rewarded for their effort and their ability.

Shared preferences for piece-rate contracts do not imply that farmers and laborers have entered into a cooperative arrangement. Farmers are distrusted and are accused of unwarranted deductions and faulty scales. In turn, laborers are accused of destroying trees and picking unripe beans. Supervision is considered essential, as is the need to fire laborers on the spot when they consistently bring green berries and leaves. This second method of controlling performance can be problematic when the market is tight.

By rewarding productivity, these contracts explicitly encourage laborers to optimize earning prospects but do so at the expense of cooperation with other crew members. The piece rate pits laborers' self-interests (to earn as much as possible) against farmers' interests (to produce quality beans), encouraging laborers to challenge the rate payment that limits their earning capacity. The use of piece-rate contracts adds to the tension of the harvest.

Not surprisingly, piece-rate contracts are avoided when productivity is not so closely linked to work rhythm or on small farms where the owner sets the work rhythm by picking alongside a crew of kinsmen and friends. During the maintenance season, farmers, for the most part, prefer to pay day wages. Slightly more than half of the employed laborers received this form of payment. As the term implies, laborers are both paid and hired by the day. The customary term of employment is one week, which may be extended when the week comes to an end. Even when the contract is extended several times, no expectations of permanency are conveyed.

Many farmers outline as carefully as possible the tasks to be performed, the work rules, and the remuneration the laborer will receive. These explicit contracts in theory allow bargaining and are more likely to elicit higher performance and reliable attendance. Commitment can also be enhanced by offering yearlong contracts that are usually explicit but unnegotiated. To better understand how these contracts operate in the market, it is important to determine empirically who sets the terms of the contract, whether bargaining is allowed, and how the terms are conveyed to laborers, since this process will affect the outcome. In the models proposed in some contract theories, the principal (in this case the farmer) is assumed to set the terms of the contract. It is left to the agent to decide to accept them or look for another offer. But in these models the principal does not allow the agent to bargain. The latter can only accept or reject the offer. In other models, the principal and the agent are expected to discuss and bargain to reach a collaborative agreement. Each model arrives at a different contractual solution. In a study of fruit growers in Chile, a quarter of the farmers questioned responded that they fixed salaries unilaterally. A similar percentage negotiated individually with each laborer. The rest negotiated collectively, either with a group of laborers or with union representatives (Jarvis, Montero, and Hidalgo 1993: 33–34). The coffee farmers of our study set terms and expected laborers to either accept or reject them. Whatever bargaining did occur took place during the course of the employment, usually over the specifics of the assigned job, working conditions, or food quality. In other words, the bargaining concerned the tacit aspects of the explicit contracts.

Not all farmers made explicit contractual offers. Farmers with financial constraints are more concerned with cash-flow problems and want to pay as little as possible. During the maintenance season, even cash-strapped farmers have enough market power to manipulate the hiring process to their advantage. If they do not spell out any terms of the contract, including the wage, they can get away with paying below the minimum wage and retain uncomplaining laborers, at least until the first payday. These unbargained, undisclosed contracts contain too many potential misunderstandings to lead to transactions that are satisfactory to both parties (see section 7.3). Short-term undisclosed contracts are best suited for later in the season, when laborers are so desperate for jobs that they will return even if they believe that they will receive an inappropriate remuneration. Some farmers who are heavily indebted try to schedule as many tasks as they can late in the season, when demand is lean and when laborers are hungry. Farmers can minimize the effect of disappointing contractual exchanges with gift offers of plantains and services. Sometimes these exchanges, particularly if they have extended over a number of years, balance the effects of lower pay. More often than not, animosity remains (Cohen 1991: 97–107). For this reason, these poorer medium farmers, who hire about a quarter of the occasional laborers, sometime are more explicit in the hiring process. Alternatively, they hire a few trusted workers at competitive wages while offering other workers undisclosed, low-wage contracts. Since both types of contracts coexist on the same farm, it is very difficult to determine the prevalence and seasonality of each. They could not have amounted to more than 25 percent of all maintenance contracts during 1985–86. In some labor markets or under specific competitive conditions, undisclosed contracts may predominate. The reality of this contract is often not reflected in average wage statistics and hence it is not considered by most analysts.

When laborers are contracted and paid for specific tasks, they are not supervised. Farmers can reduce the costs of weeding by driving a cheap bargain, which they can easily do since they are more familiar with the land and condition of the coffee trees than are the laborers hired (see section 7.4). Farmers must be prepared, however, to accept low-quality work. Subcontracting by task represents a very small share of all contracts and is used more frequently during slump periods (Arango 1993). Managers of enterprise farms who want to simplify their jobs use a less exploitative variant of this type of contract. These contracts are clearly and openly negotiated and the cost depends on the contractor's experience, the number of tasks to be performed, and their complexity. Managers use these bargained-task contracts most frequently to establish new coffee groves or to renovate old ones—that is, tasks that require experienced personnel and close supervision.

Most laborers hired must be supervised by the farmers, their managers, or their attached laborers (*agregados*). There is a tier system of attached laborers (see section 7.5). They receive housing, access to wood, water, some food resources, and almost full employment in exchange for their availability when farmers need it. On some farms attached laborers can and do work elsewhere when they are not needed, but laborers must give first priority to the farmers who hire them as *agregados.* Although most *agregados* serve as crew leaders during the harvest, few are selected for supervisory jobs during the rest of the year.[5] Farmers reward or claim to reward their *agregados* with special favors, displaying both benevolence and power in so doing. Some *agregados* are also covered by social security and other legally required fringe benefits. The *agregados'* loyalty depends on how they were hired and they and the farmers relate to each other. Initially, the contractual obligations between farmers and *agregados* are only vaguely stated; they are never openly negotiated. During this preliminary period, mutual suspicion prevails, enhanced by class differences and past experiences. The farmers must slowly build a relation of dependence and trust through gifts and fringe benefits, and laborers must convey responsibility and ability (Bazzoli, Kirat, and Villeval 1994). Only after this initial period are the full gamut of fringe benefits and privileges offered. (See Bardhan and Rudra 1981 for another example of range of variation of these contracts within villages.) It takes many years for an *agregado* contract to become fully explicit and for the two parties to engage in a collaborative agreement. These agreements cannot automatically insure compliance, as the economic literature implies. Why then do farmers continue in this practice? As Platteau (1995) suggests, they do so in part because it allows them to reward attached laborers selectively and according to the responsibility assigned to them. Farmers become patrons of their key laborers. Platteau's argument rests on the awareness that patrons' ability to exert social control does not just rest on their occasional gifts but on elite status and the political power associated with it. Thus, Platteau expects the use of attached contracts and patronage to decrease as farmers lose their elite status. I suggest that the practice may continue longer than predicted because it reflects farmers' social perceptions of what the boss-worker relation should be; disappointing loyalty only confirms their perceptions.

A review of contract options reveals several considerations. Farmers are concerned by costs, quality, control of the labor process, managerial simplicity, and flexibility. They are also concerned about retaining authority over the entire labor process and the use of technology (Torres 1997). Some farmers are also concerned about how their style may impinge on their social and political ambitions. Married laborers are concerned about security as well as fair wages. They represent the majority of laborers during the maintenance season. Some are also concerned about free housing and opportunities for the rest of the family and opt for *agregado* contracts. Most younger harvesters are more concerned about income. The gamut of contractual and managerial options serves to address some of the concerns of farmers and of particular sectors of the laboring population. Good managers know how to combine the options. However, their success also depends on how power and class difference intervene in the exchange relation (Bell 1989; Ortiz 1992). Animosity is likely to prevail in the case of undisclosed contracts between unrelated parties but is not likely to be so when the exchange is between kin or close friends. In the latter case the embeddedness of the exchange in a mutual familiarity and shared interests speaks to the implicit aspects and transforms it into a benign undisclosed contract. Work performance relies as much on the existing social network as on the nature of the contracts and remuneration received (Granovetter 1985; Bazzoli, Kirat, and Villeval 1994).

Only by incorporating all these considerations as well as the effects of power, class, and culture can the presence or disappearance of contractual preferences be fully explained. It is shortsighted to discuss the optimality of contracts out of context of the social conditions, managerial requirements, and expectations that affect the balance of the transactions (Hayami and Otzuka 1993). Efficiency is not the only soul of a contract.

8.4   Summary: The Configuration of Local Labor Markets

I have argued that it is not possible to unravel the structure of labor markets by simply focusing on supply, demand, productivity, costs, commodity prices, and risk. The relevance of these conditions depends on the degree of competition among producers and among laborers and the extent to which social and political institutions support or hinder that competition. The FNCC's internal price and purchasing policies assured farmers a buyer and protected them from price swings, though at a cost that made these policies eventually unsustainable (see section 2.4). Farmers did not have to compete with each other for a market niche. They did not have to strive to constantly reduce costs or to increase productivity. They had only to sustain reasonable profits by maintaining productive coffee groves when commodity prices were high and by balancing returns and costs of production. Furthermore, cost reduction could be attained without having to cut wages. Only after profits had dropped consistently for a number of years did farmers begin to increase the number of short-term occasional laborers used. In this labor market operating within the sociopolitical framework described in chapters 2 and 3, profit levels are more instrumental than is interfarm competition.

Laborers realize that at times only some of them will find employment. However, they do not gain a better competitive position by bidding or accepting lower wages than other laborers. After the harvest there are so many unemployed workers that competition among them for jobs has a very weak effect on employment or wages. All workers receive low wages. Job prospects depend on connections to particular farmers, breadth of information network, and residence close to a cluster of farms with high labor demand.

In chapter 1, I indicated that to understand market dynamics, it is necessary to explain the rationale behind the practices used to attract laborers. The prospect of higher wages by itself is often not enough to mobilize all workers. The supply sector is socially differentiated, with each subsector responding to different incentives. In this particular case, young men did not respond in the same way as married men, and different strategies were required to encourage women to work on farms. Search models also have created an awareness of the many considerations that impinge on the willingness or ability of laborers to find out about more rewarding prospects and about the costs of searching for them. In chapter 5, I described the social impediments to mobility and how harvesters used social networks to facilitate information flows and lower costs in about half of their job searches. The situation changes during maintenance season, when jobs are scarce and search costs are very high, as I discuss in chapter 6. Not all workers, however, are in the same position. For example, laborers with few familial responsibilities can afford to tolerate longer periods of unemployment; those with more extensive local connections may find it easier to wait to see the prevailing options. For the most part, however, laborers cannot compare prospects during maintenance season and hence cannot behave as "rational" market actors.

Even when no political strategies are used to mobilize laborers, as in the case of coffee agriculture, optimal-contract models do not explain all existing and absent practices. One reason is that these models make unrealistic assumptions about hiring conditions and the hiring process: agreements are explicit and bargained and there is no inordinate balance of power. Only during the harvest are power sufficiently balanced and market pressures strong enough that farmers have to abide by these conditions. During periods of low demand, class and power are more likely to determine exchanges between farmers and laborers. It is not that the market has failed (Binswanger and Rosenzweig 1984) but that the model of the market is then irrelevant. New models must be developed that integrate the economic conditions of farmers, the aspirations of laborers, the costs of managing the labor force, the cost of job searches, and the power imbalances during negotiations. Only then will it be possible to analyze the fluctuations in wage rates in unnegotiated exchanges.

To draw more poignant theories about labor market dynamics and more compelling and caring policies, it is necessary to avoid overreliance on optimizing contracts based on unrealistic assumptions about how markets work. This case study highlights the importance of financially viable social and political institutions and policies to support farmers in a highly competitive world market. These institutions and policies should also support the bargaining process, job search, and the flow of information to insure equitable relations in the labor market. Minimum-wage policies might give legitimacy to the demand for fair wages when laborers have little bargaining power (Lustig and McLeod 1997). Insuring the rights of laborers to organize collective action will also enhance their bargaining position when agricultural workers encounter too much oppositional power in the market. The cost of job searching can be eased by providing some form of unemployment assistance and information. These or other institutional support measures are necessary if the agricultural laborers are not to bear a disproportionate share of modernization costs as seems to be the case in the United States and probably Chile (Carter, Barham, and Mesbah 1996: 51). The welfare of rural families can also be enhanced through policies that foster agricultural diversification and/or other employment opportunities that will allow family members to be more fully employed throughout the year.

Appendix A

Labor Demand in Coffee Agriculture, Belén-Marsella, 1985–1986

Harvest

Since I have no information on yields per municipality, I cannot use Errazuriz's method to determine the demand for harvest labor. Instead, I have calculated the demand in terms of the average number of harvesters that each type of farm is said to require (see table A1). This average was derived from estimates given by owners, managers, and the local FNCC agronomist, who is familiar with most farms in the area. These estimates were checked against the number of harvesters on each farm at the time of the survey. This approach allows the taking into account of the average productivity of traditional and modernized coffee groves in each municipality during the 1985–86 harvest period. Only the account books of farms would provide more precise information.

Because trees at higher altitude ripen a bit later than those down the slope, the number of actual laborers will be smaller than the number of labor days needed to harvest all coffee in the municipalities. The laborers move up the slope, and the total harvest lasts longer. I have incorporated a correction to take into account the impact of altitude differences on demand for labor. This correction was based on the coffee census estimates for altitude variations and our information about the farms in our survey. I have estimated that a quarter of the harvest takes place a few days after it has finished at lower altitudes.

The corrected demand estimate of 13,646 men include only the individuals required to harvest the berries. To this number one must add managers, truckers, carriers, supervisors, and the men responsible for processing the berries. Since most of these people are part of the permanent personnel of the large farms and represent a small proportion compared to those hired to harvest, I have omitted them from this count. The estimates also exclude unpaid family helpers and those owners who perform these tasks on medium-size and smaller farms.

Farms with less than three hectares in coffee are likely to be run by a family that takes care of most tasks. Farms with between three and five hectares in coffee hire one or two laborers to help harvest the berries. Small coffee groves that are owned by city residents or by farmers with more than one grove are harvested by a small crew of laborers. I have averaged these small-farm labor demands to two harvesters per farm.

Maintenance Season

During the maintenance season the coffee groves must be weeded, fertilized, pruned, and cleared; during 1985, they also had to be sprayed. Berries ripen throughout the year, and sometimes there is a second small harvest; hence, a small crew of harvesters did work throughout the 1985–86 season. Table A2 lists the various labor requirements by category of farm.

I have followed the estimates suggested by the FNCC for the technified farms as quoted and used by Errazuriz (1989b: table 2). The federation estimates a per-hectare average of fifty-seven days for maintenance and ten

TABLE A1.   Harvesters Required by Type of Farm in Marsella and Belén, 1985–86

Farm Type	Harvester/Ha. or per Farm	Total Ha. in Coffee or No. of Farms	Total No. of Harvesters	% of Total of Harvesters
Large Enterprise 50+ Has.	1.6 per Ha.	1,800 (Has.)	2,880	15.83
Medium Enterprise 10.1–50 Has.	1.45 per Ha.	6,625 (Has.)	9,606	52.80
Medium Farms 5.1–10 Has.	1.40 per Ha.	3,232 (Has.)	4,524	24.87
Small Farms 2.1–5 Has.	2 per Farm	592 (Farms)	1,184	6.50
Total Harvesters Required			18,194	100

Note: The distribution of hectares in coffee by type of enterprise is based on farm census by the municipal committees of the FNCC. Most of the farms not yet converted to the high yielding variety have between 5 to 50 hectares in coffee, hence the lower average number of laborers per hectare estimated for farms in the categories of medium enterprises and medium farms.

days for spraying. This is the equivalent of 0.35 men working five days a week during the thirty-eight weeks of the maintenance period. This estimate is close to the average number of laborers (0.35 per hectare) used during the maintenance period on the one highly productive enterprise farm in Marsella. I have used the United Nations report (1958), as did Errazuriz, to estimate the labor maintenance demand in traditional coffee groves. Since labor requirements vary according to agrotechnology rather than productivity, I have categorized farms by size and by type of coffee trees.

To this demand must be added the small crews of harvesters that are required off and on throughout the year on all farms. I have used the number of laborers for that purpose on one modernized farm since this farm's account books list the tasks that the laborers were assigned. On this basis I have estimated that a modernized coffee farm needs 0.30 laborers per hectare to pick the berries that mature during the nonharvest period. Since, according to the FNCC's census (Federación Nacional 1983), the yield of traditional groves is about one-third that of modernized groves, I have calculated that these farms require only 0.10 harvesters per hectare during the maintenance season. Very few small farmers hire laborers during the maintenance season, so I have omitted them from my calculations.

To the total of 5,144 laborers required during the thirty-eight-week nonharvest period should be added the number of laborers required for renovations, expansions, and other agricultural tasks. During 1985–86 a total of 608 hectares were renovated in both municipalities. Using the FNCC's figures quoted by Errazuriz (1989b: table 2) of seventy-three days

TABLE A2. Maintenance Season Labor Demand by Farm Type and Coffee Agrotechnology, Risaralda, 1985–86

Farm Type	New Coffee Technology		Traditional Technology		
	No. of Men for Upkeep	No. of Harvesters	No. of Men for Upkeep	No. of Harvesters	Total No. of Men
Large Enterprise	323	277	148	87	835 (16.23%)
Medium Enterprise	967	828	656	386	2,837 (55.15%)
Medium Farms	554	474	280	164	1,472 (28.62%)
Total No. of Men	1,844	1,579	1,084	637	5.144 (100%)

of labor per hectare, I arrive at a figure of 0.38 men per hectare during the nonharvest season. Only eleven hectares were planted with new trees during that period. The same source indicates that 145 days of labor are required to plant one hectare, or 0.76 men per hectare during the off-season. The local FNCC agronomist calculated estimates for other agricultural activities (clearing of pasture lands and planting tomatoes). He estimated that the total demand for wage laborers for other tasks is then:

$(608 \times 0.38) + (11 \times 0.76) + 600 = 839.38$

Therefore, the total maintenance season demand is calculated as:

839 men + 5,144 men = 5,983

Probably about 1,118 of these laborers are *agregados* who reside on the farm. These calculations assume that all tasks are concentrated during the thirty-eight-week nonharvest period.

Wages and Salaries, Risaralda

Administrators

The salary paid to administrators during 1985 varied according to the responsibilities assigned, experience and training, whether bonuses were also paid, and what fringe benefits were included.

On the large enterprise farms the administrators were paid between twenty thousand and thirty thousand pesos a month plus the legally stipulated fringe benefits. They also had access to houses, sometimes transportation, and an incentive bonus based on the amount of parchment coffee produced. The usual rate in 1985 was of twelve pesos per arroba of parchment coffee produced. On these large farms, the bonus could amount to more than 150,000 pesos annually. Similar salaries and privileges were earned by the administrators of farms with at least forty-five hectares in coffee.

On the medium enterprise farms there was a wider range of salaries that corresponded more or less to differences in responsibilities and size of the enterprise. Administrators who had considerable responsibility received twenty thousand pesos per month and the legal fringe benefits but no incentive bonus. Alternatively, they were paid less but received generous bonuses ranging from three to twenty pesos per arroba of parchment coffee produced. The incentive also related to the farm's condition and potential.

Permanent Personnel

Although the basic salary received by resident laborers varied from farm to farm, the differences did not reflect differences in farm size. However, resident laborers on large farms were more likely to receive fringe benefits than those on smaller farms. All personnel who had supervisory responsibilities received more than those who did not. Crew supervisors often received bonuses amounting to about seven cents per arroba of beans harvested. On large farms the bonuses could add just enough to the basic weekly salaries (600 to 1,500 pesos) to match what harvesters were earning on a piece-rate basis. The workers responsible for processing coffee were often paid slightly higher basic salaries and received larger incentive bonuses.

Table B1 lists the range of basic salaries recorded from November 1985 to August 1986. I do not include fringe benefits because the information was incomplete and not very reliable.

Occasional Laborers—Day Wages

Errazuriz's longitudinal analysis of wage trends is based on the Departamento Nacional de Estadística's (DANE's) list of wages by department. DANE collects the data by requesting information about average wages from each municipality. These municipal averages are gathered from information given by a few farmers in each municipality. The reported information masks the considerable wage variation among farms within each municipality. Table B2 presents the range of day wages recorded in these interviews during the harvest of 1985 and in July 1986.

TABLE B1.   Weekly Salaries of Permanent Laborers, Risaralda, 1985

Weekly Salaries (Colombian Pesos)	Resident Laborer (No. of Farms)	Crew Supervisor (No. of Farms)	Coffee Processing (No. of Farms)
2,000–2,500	2		
3,000–3,200	7	3	1
3,200–3,400		4	
3,400–3,600			3
4,000–5,000		1	3

Source: Field data from interviews with farmers and laborers on the sampled farms. Some laborers refused to answer, and other farms had no resident laborers who performed these tasks.

TABLE B2.   Day Wages of Occasional Laborers in Colombian Pesos, Risaralda, 1985–86

	DANE's Information[a]	Legal Minimum Wage	Recorded Wages[b]
Harvest 1985	564	451.92	475–500–550–600–700
July 1986	500	560.38	400–500–600–700

[a]Departamento Nacional, 1985c, 1986c.
[b]From interview with laborers in Marsella and Belén.

Agregados Who Served Food to Laborers

These *agregados* who are brought to the farm for the specific purpose of preparing hot food for laborers who request it must be married, ideally have adult daughters, and have the necessary cooking equipment and eating utensils. The farmer provides housing, pays for electricity, provides wood for cooking, and contributes plantains and bananas if they are grown on the farm. The man of the family receives a salary as an *agregado* and must do the shopping and either supervise labor crews or maintain the lodgings provided to migrant harvesters. His wife and daughters cook and serve the laborers if they eat at the *agregado*'s house. The laborers must pay for the food at a price set by the farmer, who deducts the amount from their weekly earnings. The *agregado* rather than his wife receives food payments. Although farmers agree that the arrangement is very unfair, nothing has been done to change it.

The food consists of morning coffee, followed by a breakfast of coffee or chocolate with corn cakes and meat or soup. Lunch consists of a yucca, meat, and plantain stew. Dinner includes meat, rice, and perhaps beans. The menu may vary, but it is always mediocre.

Food preparation takes a considerable effort and is a risky venture. The *agregado* must purchase enough food to feed the laborers without any assurance that those who have promised to come will show up. Without refrigeration, food spoils, and costs are not recovered. When the family is assigned at least twenty laborers and all of them come, the family makes a small profit. Otherwise, the family's own food expenses are barely covered. Many of these families complain that they lose money.

Family Budget and Income Estimates, Belén-Marsella, 1985–1986

Income (1985–1986)

The estimates are based on the account book records of two highly productive farms in Belén and Marsella. Laborers' incomes on these two farms are estimated on the basis of workers' average earnings during different periods of the harvest and the wage most frequently paid in the municipality during the nonharvest period. The estimates assume that laborers are employed for fifty weeks out of the year. It was estimated that during the eight-week period of high harvest they were able to bag 750 kilograms a week and were paid ten pesos per kilogram. I estimated that during the subsequent four-week period, harvesters bagged only four hundred kilograms a week and were paid eleven pesos per kilogram. It was estimated that during the rest of the year (thirty-eight weeks), workers earned an average of three thousand pesos a week. Based on these numbers, I estimated the average weekly income throughout the year as 3,548 pesos.

To arrive at an estimate of a family income I calculated that a father earns the full average weekly income and an adult son at home earns three-quarters of that income since he is likely to be unemployed more often. I assumed that a woman's income would amount to no more than 25 percent of an adult male income, since mothers were not expected to work if young children were at home (scenario A in table C1).

These income estimates are likely to be higher than what most laborers earned and hence do not truly reflect the plight of laborers. Many workers were unemployed during August, and older men are likely to be called less often and to have to take time off for sickness. If periods of sickness and unemployment are incorporated—estimated at a total of four weeks per year—then the average weekly income would amount to only 3,338 pesos (scenario B in table C1).

Budget

The figures for weekly expenses in table C1 include only food and are based on information gathered from local women checked against what laborers specify they need to feed their family for a week. I have taken into account that the food expenditures are higher during the harvest. I have calculated that an average of 1,386 pesos was required to feed an adult per week during 1985–86. The cost of feeding a child is assumed to be half of the cost of feeding an adult. No difference is made between the costs of feeding men and women.

Family Types

I have categorized families according to the number, gender, and age of dependents as this situation changes through the family's developmental cycle. I have also taken into account that most families have an average of

TABLE C1.   Family Income and Family Expenses by Number of Dependents and Contributors (Family Types), Risaralda, 1986

Family Type	Weekly Expenses (Colombian Pesos)	Income			
		Scenario A		Scenario B	
		Only Men Work (Colombian Pesos)	Men and Women Work (Colombian Pesos)	Only Men Work (Colombian Pesos)	Men and Women Work (Colombian Pesos)
Type 1	4,158	3,548	3,548	3,338	3,338
Type 2	6,930	5,913	6,800	5,563	6,397
Type 3	7,623	8,278	9,165	7,788	8,622
Type 4	6,930	5,913	8,574	5,563	8,065
Type 5	4,158	3,548	5,322	3,338	5,006
Type 6	2,772	3,548	4,435	3,338	4,172

Note:

Type 1 family: Parents + two children below fourteen years of age.

Type 2 family: Parents + two children below fourteen years of age + one adult son + one adult daughter.

Type 3 family: Parents + one child below fourteen years of age + two adult sons + one adult daughter.

Type 4 family: Parents + one adult son + two adult daughters.

Type 5 family: Parents + one adult daughter.

Type 6 family: older parents.

five children, that daughters are likely to stay at home longer than sons, and that one son will stay at home if there are too many daughters. Table C1 lists income and expenses for each type of family depending on whether women also contribute income and whether the head of the household is employed all year (scenario A) or has trouble finding work during August (scenario B). As the table suggests, the hardest time for a family is when children are young and the husband/father is the only one contributing to household expenses. When the children grow up, the family can cover food expenses as long as all of the women help. To cover costs other than food, the sons must contribute and/or all of the women must work.

Changes in Income, 1977–1984

From the mid–1970s through 1982, real incomes were higher than in 1985–86, and families fared better. I have illustrated this point in table C2, where I estimate changes in the share that each member of the household receives. These changes are a consequence of changes in number of contributors and dependents and, more significantly, of changes in the real value of wages. To arrive at the figures listed in table C2, I have followed the same accounting procedures as for table C1 and used the average annual wage received by laborers in Marsella and Belén (Departamento Nacional 1985c, 1986c). These wages were deflated by the cost-of-food index (1978 = 100), which was derived by considering the difference between wages with food and wages without food. Shares are calculated by dividing income by number of household members, with adults receiving full shares and children a half share.

TABLE C2.   Members' Share of Family Income According to Number of Contributors and Dependents (Family Types), Risaralda, 1977–84

Year	Family Type 1	Family Type 2	Family Type 3	Family Type 4	Family Type 5
1977	63	63	80	63	63
1978	71	71	90	71	71
1979	71	71	91	71	71
1980	65	65	83	65	65
1981	58	58	74	58	58
1982	60	60	76	60	60
1983	58	58	73	58	58
1984	52	52	66	52	52

Note: Family types are the same as in table C1.

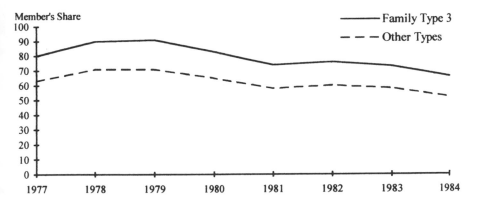

Fig. C1. **Average share of family income by each of its members, Belén-Marsella, 1977–84.** For the sake of comparison, I have estimated that all adults receive an equal share and children receive half a share.

In figure C1, I plot the changes in the shares received by each member of family type 3 against the changes in all other family types through the 1977–84 period. It is clear that laboring families did better during the 1970s than during the 1980s. As incomes fell, it is probable that more women began to work outside the home. It is also clear that only families with at least two sons contributing income would have been able to improve the quality of the family dwelling and been able to enjoy some small luxuries, even when incomes were not high.

Chapter 1

1. The remuneration previously received may have been determined by market forces as economists suggest, but it may also have been determined by a composite set of forces.

2. In 1977 the municipalities in the vanguard of technical reform offered much higher salaries to attract sufficient workers, but that increase had little effect on other municipalities: 32 percent of the coffee municipalities in the central zone, where Risaralda is located, and 56.5 percent of the coffee municipalities in the eastern zone, where La Vega is located, paid less than the annual average regional daily wage. As more farms and municipalities converted to the new agrotechnology, the year-round labor demand across municipalities became more uniform, and only 13 percent of municipalities nationwide paid below the average daily wage. Though more municipalities began to approximate the regional average wage, the deviation from this average was still significant in 1985; 71 percent of salaries did not conform to the average in the central zone and 75 percent did not conform in the eastern zone. In the central zone, 34 percent of the salaries fell below the average, and in the eastern zone 30 percent fell below the average (Errazuriz 1989a: 93–95). Within Risaralda, the intermunicipality deviation was not as great: 21 percent deviated from the average in 1977, and 37 percent did so in 1984. However, the difference is significant since it would be easy for the population of harvesters to go to a neighboring site. Arango noticed the same pattern when he contrasted the wages in Antioquia with those of departments from which harvesters came. Antioquia initially paid lower wages, but those differences eventually became smaller (Arango, Aubad, and Piedrahita 1983: 196–98).

Chapter 2

1. Various historians have studied the militancy of the 1930s. The most incisive sources are Bergquist 1973, 1986; Tovar 1975; Palacios 1983; Fajardo 1977; Machado 1977; and Jimenez 1981.

2. According to Jimenez (1989: 211–14), despite the risk involved, wage laborers predominated on some of the smaller estates in Cundinamarca that were owned by farmers who had access to credit. Using data collected by Marcos Palacios, I documented that on one estate in Antioquia, wage laborers did most of the tending and harvesting of coffee trees in 1889 and their presence was noticeable

until 1907. After that time, tenants and attached resident laborers (*agregados*) regained their preeminence (Ortiz 1989).

3. Machado and Urrea used two separate farm censuses for their estimates. Each census used a different methodology and reported different information: the 1938 census reports the number of agricultural workers and the number of independent laborers; the 1955 figures were derived from the 1951 census information on farm-size distribution and from a 1955 survey of agricultural employment that was taken during harvesting season, when there is a high ratio of workers to farms.

4. Bergquist (1986) proposed that one of the multifaceted aspects of the *violencia* was the ongoing struggle for land and social mobility in the coffee region.

5. The absence of census information during the intervening period and the disparity in the criteria used to compile information about production before and after the *violencia* make it very difficult to estimate the impact of the events on local economies.

6. The estimates given by Fedesarrollo are a bit higher and probably more accurate than the FNCC figures. The FNCC estimates a growth in acreage of 1.3 percent between 1970 and 1980 (Federación Nacional 1985: 6); Fedesarrollo estimates an expansion of 5.5 percent for the same period (Ocampo 1987: 282). Errazuriz (1989: 7) estimates that between 1960 and 1985 the amount of land in Colombia dedicated to coffee was enlarged by about two hundred thousand hectares. The growth change is visible when traveling through some major coffee areas, such as Risaralda, and is corroborated by informants who point to farms that gave up production of sugarcane, corn, and beans, which are now imported from other areas of Colombia.

7. Each sack weighs sixty kilograms. Coffee statistics are recorded in terms of weight in berries, parchment coffee, or green coffee. Berries are the unprocessed beans, still surrounded by flesh and skin. Parchment coffee has been dried but is still enclosed within a fine, brittle husk. Green coffee is ready for roasting and is exported in this form. Export figures are usually for green coffee. Farm production figures are given in parchment coffee, and harvest figures are usually in weight of berries.

8. The fungus (*Heneileia vastratix*) (referred to as *rust* in English and *roya* in Spanish) attacks the coffee leaves and causes eventual defoliation. In 1980, 5.2 percent of all hectares of coffee in Colombia were affected by the fungus.

9. Errazuriz 1989b: table 9. These estimates are based on annual national harvest yields and recorded data on hectares renovated. For details of the methodology used, see Errazuriz 1989b. Her estimates are much more conservative than those offered by other researchers (see Junguito and Pizano 1991: 158–65).

10. In a national survey by the FNCC in 1984, 57 percent of farmers surveyed said that with appropriate financial help they would modernize their coffee groves (Federación Nacional 1984a).

11. The criteria used to collect census information have shifted over the years so that figures are not exactly comparable. The most drastic change occurred in 1980, when the FNCC opted for a technology of aerial photography that blurs farm boundaries. This census thus gives only information on hectares per munici-

pality planted in coffee (with varying amounts of shade coverage) and hectares in other crops, pasture, and scrub land. At the municipal level, the FNCC's offices keep a listing of members that indicates acreage in coffee, pasture, and other crops, but no records are kept on turnover in ownership. It was impossible to comprehensively track down sales for the region studied. A 1984 FNCC survey indicates that only 38 percent of farms measure less than five hectares. If no biases were introduced in the sampling, this figure would indicate a serious drop in the number of small farms.

12. The number of farms below two hectares dropped by 73.3 percent, and those between 2.1 and 5 hectares by 26.2 percent. The number of farms in each subsequent five-hectare category increased by 28.6 percent, 39.7 percent, 60 percent, 43.1 percent, 58.8 percent, and 36.3 percent. Most of the farms now have between five and fifteen hectares.

13. In Antioquia there was little change in the proportion of farms with less than three hectares in coffee: 38.6 percent in 1975 and 38.5 percent in 1980.

14. To be a member, a farmer need only produce 375 kilograms of parchment coffee annually, which now can be done on a farm of between half a hectare and one hectare. In fact, 82 percent of producers with traditional coffee groves are members of the FNCC (Federación Nacional 1984a).

15. For a succinct review of FNCC's increasing power and relations with the government, see Bates 1997. For a more detailed analysis of the significance of the agreement for Colombia, see Junguito and Pizano 1993. These sources discuss at great length how the signing of the International Coffee Agreement restructured the relation between government and export agriculture as well as the relation between growers and the FNCC. Montenegro (1993: 151–95) discusses the agreement's implications for production.

16. There is a vast literature about the FNCC's internal politics as well as the appropriateness of its policies. Some of the most significant sources that describe the structure and internal politics of this organization are Bates 1997; Errazuriz 1986; Palacios 1983. Price and export policies of the FNCC have been evaluated by Junguito and Pizano 1997; Montenegro 1993; Zuleta et al. 1989; and several of the contributors in Ocampo 1987.

17. There is a vast literature by Colombian economists about the implications of the FNCC price and subsidy policies on production and for the viability of the Fondo Nacional del Café. These controversies are summarized by Junguito and Pizano 1993; Zuleta et al. 1989; Montenegro 1993.

18. Farmers process and dry the coffee on their farms. They then transport it to the closest town, where they sell either to agencies connected with FNCC or to private buyers. In 1984, 3.3 percent of the coffee growers with traditional groves sold their harvest to ALMACAFE, 67.5 percent of these producers sold it to coffee cooperatives, and 27.5 percent sold it to private buyers (Federación Nacional 1984a). At that time the FNCC, through its various subsidiaries, purchased about 35 percent of the coffee produced in Risaralda.

19. Until the middle of 1989, the FNCC distributed fumigants free of charge and gave a small subsidy to pay for the labor cost of spraying. In 1988 the cost of

this program amounted to 4 percent of the cost of the harvest. The program was terminated and replaced by an indirect subsidy incorporated into the internal price of coffee.

20. The FNCC serves 73 percent of the producers. Two-thirds of them received some technical assistance and attended training workshops, but only one-third of the farmers participated in friendship groups. At one time or another, 81 percent of farmers have received credit.

Chapter 3

1. In 1925, Old Caldas (which encompassed the present departments of Risaralda, Caldas, and Quindío), Cundinamarca, Antioquia, and Tolima were the four major coffee-producing regions (Arango 1981: 161).

2. In Risaralda, 63 percent of land under cultivation is planted with coffee. This percentage is based on estimates for 1981 by the Departamento Nacional de Estadística (1985b: 287–96) and FNCC (Federación Nacional 1981). The amount of land dedicated to coffee has continued to grow at an annual rate of 1.2 percent (Vallejo Mejía 1993: 252). Although cattle is an important industry, it is not as important as in Cundinamarca. Three times as many head of cattle are slaughtered annually in Cundinamarca as in Risaralda. Cundinamarca also has an important milk and cheese industry.

3. In Cundinamarca, only 35.47 percent of the agricultural land was planted in coffee in 1980, 13 percent less than in 1970 (Federación Nacional 1973, 1983). Furthermore, many coffee groves have recently been allowed to deteriorate, and conversion to new varieties has been slower than in Risaralda. According to FNCC's 1980–81 coffee census, 23 percent of land in coffee in Cundinamarca and 35 percent in Risaralda was planted with the new variety of coffee. Average coffee yields per hectare in Cundinamarca fell below the norm in other major coffee departments, while Risaralda compared favorably with Antioquia.

4. By 1981, Risaralda farmers were ahead of the Cundinamarca farmers in converting coffee groves to the new coffee variety: 35 percent of the coffee hectares had already been planted with the *caturra* variety in Risaralda, while only 23 percent of coffee hectares in Cundinamarca had the new variety (Federación Nacional 1983). Furthermore, in Risaralda 8,903 more hectares were planted with coffee, whereas in Cundinamarca the expansion included only 5,959 hectares (Federación Nacional 1981). As a result, production per hectare was higher in Risaralda (1,281 kilograms per hectare) than in Cundinamarca (951.25 kilograms per hectare).

5. Although a decrease in coffee prices affects the economic health of Risaralda's agriculture, it is not always clear how closely related the fate of this sector is to that of Pereira's industrial and commercial sectors (Vallejo Mejía 1993).

6. Only 7.4 percent of Risaralda's traditional farms were either poorly managed or in a state of decay, according to the preliminary results of the 1980–81 census. This figure compares favorably with the statistics in the other major coffee-producing areas. It is possible that some farmers with between five and ten hectares in coffee may own more than one farm. We were able to trace double ownership for 9 percent of farms in Marsella and 12 percent in Belén. The number may be

higher but is probably not significantly so. Multiple-farm ownership is common among wealthy farmers, but in these cases the farms are often not in the same municipality and are dedicated to different activities.

7. Between 1960 and 1970 the surface planted with permanent crops that was controlled by farmers with less than five hectares was reduced by 17.2 percent, while the amount of such land controlled by farmers with between five and ten hectares decreased by 6.7 percent (Urrea 1976: 46). It is too early to know the impact of the 1992 crisis on land distribution, but Arango has reported that small farmers are having serious difficulties in Antioquia (Arango 1993: 192).

8. This information is based on the farm census kept in the municipal offices of the FNCC. It does not include some farms on the higher slopes of these municipalities, beyond the coffee belt.

9. This characterization of farms corresponds to what Ruíz Niño (1972: 275) suggests for Tolima.

10. *Agregado* is still used to refer to a resident laborer. The word relates the present form of permanent day-labor contract with residential privileges to the older version of attaching laborers to farms by obliging them to work for as long as they resided on the farms and cultivated assigned plots of land (see section 2.2). *Agregados* did receive wages, as they do now. However, at present they are offered houses but have no access to land for their own subsistence (see section 7.5).

11. Arango is quite aware that farmers respond to prices or incomes when deciding how much fertilizer to use. He discusses this point when he reviews farmers' reactions to the 1992 coffee crisis (Arango 1993). A survey in Caldas during this period indicates that farmers purchased 33.5 percent less fertilizer and reduced labor use during maintenance season by 20 percent in response to the crisis (Saldías Barreneche 1993: 252).

Chapter 4

1. This chapter is based largely on Risaralda, where most of the fieldwork was done and where extensive interviews of families were carried out in their homes to supplement the information gained from the harvest survey. The social organization of families in 1985 still conformed very closely to the prototypical patriarchal Antioqueño family discussed by Gutierrez de Pineda (1976) in her careful and detailed study of Colombian families. Familial relations in Cundinamarca were more informal than those in Antioquia, and women participated more actively in labor markets. When pertinent, these differences are noted.

2. In fact, about half of the rural laborers who settled in these neighborhoods remained there or in the same municipality for at least nine years, and nearly a third of them have never been away (Velez, Becerra, Gomez et. al. 1986). Of the harvesters surveyed, 41 percent had always lived in the municipality in which they resided at the time of the study, and another 7.95 percent had been there longer than five years. Continuity of residence was more striking for the local population of harvesters: 67 percent had always lived in the area, and an additional 14 percent had done so for more than five years. But length of time in a particular residence or neighborhood may be shorter. It is probable that in the municipality of La Vega

(Cundinamarca) there were more frequent migratory movements since it was close to a number of industrial centers and cities where women could find appropriate employment.

3. During the harvest of 1985, we administered questionnaires to harvesters working in sampled farms. All figures citing harvesters refer to the results of this survey. During the summer months, we visited rural areas and urban districts of Risaralda, where landless laborers lived, and interviewed one or more members of each family. Any mention of visits or interviews refers to nonsampled families visited during the nonharvest season.

4. SENA (the national training service) was organized in 1957 as an independent central government agency to help train and educate laborers in both the rural and urban sectors. This agency has also taken on a more general educational role by organizing courses and campaigns to improve the welfare of rural families. It has also helped to finance housing projects for many rural families.

5. Rents range from 1,000 pesos to 1,500 pesos, or 12 percent of monthly income.

6. According to Echeverri de Ferrufino (1984: 98–99), in the rural areas of Antioquia and Caldas, these alliances now tend not to end in marriage; rather, people engage in a series of free unions. A study of women in Marsella (Saxena 1995) indicates that women are currently more reluctant to commit themselves to marriage until they find reliable companions after experimenting with several free unions. Since there is more access to birth control and more acceptance of it, women are now less likely to be trapped in a relationship or trapped into needing men to support them.

7. In 1991 Saxena (1995: 174) interviewed young women in one of the municipalities covered in this study and found that 80 percent of the rural women in her sample acknowledged using some form of birth control without their husbands' knowledge. In towns, information about birth control from government campaigns and access to hospitals has made it easier for women to use birth control pills or IUDs. However, women over forty years of age were more likely to terminate their fertility surgically.

8. A survey of rural residents in coffee regions (Velez, Becerra, Gomez et al. 1986: 50) indicates that only 52.6 percent finished primary school. Similar figures emerged from our survey. There is a big drop in school attendance for boys after they reach the age of ten, when they begin to help their fathers: 84 percent of boys younger than ten attended school, while only 57.39 percent of those in the next age bracket (ages ten to fourteen) did so. While fewer girls go to school (only 61 percent of girls younger than ten were in school in Risaralda), they are more likely to finish primary school, since they face no similar labor demands (see table 4.2). It is important to remember that these percentages refer to the population of harvesters studied and excludes well-off farmers and middle-class urban families. Other studies indicate that more boys are likely to finish primary school in Cundinamarca than in Risaralda.

9. A survey of rural coffee regions (Velez, Becerra, Gomez et al. 1986) indicated that 23.9 percent of homes, regardless of class or wealth, had at least one person emigrate permanently.

10. In the local towns in 1985, domestics received between two thousand and three thousand pesos a month plus food and lodging; that sum represents about what a man would earn in a week. Only if young women went to the capital of the department were they likely to receive four thousand pesos a month; if they went to Bogotá, they earned seven thousand pesos a month in 1985. The Colombian Household Census lists domestic service as the most common occupation for women in Marsella in 1985 (37 percent of those who held jobs). The next most frequent occupation was agricultural laborer (12 percent of employed women). The rest reported a variety of occupations, including teachers and self-employed artisans.

11. In Cundinamarca, women are more engaged with the world outside of the home. They do the shopping and are more likely to work on their own farms or for wages.

Chapter 5

1. According to Ruíz Niño (1972: 275), three family members can handle a harvest of up to 7,500 kilograms of dry coffee beans a year.

2. This estimate is confirmed by a survey of 832 coffee farms in Risaralda that indicated that 19.1 percent of farms did not hire harvesters, 15.9 percent hired only one harvester, and 14.5 percent hired two. These figures match our estimates and approximate the pattern of land distribution for Risaralda. In the two municipalities studied in this department, 31.6 percent of the farms had less than 2.9 hectares in coffee (which could be worked by a family without outside help). We rarely interviewed small holders who regularly hired harvesters (Federacion Nacional 1980).

3. A survey indicated that only 22 percent of females between the ages of fourteen and fifty in both landless and farm-owning households are involved in any remunerated or unremunerated agricultural activity (Velez, Becerra, Gomez et al. 1986).

4. A laborer for a week can cost from four thousand to ten thousand pesos, depending on the amount harvested. In 1985 the internal price for coffee was 165.6 pesos per kilo; hence, a farmer had to sell between twenty-four and sixty kilograms of coffee to cover the cost of a laborer for a week. Given that one kilo of dried coffee is equivalent to 4.5 kilos of coffee berries and that the harvesting yields are lower at the beginning, it would take a farmer two to four days to harvest that amount on his own. By the end of the first week he would be drying enough coffee to hire 1.5 laborers for a week, and by the second week he would be selling the coffee.

5. Using the farm census available at each of the Risaralda municipalities from the local representative of the FNCC, I calculated that the maximum number of field hands required could reach 13,646 (see appendix A). I based this estimate on the number of hectares in each farm type, considering only those farms that hired wage laborers. I took into account the average size crew that both farmers and agronomists considered necessary. My estimate also incorporates differences in the timing of the harvest. One limitation of this estimate is that it is based on

acreage rather than coffee yields. Information on yields is not available by municipality, at least not to the public.

6. There were 12,550 men between the ages of fifteen and fifty-nine residing in the two municipalities. However, many of them were farmers or had other busy jobs during the harvest. I considered only those among the 8,613 men of all ages who identified themselves as laborers.

7. This percentage excludes the one farm that recruited mostly women. It was added to the survey to interview a fair number of female harvesters.

8. Only seven local male harvesters (3.7 percent) were working elsewhere just before the harvest started in Risaralda; many others were probably unemployed at the time. Thus, most of the locals are readily available to shoulder the initial stages of the harvest.

9. Even if all sons of peasants had participated in the harvest labor market, their presence would have amounted to only 11.3 percent of the labor force. This estimate is based on an average of 4.2 children living at home, of whom half are males and 1.5 are likely to be old enough to be laborers. If these sons are older and married, they either own a farm or have become landless laborers no longer connected with the family enterprise. If the labor demand at the height of the harvest is for 13,646 individuals, then the 1,030 sons of peasants still living at home and the 687 fathers would amount to only 12.58 percent of the labor force. This is a generous estimate that assumes full participation by all able male members of these families. In fact, very few of the small farmers interviewed acknowledged working on someone else's farm. We visited forty-four small farmers whose major income came from their farm enterprises, which entailed mostly family labor. Of these families, only three fathers worked regularly on other farms at least a few weeks during the harvest; seven others did so irregularly either because of a poor harvest or because they had large families of dependent children. Sons are more ready to participate than their fathers but usually do so only after they help at home. Only in four of the forty-four families did the sons work exclusively for wages without helping their fathers. Thus, the peasant or small-farm population made no significant contribution toward the labor needs of larger farmers.

10. According to the 1985 census (taken just before harvest time) for the two Risaralda municipalities studied, 4,604 males over ten years of age (34.8 percent) said that their full-time occupation (for more than eight months of the year) was as employee, boss, or other. In Cundinamarca, 39.9 percent gave the same answer. Some of these occupational categories, for example, "boss," may encompass agricultural activities, but it is not possible to tell from the census.

11. The actual percentage in our sample was 43.3 percent. It was then corrected for a bias introduced as a result of the location of the farms with respect to the town. The correction is based on the average ratio of urban to total population on farms in distance zones 1 and 2 and the average ratio in farms in zone 3 times the proportion of land in coffee for each zone (assumed to be half): Urban/total = $(0.5 \times 0.52) + (0.5 \times 0.34) = 0.43$.

12. It is possible that there is an underreporting of helpers on many farms. When wives of local, landless laborers were interviewed after the harvest, only a few indicated that they had helped their husbands with the harvest. When asked in the harvest survey whether they bagged together with other family members on the

farm where they were working, 17 percent of the women answered in the affirmative. This figure is much higher than the one derived from the account books of selected farms. It is also impossible to determine the number of women per department who participated in the harvest from the 1985 census since the region was surveyed before the harvest.

13. Of the seventy-two female harvesters (migrants and locals) in our survey (including the farm that was added because it had female crews), sixteen were heads of households, twenty-six were spouses, eighteen were daughters, and six lived with other kin. We had no information about the status of the other six women.

14. Among all harvesters, 30.86 percent had heard about the progress of the harvest from friends, 11.2 percent from relatives, and 8.5 percent over the radio. Others harvesters were local and did not need progress information.

15. The regionalization of supply areas was first noted by Urrea in his 1975 national survey of harvest markets (Urrea 1976: 112–14). At that time, Marsella provided harvesters to farms surrounding the capital of the department—that is, to its neighboring municipality—and Belén served as a reserve area for nearby areas in the department of Caldas. By 1985 the interlinkage among a specific set of socially related local coffee labor markets became more obvious as the proportion of ambulant laborers decreased from the 71.36 percent in 1975 to 24.24 percent in our 1985 survey. At that time, Marsella provided and drew laborers not only from its neighboring municipality of Pereira but also from noncontiguous municipalities. See Arango 1983: 140–41; Cuellar 1976: 65; Medrano 1985: 85 for other references to supply sources for laborers. Geographic distance and travel costs are only partially relevant to distance and direction of harvest job searches.

16. These percentages exclude men and women who reside on farms.

17. This quitting rate is comparable to the one reported by Sosnick (1978: 181) for North American agriculture. Quitting rates hide demand oscillations, which Sosnick does not take into account.

18. There is some difference in the percentage of urban residents in these two departments, which is not surprising given that there are more urbanized areas in Cundinamarca and consequently more opportunities. In Risaralda, 45 percent of the male harvesters said they lived in towns or cities; in Cundinamarca, 56 percent answered the same way. However, the difference may not be significant given the disparity in the population surveyed in each department.

19. Emerson (1989) warns that migrants probably follow the crops in the United States not because such workers are attached to an ambulatory lifestyle but because they find it difficult to extricate themselves from seasonal agricultural labor. It is quite possible that the United States has some migrants who share the characteristics of the *andariegos* since, as Whitener (1985) has pointed out, the migrant stream in U.S. agriculture includes a very diversified group of people.

Chapter 6

1. This chapter is based only on the two municipalities in Risaralda because I did not have enough follow-up data for Cundinamarca to interpret those responses to the questionnaires. After interviewing younger male, older male, and

female coffee laborers during the nonharvest season, I made sense of some of the cross-tabulations. I also examined responses to the original questionnaires and retraced some sequences of jobs that workers had held. Harvesters were not surveyed about job searches, with the exception of how they found the particular jobs held at the time of the interviews. The topic of job searches was discussed in open-ended interviews during the off-season.

2. Information on availability of workers is based on the 1985 census, which lists age groups and occupations. I considered only those people listed as workers who said they worked during the previous two weeks. The census was taken just before the harvest, when many men and women were unemployed; hence, it does not fully capture the number of potential agricultural laborers. Also included are family helpers, who receive no remuneration. However, since many of these helpers are also maintenance-season wage laborers, their inclusion is relevant.

3. According to the 1985 census for the two municipalities of Risaralda, 47 percent of the laborers were married men (Departamento Nacional 1985a). It refers to the percentage of men between ages thirty and fifty-nine, hence likely to be married, who participated in the labor market. After the harvest started, when many young men joined the labor force, the share of married workers was reduced to 32 percent.

Chapter 7

1. On only one farm in Risaralda and one in Cundinamarca, both growing coffee under shade trees, were harvesters paid a day wage rather than per kilo of berries harvested. On all other farms, only supervisors and nonharvesting personnel were paid a day wage. Some supervisors received a day wage in addition to a bonus according to how many kilos of berries their crews harvested. The general impression is that the day wage during harvest is the highest prevailing wage just before the harvest. There was a slight range in day wages quoted by laborers, and I am not clear about what was discounted from the quoted wages.

2. This phenomenon resembles what Sosnick reported for agricultural workers in the United States. Growers informed him that they set the rates after considering the associations' recommendations, the previous year's rates, what neighboring farmers said they were paying, rates in other seasonal work, field conditions on particular farms, and the U.S. Department of Labor's minimum wage for growers employing foreign contract workers (Sosnick 1978: 26). In Chile's fruit industry, 25 percent of the growers set the rate unilaterally (Jarvis, Montero, and Hidalgo 1993).

3. Although the large enterprise farms paid the highest piece rate, it is important to keep in mind that these large farms engage only 18 percent of the wage-labor force, while the medium enterprise farms engage 51 percent. Rates varied greatly among other farms according to the issues discussed in the text. In one of the Risaralda municipalities, during a two-week period at the height of the harvest, 38 percent of the laborers surveyed received ten pesos per kilo, 27 percent received nine pesos, and the remainder were evenly distributed among the rates of eight, eleven, and twelve pesos per kilo. Several months later, when the main harvest

took place in Cundinamarca, 61 percent of the laborers received ten pesos per kilo; otherwise, the rate of payment was evenly distributed between six and sixteen pesos per kilo.

4. In 1977 32 percent of the municipalities in the central coffee region, where Risaralda is located, paid below the annual average wage for the zone. Within Risaralda itself there were considerable intermunicipal variations in 1977: 21 percent of the municipalities paid below the annual department average. Within the eastern region, where La Vega is located, 56 percent of the municipalities paid below the regional average. The greater variation in this second region probably results from the more diversified character of its agriculture.

5. This phenomenon is similar to what has been reported in other parts of the world (Ahmed 1981: 310). In India, wage changes have been associated with population changes (Evenson and Binswanger 1984: 274). No one has claimed that rural wages can be explained by productivity.

6. These benefits could be incorporated as fringe benefits with a financial cost. It could be argued that once the total wage packet is estimated, real wages are higher than they appear. It was impossible to gather information on frequency and value of these exchanges. My general impression is that they do not significantly alter occasional laborers' day-wage rates.

Chapter 8

1. The census figure for Manizales is much lower, with only 5.6 percent of all city residents listed as agricultural laborers. While this figure reflects more closely the extent of the urban-rural articulation than the figures from selected working-class areas, the Manizales number excludes the seasonal participation of urban residents during the harvest; in 1985, the census was taken just before the harvest started.

2. There are no annual harvest yield records available for each municipality or department. It will have to be assumed that the increase in yield for Risaralda reflected the national increase, which was about 25 percent. During that year, only 10 percent extra field hands from outside the area were needed. Since the productivity per hectare was above the national average and kept pace with other major departments in extent of annual renovations, the estimate of 25 percent increase is probably conservative.

3. The same applies to Cundinamarca, but the rural areas are still losing some population that moves either out of the region or to urban areas. In our sample only 5 percent of the laboring families had settled in Cundinamarca during the past five years.

4. Share contracts have remained unpopular in Risaralda. According to the 1970 census, only 11.2 percent of the farms were exploited under share contracts, and a 1977 FNCC survey revealed that such was only the case for 9.2 percent of the coffee farms (Comité de Cafeteros de Risaralda 1980). Although there are no figures for the municipalities studied, local residents insisted that these contracts were rare and insignificant. They are now used only in a few circumstances: in old coffee groves where owners are not considering renovations; when an entrepreneur

has invested in a number of separate parcels that he cannot manage directly on his own; in farms in the process of subdivision through succession; and when parents want to begin to pass a neglected farm to their children. In the first two instances, the landlord has to offer a parcel of no less than two hectares to attract a share tenant. Thus, it is unlikely that sharecropping contracts will regain their popularity in the near future. Legal constraints, social uncertainties, and changes in the economic environment have increased the transactional costs of these contracts. Yet according to Arango, once the bonanza began to ebb in Antioquia, the land exploited using share-contract arrangements began to increase once again, though not evenly throughout the state. While in most of Antioquia the land under share contract increased from 2.7 percent to 15.5 percent of total hectares, in the southeast it decreased from 10 percent to 7 percent. Arango offers no explanation for the regionalization of sharecropping contracts (Arango, Aubad, and Piedrahita 1983).

5. During 1985–86 *agregados* who were crew supervisors earned on average 533 pesos a day. The average daily wage was 550 pesos. But the sample used to determine the average is small and heterogeneous. When fringe benefits and bonuses are included, the *agregados* received above the going wage. *Agregados* not known to have supervisory responsibilities earned only 516 pesos a day plus housing but no other fringe benefits. These men might be able to earn more as day laborers. They had other reasons for accepting the jobs.

References

Aguilera, María Eugenia. 1997. Modalidades de Intermediación en la Contratación de Cosecheros Citrícolas en Tucumán. Paper presented at the workshop on "Rural Employment during a Period of Deregulation," University of Buenos Aires.

Ahmed, Iqbal. 1981. Wage Determination in Bangladesh Agriculture. *Oxford Economic Papers* 33:298–322.

Akerloff, George A. 1980. The Theory of Social Custom, of Which Unemployment May Be One Consequence. *Quarterly Journal of Economics* 94:543–70.

———. 1982. Labor Contracts as Partial Gift Exchange. *Quarterly Journal of Economics* 97:543–69.

———. 1990. The Fair Wage–Effort Hypothesis and Unemployment. *Quarterly Journal of Economics* 105:255–83.

ANIF, Biblioteca de Economía. 1974. *Legislación Cafetera.* Bogotá: Tercer Mundo.

ANUC. 1975. El Café y el Movimiento Campesino. *Latin American Perspectives* 2:53–84.

Aparicio, Susana, and Roberto Benencia. 1997. El Empleo Rural en la Argentina: Viejos y Nuevos Actores Sociales en el Mercado de Trabajo. Paper presented at the workshop on "Rural Employment during a Period of Deregulation," University of Buenos Aires.

Aparicio, Susana, and Carla Gras. 1997. El Mercado de Trabajo Tabacalero en Jujuy: Un Análisis en los Cambios de la Demanda. Paper presented at the workshop on "Rural Employment during a Period of Deregulation," University of Buenos Aires.

Arango, Mariano. 1981. *Café e Industria, 1850–1940.* CIE, Universidad de Antioquia. Bogotá: Carlos Valencia Editores.

———. 1982. *El Café en Colombia, 1930–1958: Producción y Política.* CIE, Universidad de Antioquia. Bogotá: Carlos Valencia Editores.

———. 1993. La Caficultura Antioqueña Frente a la Crisis Cafetera. In *Economía Cafetera: Crisis y Perspectivas,* 189–238. Santafe de Bogotá: Centro Editorial Javeriano.

Arango, Mariano, Rafael Aubad, and Jaime Piedrahita. 1983. *Bonanza de Precios y Transformaciones en la Industria Cafetera. Antioquia, 1975–1980.* CIE, Universidad de Antioquia. Medellin: Carlos Valencia Editores.

Attanasio, Orazio P., and Fiorella Paddoa Schioppa. 1991. Regional Inequalities, Migration, and Mismatch in Italy, 1960–1986. In *Mismatch and Labour*

Mobility, ed. Fiorella Paddoa Schioppa, 230–320. Cambridge: Cambridge University Press.

Bardhan, Pranab K. 1979. Wages and Unemployment in a Poor Agrarian Economy: A Theoretical and Empirical Analysis. *Journal of Political Economy* 87:479–500.

———. 1980. Interlocking Factor Markets and Agrarian Development: A Review of Issues. *Oxford Economic Papers* 32:82–98.

———. 1984. *Land, Labour, and Rural Poverty: Essays in Development Economics.* New York: Columbia University Press.

———. 1989. A Note on Interlinked Rural Economic Arrangements. In *The Economic Theory of Agrarian Institutions,* ed. P. K. Bardhan, 237–42. Oxford: Clarendon.

Bardhan, Pranab K., and Ashok Rudra. 1981. Terms and Conditions of Labour Contracts in Agriculture: Results of a Survey in West Bengal. *Oxford Bulletin of Economics and Statistics* 43:89–111.

———. 1986. Labour Mobility and the Boundaries of Village Moral Economy. *Journal of Peasant Studies* 13:90–115.

Barlett, Peggy. 1986. Profile of Full-Time Farm Workers in a Georgia County. *Rural Sociology* 51:78–96.

Barnett, Paul. 1978. Labor's Dwindling Harvest. Report, California Institute for Rural Studies.

Bates, Robert H. 1997. *Open-Economy Politics: The Political Economy of the World Coffee Trade.* Princeton: Princeton University Press.

Bazzoli, Laure, Thierry Kirat, and Marie Claire Villeval. 1994. Rules, Contracts, and Institutions in the Wage-Labor Relationship: A Return to Institutionalism? *Journal of Economic Issues* 28:1137–71.

Bell, Clive. 1989. A Comparison of Principal-Agent and Bargaining Solutions: The Case of Tenancy Contracts. In *The Economic Theory of Agrarian Institutions,* ed. P. K. Bardhan, 73–93. Oxford: Clarendon.

Bendini, Mónica. 1997. Las Trabajadoras del Empaque de Fruta en el Alto Valle: Perfil y Trayectoria. Paper presented at the workshop on "Rural Employment during a Period of Deregulation," University of Buenos Aires.

Benencia, Roberto. 1997. La Mediería. In *Area Hortícola Bonaerense: Cambios en la Producción y su Incidencia en los Sectores Sociales,* ed. Roberto Benecia, 151–77. Buenos Aires: Editorial La Colmena.

Bergquist, Charles. 1973. *Coffee and Conflict in Colombia, 1886–1904: Origin and Outcome of the War of a Thousand Days.* Stanford, Calif.: Stanford University Press.

———. 1986. *Labor in Latin America: Comparative Essays on Chile, Argentina, Venezuela, and Colombia.* Stanford, Calif.: Stanford University Press.

Binswanger, Hans P., and M. Rosenzweig, eds. 1984. *Contractual Arrangements, Employment, and Wages in Rural Labor Markets in Asia.* New Haven: Yale University Press.

Bonilla C., Elssy, comp. 1985. *Mujer y Familia en Colombia.* Bogotá: Plaza y Janes Editores.

Bossen, Laurel. 1982. Plantations and Labor Force Discrimination in Guatemala. *Current Anthropology* 23:263–68.

Bourgois, Philippe I. 1989. *Ethnicity at Work: Divided Labor on a Central American Banana Plantation.* Baltimore: Johns Hopkins University Press.

Breman, Ian. 1974. *Patronage and Exploitation: Changing Agrarian Relations in South Gujarat, India.* Berkeley: University of California Press.

———. 1985. *Of Peasants, Migrants, and Paupers: Rural Labour Circulations and Capitalist Production in South India.* Oxford: Oxford University Press.

———. 1996. *Footloose Labour: Working in India's Informal Economy.* Cambridge: Cambridge University Press.

Brown, Martin, and Peter Phillips. 1986. The Decline of the Piece-Rate System in California Canning: Technological Innovation, Labor Management, and Union Pressure, 1890–1947. *Business History Review* 60:565–601.

Buttel, Frederick H., Olaf F. Larson, and Gilbert W. Gillespie Jr. 1990. *The Sociology of Agriculture.* New York: Greenwood.

Calderon de Cuellar, Gloria. 1976. *Características Sociolaborales de los Recolectores de Café en una Area de Cersi.* SENALDE, Migraciones Laborales no. 20. Bogotá: Ministerio de Trabajo y Seguridad Social.

Cambranes, Julio Castellanos. 1985. *Coffee and Peasants: The Origins of the Modern Plantation Economy in Guatemala, 1853–1897.* Monograph no. 10. Stockholm: Institute of Latin American Studies.

Campillo, Fabiola C. 1985. Modernización Agrícola y Desarrollo Rural: El Caso del Café en Colombia. Unpublished manuscript.

Carter, Michael R., Bradford L. Barham, and Dina Mesbah. 1996. Agricultural Export Booms and the Rural Poor in Chile, Guatemala, and Paraguay. *Latin America Research Review* 31: 33–66.

Chomitz, Kenneth. 1990. *Technological Determinants of Non-Market Clearing Wages.* Boston University Institute for Development Economics, Discussion Paper No. 10.

Christaller, W. 1966. *Central Places in Southern Germany.* Englewood Cliffs, N.J.: Prentice Hall.

CIDSE, Facultad de Ciencias Sociales y Económicas. 1989. *Mercados Rurales de Trabajo: Informe Final Presentado a la Misión de Estudios del Sector Agropecuario.* Cali: Universidad del Valle.

Cohen, Robin. 1991. *Contested Domains: Debates in International Labor Studies.* London: Zed Books.

Collins, Jane L. 1993. Gender, Contracts and Wage Work: Agricultural Restructuring in Brazil's São Francisco Valley. *Development and Change* 24:53–82.

———. 1995. Transnational Labor Process and Gender Relations. *Journal of Latin American Studies* 1:178–99.

Comité de Cafeteros de Risaralda. 1980. Estudios y Proyectos Básicos. Unpublished manuscript.

Daniel, Cletus E. 1981. *Bitter Harvest: A History of California Farmworkers, 1870–1941.* Berkeley: University of California Press.

Deas, Malcolm. 1977. A Colombian Coffee Estate: Santa Barbara, Cundinamarca, 1870–1912. In *Land and Labour in Latin America,* ed. K. Duncan and I. Rutledge, 118–40. Cambridge: Cambridge University Press.

de Janvry, Alain, Elizabeth Sadoulet, and Linda Wilcox Young. 1989. Land and Labour in Latin American Agriculture from 1950s to the 1980s. *Journal of Peasant Studies* 16:396–424.

Departamento Nacional de Estadística. 1951. *Censo de la Población.* Bogotá: Departamento Nacional de Estadística

———. 1964. *Censo Nacional de Población.* Bogotá: Departamento Nacional de Estadística.

———. 1973. XIV Censo Nacional de la Población y Vivienda. Database. Unpublished manuscript.

———. 1981. *Anuario Estadístico de Quindío y Caldas.* Bogotá: Departamento Nacional de Estadística.

———. 1985a. Censo Nacional de Población y Vivienda: Banco de datos por municipalidad. Database. Unpublished manuscript.

———. 1985b. *Colombia Estadística.* Bogotá: Departamento Nacional de Estadística.

———. 1985c. Jornales Agropecuarios en Agricultura. Risaralda. Unpublished manuscript.

———. 1986a. *Avances de los Resultados Preliminares del Censo de 1985.* Bogotá: Departamento Nacional de Estadística.

———. 1986b. *Colombia Estadística.* Bogotá: Departamento Nacional de Estadística.

———. 1986c. Jornales Agropecuarios en Agricultura. Risaralda. Unpublished manuscript.

———. 1990. *Colombia Estadística: 1989.* Vol. 2, *Municipal.* Bogotá: Departamento Nacional de Estadística.

Devine, Theresa J., and Nicholas Kiefer. 1991. *Empirical Labor Economics: The Search Approach.* Oxford: Oxford University Press.

Deygout, Phillipe. 1980. La Fuerza del Trabajo en la Zona Algodonera de Espinal. CIE, Universidad de Antioquia, Medellin. Unpublished manuscript.

Downs, Laura Lee. 1995. *Manufacturing Inequality: Gender Division in the French and British Metalworking Industries, 1914–1939.* Ithaca: Cornell University Press.

Dunlop, John. 1988. Labor Markets and Wage Determination: Then and Now. In *How Labor Markets Work: Reflections on Theory and Practice,* ed. Bruce E. Kaufman, 47–87. Lexington, Mass.: Lexington Books.

Durkheim, Emile. 1957. *Professional Ethics and Civic Morals.* London: Routledge and Kegan Paul.

Echavarría, Juán José, Alejandro Gaviria, and Carlos Téllez. 1993. Modelos de Producción y Pronósticos de la Cosecha Cafetera. In *Economía Cafetera: Crisis y Perspectivas,* 115–53. Santafe de Bogotá: Centro Editorial Javeriano.

Echeverri de Ferrufino, Ligia. 1984. *La Familia de Hecho en Colombia.* Bogotá: Tercer Mundo.

Economists' Intelligence Unit. 1988. Country Report. London.

Ekboir, Javier M., Raul Fiorentino, and Liliana Lunardelli. 1990. La Ocupación de la Mano de Obra Rural en Argentina. *Desarrollo Económico* 30:367–93.

Emerson, Robert D. 1989. Migratory Labor in Agriculture. *American Journal of Agricultural Economics.* 71:617–30.

Errazuriz, María. 1986. *Cafeteros y Cafetales del Líbano.* Bogotá: Universidad Nacional.

———. 1989a. Colombia, Costa Rica, y Guatemala: Países Cafeteros de la Cuenca del Caribe. Unpublished manuscript.

———. 1989b. *Mercado del Trabajo y Empleo en la Caficultural.* Bogotá: Fedesarrollo.

———. 1993. El Empleo y los Salarios Durante la Crisis: Que Muestra la Evidencia Empírica? In *Economía Cafetera: Crisis y Perspectivas,* 159–88. Santafe de Bogotá: Centro Editorial Javeriano.

Eswaran, M., and A. Kotwal. 1985. A Theory of Contractual Structure in Agriculture. *American Economic Review* 75:352–67.

Etxezarreta, Miren. 1992 Transformation of the Labour System and Work Process in a Rapidly Modernizing Agriculture: The Evolving Case of Spain. In *Labour and Locality: Uneven Development and the Rural Labour Process,* ed. Terry Marsden, Phillip Lowe, and Sarah Whatmore, 44–67. London: David Fulton.

Evenson, Robert E., and Hans P. Binswanger. 1984. Estimating Labor Demand Functions for Indian Agriculture. In *Contractual Arrangements, Employment, and Wages in Rural Labor Markets in Asia,* ed. Hans P. Binswanger and Mark R. Rosenzweig, 263–79. New Haven: Yale University Press.

Fajardo, Darío. 1977. Violencia y Desarrollo: Transformaciones Sociales en Tres Regiones Cafeteras del Tolima, 1936–1979. In *El Agro en el Desarrollo Histórico Colombiano,* ed. F. Leal Buitrago, et al., 265–301. Bogotá: Editora Guadalupe.

Federación Nacional de Cafeteros de Colombia. 1973. Censo Cafetero de 1970.

———. 1980. Estudio Sobre los Cafeteros Atendidos y no Atendidos. Departamento de Risaralda, División Técnica. Unpublished manuscript.

———. 1981. Renovaciones y Nuevas Siembras de Café por Departamento 1970–71, 1979–80. Unpublished manuscript.

———. 1983. *Censo Cafetero Nacional 1980–1981.*

———. 1984a. El Empleo y los Salarios en el Sector Cafetero. División de Planeación y Proyectos Especiales. Unpublished manuscript.

———. 1984b. La Estructura de la Caficultura Tradicional en Colombia. Unpublished manuscript.

———. 1985. Marco General del Plan de Desarrollo de las Fincas Cafeteras. Unpublished manuscript.

———. 1992. XLX Congreso Nacional de Cafeteros, Informe del Gerente General.

Fisher, Lloyd. 1953. *The Harvest Labor Market in California.* Cambridge: Harvard University Press.

Friedland, William H. 1984. Commodity Systems Analysis: An Approach to the

Sociology of Agriculture. *Research in Rural Sociology and Development* 1:221–35.

Friedland, William H., Amy Barton, and Robert J. Thomas. 1981. *Manufacturing Green Gold: Capital, Labor, and Technology in the Lettuce Industry.* New York: Cambridge University Press.

Galarza, Ernesto. 1964. *Merchants of Labor: The Mexican Bracero Story.* Santa Barbara, Calif.: McNally and Loftin.

Gilhodes, P. 1972. *Las Luchas Agrarias en Colombia.* Bogotá: Editorial Tigre de Papel.

Gomez, Ciro Martinez, and Gladys Escobar Morant. 1987. Tendencias Recientes de la Población en Colombia. *Boletín de Estadística* 413:214–37.

Gomez, Jaime. 1976. *El Cumplimiento de la Legislación Laboral en Cultivos Temporales.* Migraciones Laborales no. 7. Bogotá: SENALDE, Ministerio de Trabajo y Seguridad Social.

Gomez, Sergio, and Jorge Echenique. 1988. *La Agricultura Chilena: Las Dos Caras de la Modernización.* Santiago de Chile: FLACSO.

Gonzalez, Michael. 1985. *Plantation Agriculture and Social Control in Northern Peru, 1875–1933.* Austin: University of Texas Press.

Granovetter, Mark. 1981. Toward a Sociological Theory of Income Differences. In *Sociological Perspectives in Labor Markets,* ed. Ivan Berg, 12–47. New York: Academic Press.

———. 1985. Economic Action and Social Structure: The Problem of Embeddedness. *American Journal of Sociology* 91:481–510.

———. 1995. *Getting a Job: A Study of Contacts and Careers.* Chicago: University of Chicago Press.

Gregory, C. A. 1982. *Gifts and Commodities.* London: Academic Press.

Gregory, Peter. 1986. *The Myth of the Market Failure: Employment and the Labor Market in Mexico.* Baltimore: Johns Hopkins University Press.

Grieco, Margaret. 1996. *Workers' Dilemmas: Recruitment, Reliability, and Repeated Exchange: An Analysis of Urban Social Networks and Labour Circulation.* London: Routledge.

Griffith, David. 1993. *Jones's Minimal: Low-Wage Labor in the United States.* Albany: State University of New York Press.

Griffith, David, and Ed Kissam. 1995. *Working Poor: Farmworkers in the United States.* Philadelphia: Temple University Press.

Gudmundson, Lowell. 1995. Peasant, Farmer, Proletarian: Class Formation in a Smallholder Coffee Economy, 1850–1950. In *Coffee, Society, and Power in Latin America,* ed. W. Roseberry, L. Gudmundson, and M. Samper Kutschbach, 112–51. Baltimore: Johns Hopkins University Press.

Gutierrez de Pineda, Virginia. 1976. *Estructura, Función, y Cambio de la Familia en Colombia.* Bogotá: Asociación Colombiana de Facultades de Medicina.

Hanson S. 1992. Geography and Feminism: Worlds in Collision? *Annals of the Association of American Geographers* 82:569–86.

Hanson, S., and G. Pratt. 1995. *Gender, Work, and Space.* New York: Routledge.

Hart, Gillian. 1986. Interlocking Transactions: Obstacles, Precursors, or Instruments of Agrarian Capitalism? *Journal of Development Economics* 23: 117–203.

———. 1992. Imagined Utilities: Constructions of "the Household" in Economic Theory. In *Understanding Economic Process,* ed. Sutti Ortiz and Susan Lees, 111–31. Monographs in Economic Anthropology no. 10. Lanham, Md.: University Press of America.

Hart, Oliver, and Bengt Hölstrom. 1987. The Theory of Contracts. In *Advances in Economic Theory: Fifth World Congress,* ed. Truman F. Bewley, 71–157. Cambridge: Cambridge University Press.

Hataya, Noriko. 1992. Urban-Rural Linkage of the Labor Market in a Coffee Growing Zone in Colombia. *Developing Economies* 30:63–83.

Hayami, Yujiro, and Keijiro Otsuka. 1993. *The Economics of Contract Choice.* Oxford: Clarendon.

Hefner, Robert. 1990. *The Political Economy of Mountain Java.* Berkeley: University of California Press.

Helmsing, A. H. J. 1986. *Firms, Farms, and the State in Colombia.* Boston: Allen and Unwin.

Herrera, Fernando Boreo, and Diego Sierra Botero. 1981. *El Mercado de la Fuerza de Trabajo en la Zona Bananera de Urabá.* Medellin: Universidad de Antioquia, CIE.

Horan, Patrick M., and Charles M. Tolbert. 1984. *The Organization of Work in Rural and Urban Labor Markets.* Boulder, Colo.: Westview.

International Labour Office. 1970. *Towards Full Employment: A Programme for Colombia.* Geneva: International Labour Office.

Jarvis, Lovell, Cecilia Montero, and Mauricio Hidalgo. 1993. El Empresario Fruticultor: Fortalezas y Debilidades de un Sector Heterogéneo. Notas Técnicas no. 154. Santiago de Chile: CIEPLAN.

Jenkins, J. Craig. 1978. The Demand for Immigrant Workers: Labor Scarcity or Social Control? *International Migration Review* 12:514–35.

Jimenez, Margarita, and Sandro Sideri. 1985. *Historia del Desarrollo Regional en Colombia.* CIDER, Universidad de los Andes. Bogotá: Fondo Editorial CEREC.

Jimenez, Michael. 1981. Red Viotá: Authority and Rebellion in a Coffee Municipality in Colombia, 1928–1938. Paper presented at the annual meeting of the American Historical Association, Los Angeles.

———. 1989. Traveling Far in Grandfather's Car: The Life-Cycle of Central Colombian Estates. The Case of Viotá, Cundinamarca (1900–1930). *Hispanic American Historical Review* 69:205–19.

———. 1995a. At the Banquet of Civilization: The Limits of Planters' Hegemony in Early-Twentieth-Century Colombia. In *Coffee, Society, and Power in Latin America,* ed. W. Roseberry, L. Gudmundson, and M. Samper Kutschbach, 262–93. Baltimore: Johns Hopkins University Press.

———. 1995b. "From Plantation to Cup": Coffee and Capitalism in the United States, 1830–1930. In *Coffee, Society, and Power in Latin America,* ed. W. Roseberry, L. Gudmundson, and M. Samper Kutschbach, 38–64. Baltimore: Johns Hopkins University Press.

Junguito, Roberto, and Diego Pizano. 1991. *Producción de Café en Colombia.* Bogotá: Fondo Cultural Cafetero, Fedesarrollo

———. 1993. *El Comercio Exterior y la Política Internacional del Café.* Bogotá: Fondo Cultural Cafetero, Fedesarrollo.

———. 1997. *Instituciones e Instrumentos de la Política Cafetera Colombiana.* Bogotá: Fondo Cultural Cafetero, Fedesarrollo.

Kalmanoff, George. 1968. *The Coffee Economy of Colombia.* International Bank of Reconstruction and Development Economics Department Working Paper no. 15. [Washington, D.C.]: World Bank.

Kalmanovitz, Salomon. 1982. *El Desarrollo de la Agricultura en Colombia.* Bogotá: Carlos Valencia Editores.

Kevane, Michael. 1994. Village Labor Markets in Sheikan District, Sudan. *World Development* 22:839–57.

Knight, Rolf. 1972. *Sugar Plantations and Labour Patterns in the Cauca Valley, Colombia.* Anthropological Series no. 12. Toronto: University of Toronto, Department of Anthropology.

Landell Mills Commodity Studies. 1990. A World Survey of Coffee Costs and Production Costs, 1987–88. Vol. 2. Oxford. Unpublished manuscript.

LeGrand, Catherine. 1984. Labor Acquisition and Social Conflict on the Colombian Frontier, 1850–1936. *Journal of Latin American Studies* 16:27–49.

Leibovich, José, and José Ocampo. 1985. La Política de Comercialización Externa del Café Colombiano. In *Lecturas de Economía Cafetera,* ed. José Antonio Ocampo, 153–201. Bogotá: Tercer Mundo.

London, Christopher E. 1977. Class Relations and Capitalist Development: Subsumption in the Colombian Coffee Industry. *Journal of Peasant Studies* 24: 269–95.

Lösch, August. 1959. *The Economics of Location.* New Haven: Yale University Press.

Lukes, Steven, and Andrew Scull, eds. 1983. *Durkheim and the Law.* New York: St. Martin's.

Lustig, Nora Claudia, and Darry McLeod. 1997. Minimum Wages and Poverty in Developing Countries. In *Labor Markets in Latin America,* ed. Sebastian Edwards and Nora Claudia Lustig, 62–103. Washington, D.C.: Brookings Institution Press.

Machado, Absolon. 1977. *El Café: De la Aparcería al Capitalismo.* Bogotá: Punta de Lanza.

Mann, Susan Archer. 1990. *Agrarian Capitalism in Theory and Practice.* Chapel Hill: University of North Carolina Press.

Mann, Susan Archer, and James M. Dickinson. 1978. Obstacles to the Development of Capitalist Agriculture. *Journal of Peasant Studies* 5: 466–81.

Marmora, Lelio. 1980. *Centros Rurales de Servicios Integrados.* SENALDE, Migraciones Laborales no. 12. Bogotá: Ministerio de Trabajo y Seguridad Social.

Marsden, David. 1986. *The End of Economic Man?* New York: St. Martin's.

Martin, Phillip L. 1988. *Harvest of Confusion: Migrant Workers in U.S. Agriculture.* Boulder, Colo.: Westview.

Marx, Karl. 1977. *Capital.* Vol 1. New York: Random House.

Mauss, Marcel. 1954. *The Gift.* London: Cohen and West.

Mazumdar, Dipak. 1959. The Marginal Productivity Theory of Wages and Disguised Unemployment. *Review of Economic Studies* 26:190–97.

Medrano, Diana. 1980. La Mujer en la Región Cafetera del Suroeste Antioqueño. In *Mujer y Capitalismo Agrario Estudio de Cuatro Regiones Colombianas,* ed. Magdalena León de Leal and Carmen Diane Deere, 53–90. Bogotá: ACEP.

Mirlees, J. 1975. A Pure Theory of Underdeveloped Economies. In *Agriculture in Development Theory,* ed. L. Reynolds, 84–106. New Haven: Yale University Press.

Moberg, Mark. 1996. Myths that Divide: Immigrant Labor and Class Segmentation in the Belizean Banana Industry. *American Ethnologist* 23:311–30.

Montenegro, Armando. 1993. *Café, Dinero, y Macroeconomia en Colombia.* FESCOL. Bogotá: Tercer Mundo.

Morgan, David Hoseason. 1982. *Harvesters and Harvesting, 1840–1900: A Study of the Rural Proletariat.* London: Croom Helm.

Nash, John. 1950. The Bargaining Problem. *Econometrica* 18:155–62.

Nelson, Arthur. 1986. Urban Growth Management and Decline of Available Housing for Migrant Farmworkers. *Rural Sociologist* 6:80–87.

Nemirovsky, Ada Svelitza, Rosana Gonzalez, and Gabriela Beordi. 1997. Empleo y Conflicto en el Sector Hortícola de Matanza, Provincia de Buenos Aires. Paper presented at the workshop on "Rural Employment during a Period of Deregulation," University of Buenos Aires.

Newby, Howard, Colin Bell, and Peter Saunders. 1978. *Property, Power, and Paternalism: Class Control in Rural England.* Madison: University of Wisconsin Press.

Ocampo, José Antonio, ed. 1987. *Lecturas de Economía Cafetera.* Bogotá: Tercer Mundo.

Ocquist, P. 1978. *Violencia, Conflicto, y Política en Colombia.* Instituto de Estudios Colombianos. Bogotá: Biblioteca Banco Popular.

Ortega Torres, Jorge. 1980. *Legislación Obrera Colombiana.* Bogotá: Temis.

Ortiz, Sutti. 1983. What Is Decision Analysis About? The Problems of Formal Representations. In *Economic Anthropology: Topics and Theories,* ed. Sutti Ortiz, 43–61. Lanham, Md.: University Press of America.

———. 1989. Uncertainty-Reducing Strategies and Unsteady States: Labor Contracts in Coffee Agriculture. In *Risk and Uncertainty in Economic Life,* ed. E. Cashdan, 303–17. Boulder, Colo.: Westview.

———. 1992. Market Power and Culture as Agencies in the Transformation of Labor Contracts in Coffee Agriculture. In *Understanding Economic Process,* ed. Sutti Ortiz and Susan Lees, 43–69. Monographs in Economic Anthropology no. 10. Lanham, Md.: University Press of America.

Ortiz Sarmiento, Carlos Miguel. 1985. *Estado y Subversión en Colombia: La Violencia en el Quindio Años 50.* Bogotá: Fondo Editorial CEREC.

Padfield, Harland, and William E. Martin. 1965. *Farmers, Workers, and Machines.* Tucson: University of Arizona Press.

Paige, Jeffery M. 1997. *Coffee and Power: Revolution and the Rise of Democracy in Central America.* Cambridge: Harvard University Press.

Pal, Sarmistha. 1996. Casual and Regular Contracts: Workers' Self-Selection in the Rural Labour Markets in India. *Journal of Development Studies* 33:99–116.

Palacios, Marcos. 1983. *El Café en Colombia, 1859–1970: Una Historia Económica Social y Política.* Mexico City: El Colegio de México, El Ancora Editores. (First published in English as *Coffee in Colombia, 1850–1970: An Economic and Political History.* Cambridge University Press, 1980.)

Paredes Hernandez, Gonzalo, and Hernan Zambrano Ramirez. 1984. El Café en el Desarrollo de las Economías de Vertiente: Una Diferenciación Regional. CIE Universidad de Antioquia, Medellin. Unpublished manuscript.

Parsons, James J. 1968. *Antioqueño Colonization in Western Colombia.* Berkeley: University of California Press.

Peck, Jamie. 1996. *Work Place: The Social Regulation of Labor Markets.* New York: Guildford.

Perry, Guillermo. 1986. Siembra Vientos y Cosecharás Tempestades. *El Tiempo,* February 26.

Platteau, Jean Philippe. 1995. A Framework for the Analysis of Evolving Patron-Client Ties in Agrarian Economies. *World Development* 23:767–86.

Puyana, Yolanda. 1985. El Decenso de la Fecundidad por Estratos Sociales. In *Mujer y Familia en Colombia,* comp. Elssy Bonilla C., 177–204. Bogotá: Plaza and Janes Editores, Asociación Colombiana de Sociología, Departamento Nacional de Planeación, and UNICEF.

Ramirez, Juan Carlos. 1983. Los Andariegos. *Cuadernos de Agro-Industria y Economía Rural* 11:89–115.

Rao, Mohan J. 1988. Fragmented Rural Labour Markets. *Journal of Peasant Studies* 15:238–57.

Robertson, A. F. 1987. *The Dynamics of Productive Relationships: African Share Contracts in Comparative Perspective.* Cambridge: Cambridge University Press.

Roseberry, William. 1995. "Introduction." In *Coffee, Society, and Power in Latin America,* ed. W. Roseberry, L. Gudmundson, and M. Samper Kutschbach, 1–38. Baltimore: Johns Hopkins University Press.

Roseberry, William, Lowell Gudmundson, and Mario Samper Kutschbach, eds. 1995. *Coffee, Society, and Power in Latin America.* Baltimore: Johns Hopkins University Press.

Rosenzweig, Mark R. 1988. Labor Markets in Low-Income Countries. In *Handbook of Development Economics,* ed. H. Chenery and T. N. Srinivasan, 1:714–62.

Ruiz Niño, Soledad. 1972. La Fuerza de Trabajo en la Zona Cafetera del Tolima. Bogotá, Departamento Nacional de Estadísticas. Unpublished manuscript.

———. 1983. Café, Tecnología, y Sociedad Municipal: Montenegro, Villarica, Viotá. Unpublished manuscript.

Rutledge, Ian. 1987. *Cambio Agrario e Integración: El Desarrollo del Capitalismo en Jujuy 1550–1960.* Buenos Aires: Facultad de Filosofía y Letras, Serie Monográfica.

Saldías Barreneche, Carmenza. 1993. El Café en el Departamento de Caldas: Crisis o Transformación? In *Economía Cafetera: Crisis y Perspectivas,* 239–62. Santafe de Bogotá: Centro Editorial Javeriano.

Samper Kutschbach, Mario. 1995. In Difficult Times: Colombian and Costa Rican Coffee Growers from Prosperity to Crisis, 1929–1936. In *Coffee, Society, and Power in Latin America,* ed. W. Roseberry, L. Gudmundson, and M. Samper Kutschbach, 151–81. Baltimore: Johns Hopkins University Press.

Sanabria, Harry. 1993. *The Coca Boom and Rural Social Change in Bolivia.* Ann Arbor: University of Michigan Press.

Sanchez, Gonzalo G. 1976. *Los "Bolcheviques del Líbano" Tolima.* Bogotá: Ecoe Editores.

Saxena, Anuradha. 1995. The Dynamics of a Changing Gender Terrain: Gender, Culture, and Economy in Two Western Coffee Growing Areas of Colombia. Ph.D. diss., Boston University.

Schaffner, Julie Anderson. 1993. Rural Labor Legislation and Permanent Labor Employment in Northeastern Brazil. *World Development* 21:705–19.

Schultz, Paul T. 1971. Rural-Urban Migration in Colombia. *Review of Economics and Statistics* 53:157–63.

Skinner, William. 1964. Marketing and Social Structure in Rural China. *Journal of Asian Studies* 24:3–43, 195–228, 363–99.

Smith, Carol A. 1974. Economics of Marketing Systems: Models from Economic Geography. *Annual Review of Anthropology* 3:167–201.

Solow, Robert M. 1990. *The Labor Market as a Social Institution.* Oxford: Basil Blackwell.

Sosnick, Stephen H. 1978. *Hired Hands: Seasonal Farm Workers in the United States.* Santa Barbara, Calif.: McNally and Loftin, West.

Stiglitz, Joseph E. 1976. The Efficiency Wage Hypothesis, Surplus Labor, and the Distribution of Income in L.D.C. *Oxford Economic Papers* 28:185–207.

Stolcke, Verena. 1988. *Coffee Planters, Workers, and Wives: Class Conflict and Gender Relations on São Paulo Plantations, 1850–1980.* New York: St. Martin's.

El Tiempo. 1997. La Bonanza Cafetera se Mantiene Firme. March 23.

Thomas, Robert J. 1985. *Citizenship, Gender, and Work: Social Organization of Industrial Agriculture.* Stanford, Calif.: Stanford University Press.

Thomas, Vinod. 1985. *Linking Macroeconomic and Agricultural Policies for Adjustment with Growth: The Colombian Experience.* Baltimore: Johns Hopkins University Press for the World Bank.

Tootle, Deborah M., and Sara E. Green. 1989. The Effect of Ethnic Identity on Support for Farm Worker Unions. *Rural Sociology* 54:83–91.

Torres, Gabriel. 1997. *The Force of Irony: Power in the Everyday Life of Mexican Tomato Workers.* Oxford: Berg.

Tovar, Hermes. 1975. *El Movimiento Campesino en Colombia Durante los Siglos XIX y XX.* Bogotá: Editorial Libres.

United Nations, Economic Commission for Latin America. 1958. *Coffee in Latin America: Colombia and El Salvador.* New York: United Nations.

Urrea, Fernando. 1976. *Mercados de Trabajo y Migraciones en la Explotación Cafetera.* SENALDE, Migraciones Laborales no. 9. Bogotá: Ministerio de Trabajo y Seguridad Social.

————. 1986. Estudio Comparativo de los Mercados Laborales Urbanos y Rurales en Colombia en el Período 1960–1984. *Cuadernos de Agroindustria y Economía Rural* 17:9–55.

Urrutía, Miguel. 1969. *The Development of the Colombian Labor Movement.* New Haven: Yale University Press.

Valdés, Dennis Nodín. 1991. *Al Norte: Agricultural Workers in the Great Lakes Region, 1917–1970.* Austin: University of Texas Press.

Vallejo Mejía, César. 1983. Política Cafetera y Desarrollo Regional: El Caso de Risaralda. In *Economía Cafetera: Crisis y Perspectivas,* 277–96. Santafe de Bogotá: Centro Editorial Javeriano.

Van der Ploeg, Jan Douwe. 1992. The Reconstitution of Locality: Technology and Labour in Modern Agriculture. In *Labour and Locality,* ed. Terry Marsden, Philip Lowe, and Sarah Whatmore, 19–44. London: David Fulton.

Velez E., E. P. Becerra, C. B. L. Gomez, et al. 1986. Estudio Socio-económico de las Familias de la Zona Cafetera Colombiana. Instituto SER de Investigaciones, Bogotá. Unpublished manuscript.

Venegas, Sylvia. 1987. Family Reproduction in Rural Chile: A Socio-Demographic Study of Agrarian Change in the Aconcagua Valley, 1930–1986. Ph.D. diss., University of Texas at Austin.

————. 1995. Las Temporeras de la Fruta en Chile. In *El Rostro Femenino del Mercado de Trabajo Rural en America Latina,* ed. Sara María Lara Flores. United Nations Institute for Social Rearch. Caracas: Nueva Sociedad.

Weber, Max. 1978. *Economy and Society.* Berkeley: University of California Press.

Welch, Clifford. 1990. Rural Labor and the Brazilian Revolution in São Paulo, 1930–1964. Ph.D. diss., Duke University.

Wells, Miriam J. 1984. The Resurgence of Sharecropping: Historical Anomaly or Political Strategy? *American Journal of Sociology* 90:1–29.

————. 1996. *Strawberry Fields: Politics, Class, and Work in California Agriculture.* Ithaca: Cornell University Press.

White, Sally Blount, and Margaret A. Neal. 1994. The Role of Negotiator Aspirations and Settlement Expectancies in Bargaining Outcomes. *Organizational Behavior and Human Decision Process* 57:303–17.

White, Sally Blount, Kathleen L. Valley, Max Basserman, Margaret A. Neal, and Sharon R. Peck. 1994. Alternative Models of Price Behavior in Dyadic Negotiations: Market Prices, Reservation Prices and Negotiation Aspirations. *Organizational Behavior and Human Decision Process* 57:430–47.

Whitener, Leslie A. 1985. The Migrants' Farm Work Force: Differences in Attachment to Farm Work. *Rural Sociology* 50:163–80.

Whiteford, Scott. 1981. *Workers from the North: Plantations, Bolivian Labor, and the City in Northwest Argentina.* Austin: University of Texas Press.

Williams, Robert G. 1994. *States and Social Evolution. Coffee and the Rise of*

National Governments in Central America. Chapel Hill: University of North Carolina Press.

Woodiwiss, Anthony. 1987. The Discourses of Production: Part 2, The Contract of Employment and the Emergence of Democratic Capitalist Law in Britain and the United States. *Economy and Society* 16:441–525.

Zamosc, Leon. 1986. *The Agrarian Question and the Peasant Movement in Colombia: Struggles of the National Peasant Association, 1967–1981.* Cambridge: Cambridge University Press.

Zuleta, Luis Alberto, et al. 1989. *Bases para Evaluar el Convenio Gobierno-Federación Nacional de Cafeteros.* Bogotá: FNCC.

Index

Administrator: of enterprise farms, 68–73, 116–18; negotiating benefits with attached laborers, 185; ownership of small farms, 77; salaries, benefits, and incentives, 22

Agregado: as administrator, 119; coffee prices and, 199; contracts and labor legislation, 181–83, dependents of, 70, 91, 153–54, 185; early history of, 34, 122–23, 180, 200; as food preparers, 70, 115, 185, 223; fringe benefits, 154, 183–85, 212; ownership of small farms, 77; patron-clientage, 185–86, 212; relationships with farmers, 153–54, 212; responsibilities, 73; as supervisors, 71, 181, 212; theories explaining persistence of *agregados* on enterprise farms, 198; during the *violencia,* 36; wages, 183–85. See also *Alimentador;* Attached laborers; Laborers, resident

Akerloff, George, 9–10

Alimentador, 70. See also *Agregado,* as food preparers

ALMACAFE, 49–50

Andariego. See Harvesters, ambulant, description of

Antioqueño colonization, 32, 62

Antioquia, 32, 36–37, 44–45, 197, 200–201

Arango, Mariano, 25, 32–33, 37, 44–45, 80, 170, 178, 180, 197, 199, 201, 208, 212

Attached laborers: attraction for farmers, 185, 198; in Brazil, 25; as clients of farmers, 212; as a force in Colombian labor and land rights movements, 34–35, 52, 181; fringe benefits, 182–83; theories explaining persistence of employment on enterprise farms, 198–99

Aubad, Rafael, 44, 80, 201

Bardhan, Pranab K., 6, 17, 159, 177, 184–86, 198, 206, 212

Bates, Robert H., 20, 26, 48, 189

Bazzoli, Laure, 11, 212–13

Belén, 27–30, 61–64, 74, 127, 139, 165–66, 169, 179, 180, 202, 217–20, 224–27

Bergquist, Charles, 33, 35

Bonanza of the 1970s: causes of, 40; decline of, 43–44; impact on labor markets, 41, 191; impact on local production systems, 40–41; impact on small farmer, 43–44. *See also* Coffee, boom

Breman, Ian, 10

Caldas, 32, 36–37, 39, 53, 126, 131, 192

Campillo, Fabiola, 44, 50, 51

Capitalist agriculture, 18, 24

Caturra coffee: adoption by various types of farms, 74–80; coffee boom of the 1970s, 40–44; competitiveness of traditional farms, 119; introduction to Colombia, 25, 40; labor management, 108–9, 197; and the maintenance of